ACCA

Applied Knowledge
Diploma in Accounting and Business

Management Accounting (MA-FMA)

EXAM KIT

KAPLAN

PUBLISHING

British Library Cataloguing-in-Publication Data

A catalogue record for this book is available from the British Library.

Published by:

Kaplan Publishing UK
Unit 2 The Business Centre
Molly Millar's Lane
Wokingham
Berkshire
RG41 2QZ

ISBN: 978-1-78740-410-6

Printed and bound in Great Britain

Acknowledgements

These materials are reviewed by the ACCA examining team. The objective of the review is to ensure that the material properly covers the syllabus and study guide outcomes, used by the examining team in setting the exams, in the appropriate breadth and depth. The review does not ensure that every eventuality, combination or application of examinable topics is addressed by the ACCA Approved Content. Nor does the review comprise a detailed technical check of a the content as the Approved Content Provider has its own quality assurance processes in place in this respect.

We are grateful to the Chartered Institute of Management Accountants and the Institute of Chartered Accountants in England and Wales for permission to reproduce past examination questions. The answers have been prepared by Kaplan Publishing.

CONTENTS

Features in this edition

In addition to providing a wide ranging bank of practice questions, we have also included in this edition:

- Details of the examination format.

- Examples of 'objective test' and 'multi-task' questions that will form part of the examination format.

- Exam-specific information and advice on exam technique.

- Our recommended approach to make your revision for this particular subject as effective as possible.

This includes step-by-step guidance on how best to use our Kaplan material (Study Text, Pocket Notes and Exam Kit) at this stage in your studies.

You will find a wealth of other resources to help you with your studies on the following sites:

www.MyKaplan.co.uk and www.accaglobal.com/students/

Quality and accuracy are of the utmost importance to us so if you spot an error in any of our products, please send an email to mykaplanreporting@kaplan.com with full details.

Our Quality Co-ordinator will work with our technical team to verify the error and take action to ensure it is corrected in future editions.

INDEX TO QUESTIONS AND ANSWERS

SECTION B-TYPE QUESTIONS

Budgeting	131	233
Standard costing	139	238
Performance measurement	144	240

KAPLAN PUBLISHING

EXAM TECHNIQUE

- **Do not skip any of the material** in the syllabus.

- **Read each question** *very* carefully.

- **Double-check your answer** before committing yourself to it.

- Answer **every** question – if you do not know an answer, you don't lose anything by guessing. Think carefully before you **guess**. The examiner has indicated that many candidates are still leaving blank answers in the real exam.

- If you are answering a multiple-choice question, **eliminate first those answers that you know are wrong.** Then choose the most appropriate answer from those that are left.

- Remember that **only one answer to a multiple-choice question can be right**. After you have eliminated the ones that you know to be wrong, if you are still unsure, guess. Only guess after you have double-checked that you have only eliminated answers that are *definitely* wrong.

Computer-based exams – tips

- Do not attempt a CBE until you have **completed all study material** relating to it.

- On the ACCA website there is a CBE demonstration. It is **ESSENTIAL** that you attempt this before your real CBE. You will become familiar with how to move around the CBE screens and the way that questions are formatted, increasing your confidence and speed in the actual exam.

- Be sure you understand how to use the **software** before you start the exam. If in doubt, ask the assessment centre staff to explain it to you.

- Questions are **displayed on the screen** and answers are entered using keyboard and mouse. At the end of the exam, you are given a certificate showing the result you have achieved.

- The CBE question types are as follows:

    - Multiple choice – where you are required to choose one answer from a list of options provided by clicking on the appropriate 'radio button'

    - Multiple response – where you are required to select more than one response from the options provided by clicking on the appropriate tick boxes (typically choose two options from the available list

    - Multiple response matching – where you are required to indicate a response to a number of related statements by clicking on the 'radio button' which corresponds to the appropriate response for each statement

    - Number entry – where you are required to key in a response to a question shown on the screen.

- The computer based examination will not require you to input text, although you may be required to choose the correct text from options available.

- You need to be sure you **know how to answer questions** of this type before you sit the exam, through practice.

EXAM SPECIFIC INFORMATION

THE EXAM

FORMAT OF COMPUTER BASED EXAM

	Number of marks
35 objective test questions (2 marks each)	70
3 multi-task questions (10 marks each)	30

Total time allowed: 2 hours

- Questions will usually comprise the following answer types:

    (i) Multiple choice with four options. Identify one correct answer from the four options.

    (ii) Multiple response questions. A multiple response question is basically a multiple choice question but more than one answer option is selected. For example, the question can ask 'Which two of the following statements are true?' Candidates will be expected to select the two answer options from, say four possible answers options.

    (iii) Number entry. Candidates will need to calculate an answer and input the value into the answer box

    (iv) Section B of the exam can include the above question types but also answers may be in the form of drop-down lists. Candidates will need to click on the list to choose the correct answer.

- The multi-task questions will examine Budgeting, Standard costing and Performance measurement sections of the syllabus.

    Note: Budgeting MTQs in Section B can also include tasks from B2 Forecasting techniques. B4 Spreadsheets could be included in any of the MTQs, as either the basis for presenting information in the question or as a task within the MTQ.

- The examinations contain 100% compulsory questions and students must study across the breadth of the syllabus to prepare effectively for the examination

- The examination will be assessed by a two hour computer-based examination. You should refer to the ACCA web site for information regarding the availability of the computer-based examination.

PASS MARK

The pass mark for all ACCA Qualification examination papers is 50%.

DETAILED SYLLABUS, STUDY GUIDE AND CBE SPECIMEN EXAM

The detailed syllabus and study guide written by the ACCA, along with the specimen exam, can be found at:

accaglobal.com/management-accounting

KAPLAN'S RECOMMENDED REVISION APPROACH

QUESTION PRACTICE IS THE KEY TO SUCCESS

Success in professional examinations relies upon you acquiring a firm grasp of the required knowledge at the tuition phase. In order to be able to do the questions, knowledge is essential.

However, the difference between success and failure often hinges on your exam technique on the day and making the most of the revision phase of your studies.

The **Kaplan study text** is the starting point, designed to provide the underpinning knowledge to tackle all questions. However, in the revision phase, pouring over text books is not the answer.

Kaplan Online progress tests help you consolidate your knowledge and understanding and are a useful tool to check whether you can remember key topic areas.

Kaplan pocket notes are designed to help you quickly revise a topic area, however you then need to practice questions. There is a need to progress to full exam standard questions as soon as possible, and to tie your exam technique and technical knowledge together.

The importance of question practice cannot be over-emphasised.

The recommended approach below is designed by expert tutors in the field, in conjunction with their knowledge of the examiner.

The approach taken for the Applied Knowledge exams is to revise by topic area.

You need to practice as many questions as possible in the time you have left.

OUR AIM

Our aim is to get you to the stage where you can attempt exam standard questions confidently, to time, in a closed book environment, with no supplementary help (i.e. to simulate the real examination experience).

Practising your exam technique on real past examination questions, in timed conditions, is also vitally important for you to assess your progress and identify areas of weakness that may need more attention in the final run up to the examination.

The approach below shows you which questions you should use to build up to coping with exam standard question practice, and references to the sources of information available should you need to revisit a topic area in more detail.

Remember that in the real examination, all you have to do is:

- attempt all questions required by the exam
- only spend the allotted time on each question, and
- get them at least 50% right!

Try and practice this approach on every question you attempt from now to the real exam.

ACCA SUPPORT

For additional support with your studies please also refer to the ACCA Global website.

THE KAPLAN MANAGEMENT ACCOUNTING REVISION PLAN

Stage 1: Assess areas of strengths and weaknesses

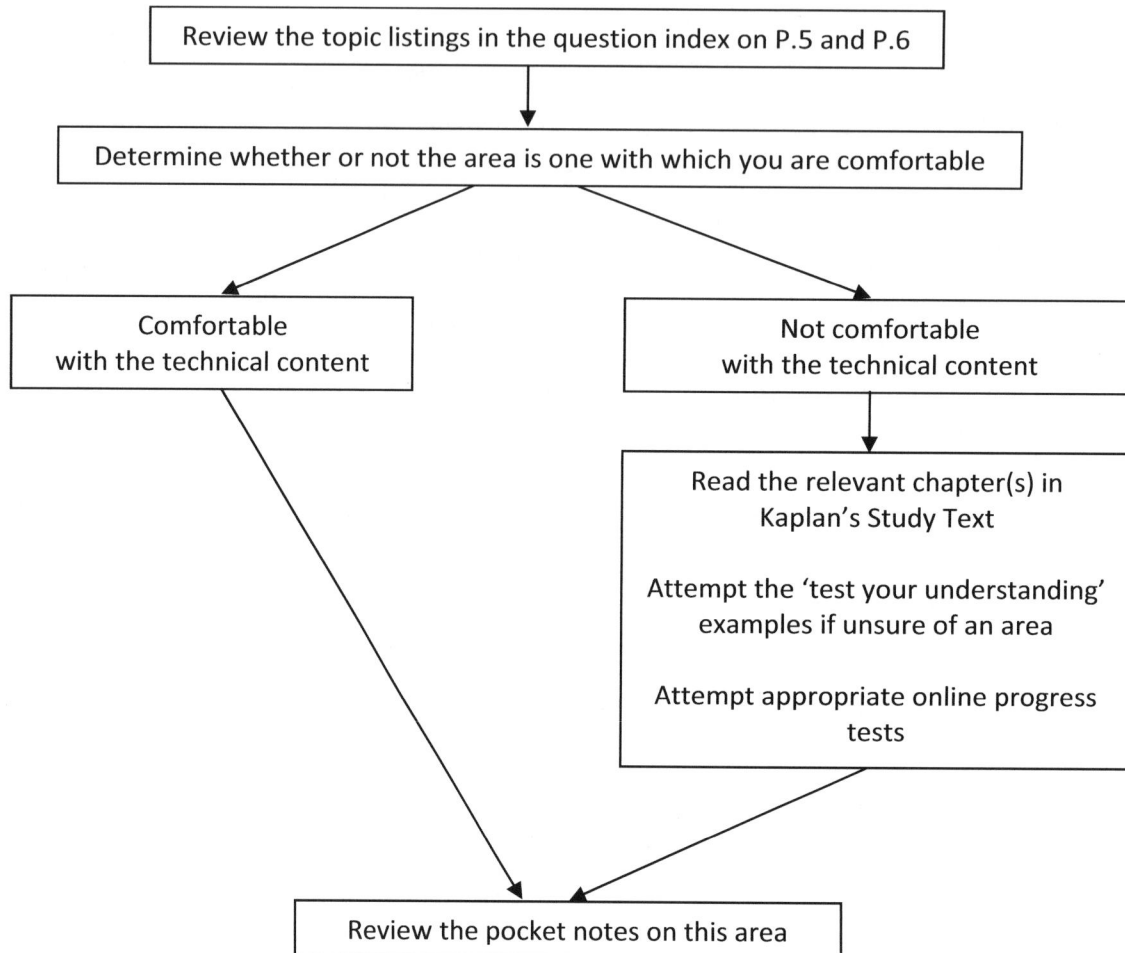

```
┌─────────────────────────────────────────────────────────────┐
│  Review the topic listings in the question index on P.5 and P.6 │
└─────────────────────────────────────────────────────────────┘
                              │
                              ▼
┌─────────────────────────────────────────────────────────────┐
│  Determine whether or not the area is one with which you are comfortable │
└─────────────────────────────────────────────────────────────┘
              ╱                                    ╲
             ▼                                      ▼
┌──────────────────────────┐          ┌──────────────────────────┐
│      Comfortable         │          │     Not comfortable       │
│  with the technical content │        │  with the technical content │
└──────────────────────────┘          └──────────────────────────┘
                                                   │
                                                   ▼
                            ┌──────────────────────────────────────┐
                            │  Read the relevant chapter(s) in       │
                            │  Kaplan's Study Text                    │
                            │                                        │
                            │  Attempt the 'test your understanding' │
                            │  examples if unsure of an area         │
                            │                                        │
                            │  Attempt appropriate online progress   │
                            │  tests                                 │
                            └──────────────────────────────────────┘
              ╲                                    ╱
               ▼                                  ▼
            ┌──────────────────────────────────────────┐
            │  Review the pocket notes on this area      │
            └──────────────────────────────────────────┘
```

Stage 2: Practice questions

Ensure that you revise all syllabus areas as questions could be asked on anything.

Try to avoid referring to text books and notes and the model answer until you have completed your attempt.

Try to answer the question in the allotted time.

Review your attempt with the model answer. If you got the answer wrong, can you see why? Was the problem a lack of knowledge or a failure to understand the question fully?

Fill in the self-assessment box below and decide on your best course of action.

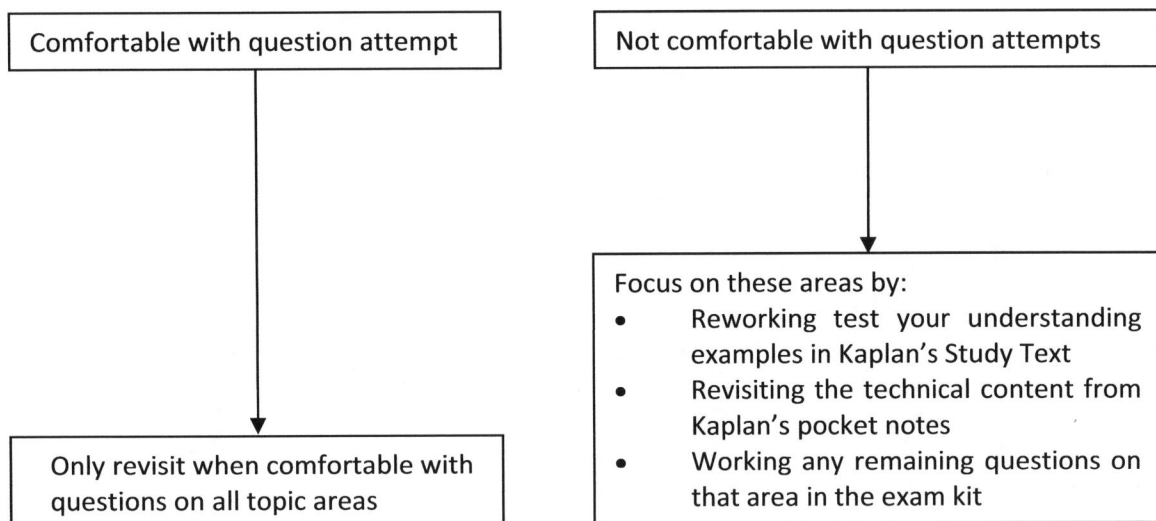

Comfortable with question attempt

Not comfortable with question attempts

Focus on these areas by:
• Reworking test your understanding examples in Kaplan's Study Text
• Revisiting the technical content from Kaplan's pocket notes
• Working any remaining questions on that area in the exam kit

Only revisit when comfortable with questions on all topic areas

Stage 3: Final pre-exam revision

We recommend that you **attempt at least one two hour mock examination** containing a set of previously unseen exam standard questions.

It is important that you get a feel for the breadth of coverage of a real exam without advanced knowledge of the topic areas covered – just as you will expect to see on the real exam day.

Ideally this mock should be sat in timed, closed book, real exam conditions and could be:

• a mock examination offered by your tuition provider, and/or

• the specimen examination in the back of this exam kit,

FORMULAE AND TABLES

Regression analysis

$$y = a + bx$$

$$a = \frac{\Sigma y}{n} - \frac{b\,\Sigma x}{n}$$

$$b = \frac{n\,\Sigma xy - \Sigma x\,\Sigma y}{n\,\Sigma x^2 - (\Sigma x)^2}$$

$$r = \frac{n\,\Sigma xy - \Sigma x\,\Sigma y}{\sqrt{\left(n\,\Sigma x^2 - (\Sigma x)^2\right)\left(n\,\Sigma y^2 - (\Sigma y)^2\right)}}$$

Economic order quantity

$$= \sqrt{\frac{2C_0 D}{C_h}}$$

Economic batch quantity

$$= \sqrt{\frac{2C_0 D}{C_h\left(1 - \dfrac{D}{R}\right)}}$$

Arithmetic mean

$$\bar{x} = \frac{\Sigma x}{n} \qquad\qquad \bar{x} = \frac{\Sigma fx}{\Sigma f} \text{ (frequency distribution)}$$

Standard deviation

$$\sigma = \sqrt{\frac{\Sigma(x - \bar{x})^2}{n}} \qquad\qquad \sigma = \sqrt{\frac{\Sigma fx^2}{\Sigma f} - \left(\frac{\Sigma fx}{\Sigma f}\right)^2} \text{ (frequency distribution)}$$

Variance

$$= \sigma^2$$

Co-efficient of variation

$$CV = \frac{\sigma}{\bar{x}}$$

Expected value

$$EV = \Sigma px$$

PRESENT VALUE TABLE

Present value of 1, i.e. $(1 + r)^{-n}$

Where r = interest rate

        n = number of periods until payment.

Periods (n)	1%	2%	3%	4%	5%	6%	7%	8%	9%	10%
1	0.990	0.980	0.971	0.962	0.952	0.943	0.935	0.926	0.917	0.909
2	0.980	0.961	0.943	0.925	0.907	0.890	0.873	0.857	0.842	0.826
3	0.971	0.942	0.915	0.889	0.864	0.840	0.816	0.794	0.772	0.751
4	0.961	0.924	0.888	0.855	0.823	0.792	0.763	0.735	0.708	0.683
5	0.951	0.906	0.863	0.822	0.784	0.747	0.713	0.681	0.650	0.621
6	0.942	0.888	0.837	0.790	0.746	0.705	0.666	0.630	0.596	0.564
7	0.933	0.871	0.813	0.760	0.711	0.665	0.623	0.583	0.547	0.513
8	0.923	0.853	0.789	0.731	0.677	0.627	0.582	0.540	0.502	0.467
9	0.914	0.837	0.766	0.703	0.645	0.592	0.544	0.500	0.460	0.424
10	0.905	0.820	0.744	0.676	0.614	0.558	0.508	0.463	0.422	0.386
11	0.896	0.804	0.722	0.650	0.585	0.527	0.475	0.429	0.388	0.350
12	0.887	0.788	0.701	0.625	0.557	0.497	0.444	0.397	0.356	0.319
13	0.879	0.773	0.681	0.601	0.530	0.469	0.415	0.368	0.326	0.290
14	0.870	0.758	0.661	0.577	0.505	0.442	0.388	0.340	0.299	0.263
15	0.861	0.743	0.642	0.555	0.481	0.417	0.362	0.315	0.275	0.239

(n)	11%	12%	13%	14%	15%	16%	17%	18%	19%	20%
1	0.901	0.893	0.885	0.877	0.870	0.862	0.855	0.847	0.840	0.833
2	0.812	0.797	0.783	0.769	0.756	0.743	0.731	0.718	0.706	0.694
3	0.731	0.712	0.693	0.675	0.658	0.641	0.624	0.609	0.593	0.579
4	0.659	0.636	0.613	0.592	0.572	0.552	0.534	0.516	0.499	0.482
5	0.593	0.567	0.543	0.519	0.497	0.476	0.456	0.437	0.419	0.402
6	0.535	0.507	0.480	0.456	0.432	0.410	0.390	0.370	0.352	0.335
7	0.482	0.452	0.425	0.400	0.376	0.354	0.333	0.314	0.296	0.279
8	0.434	0.404	0.376	0.351	0.327	0.305	0.285	0.266	0.249	0.233
9	0.391	0.361	0.333	0.308	0.284	0.263	0.243	0.225	0.209	0.194
10	0.352	0.322	0.295	0.270	0.247	0.227	0.208	0.191	0.176	0.162
11	0.317	0.287	0.261	0.237	0.215	0.195	0.178	0.162	0.148	0.135
12	0.286	0.257	0.231	0.208	0.187	0.168	0.152	0.137	0.124	0.112
13	0.258	0.229	0.204	0.182	0.163	0.145	0.130	0.116	0.104	0.093
14	0.232	0.205	0.181	0.160	0.141	0.125	0.111	0.099	0.088	0.078
15	0.209	0.183	0.160	0.140	0.123	0.108	0.095	0.084	0.079	0.065

KAPLAN PUBLISHING

ANNUITY TABLE

Present value of an annuity of 1 i.e. $\dfrac{1-(1+r)^{-n}}{r}$

Where r = interest rate

n = number of periods.

Periods (n)	Discount rate (r)									
	1%	2%	3%	4%	5%	6%	7%	8%	9%	10%
1	0.990	0.980	0.971	0.962	0.952	0.943	0.935	0.926	0.917	0.909
2	1.970	1.942	1.913	1.886	1.859	1.833	1.808	1.783	1.759	1.736
3	2.941	2.884	2.829	2.775	2.723	2.673	2.624	2.577	2.531	2.487
4	3.902	3.808	3.717	3.630	3.546	3.465	3.387	3.312	3.240	3.170
5	4.853	4.713	4.580	4.452	4.329	4.212	4.100	3.993	3.890	3.791
6	5.795	5.601	5.417	5.242	5.076	4.917	4.767	4.623	4.486	4.355
7	6.728	6.472	6.230	6.002	5.786	5.582	5.389	5.206	5.033	4.868
8	7.652	7.325	7.020	6.733	6.463	6.210	5.971	5.747	5.535	5.335
9	8.566	8.162	7.786	7.435	7.108	6.802	6.515	6.247	5.995	5.759
10	9.471	8.983	8.530	8.111	7.722	7.360	7.024	6.710	6.418	6.145
11	10.368	9.787	9.253	8.760	8.306	7.887	7.499	7.139	6.805	6.495
12	11.255	10.575	9.954	9.385	8.863	8.384	7.943	7.536	7.161	6.814
13	12.134	11.348	10.635	9.986	9.394	8.853	8.358	7.904	7.487	7.103
14	13.004	12.106	11.296	10.563	9.899	9.295	8.745	8.244	7.786	7.367
15	13.865	12.849	11.938	11.118	10.380	9.712	9.108	8.559	8.061	7.606

(n)	11%	12%	13%	14%	15%	16%	17%	18%	19%	20%
1	0.901	0.893	0.885	0.877	0.870	0.862	0.855	0.847	0.840	0.833
2	1.713	1.690	1.668	1.647	1.626	1.605	1.585	1.566	1.547	1.528
3	2.444	2.402	2.361	2.322	2.283	2.246	2.210	2.174	2.140	2.106
4	3.102	3.037	2.974	2.914	2.855	2.798	2.743	2.690	2.639	2.589
5	3.696	3.605	3.517	3.433	3.352	3.274	3.199	3.127	3.058	2.991
6	4.231	4.111	3.998	3.889	3.784	3.685	3.589	3.498	3.410	3.326
7	4.712	4.564	4.423	4.288	4.160	4.039	3.922	3.812	3.706	3.605
8	5.146	4.968	4.799	4.639	4.487	4.344	4.207	4.078	3.954	3.837
9	5.537	5.328	5.132	4.946	4.772	4.607	4.451	4.303	4.163	4.031
10	5.889	5.650	5.426	5.216	5.019	4.833	4.659	4.494	4.339	4.192
11	6.207	5.938	5.687	5.453	5.234	5.029	4.836	4.656	4.486	4.327
12	6.492	6.194	5.918	5.660	5.421	5.197	4.988	7.793	4.611	4.439
13	6.750	6.424	6.122	5.842	5.583	5.342	5.118	4.910	4.715	4.533
14	6.982	6.628	6.302	6.002	5.724	5.468	5.229	5.008	4.802	4.611
15	7.191	6.811	6.462	6.142	5.847	5.575	5.324	5.092	4.876	4.675

To find the area under the normal curve between the mean and a point Z standard deviations above the mean, use the table below. The corresponding area for a point Z standard deviations below the mean can be found through using symmetry.

$$z = \frac{x - \mu}{\sigma}$$

STANDARD NORMAL DISTRIBUTION TABLE

	0.00	0.01	0.02	0.03	0.04	0.05	0.06	0.07	0.08	0.09
0.0	0.0000	0.0040	0.0080	0.0120	0.0160	0.0199	0.0239	0.0279	0.0319	0.0359
0.1	0.0398	0.0438	0.0478	0.0517	0.0557	0.0596	0.0636	0.0675	0.0714	0.0753
0.2	0.0793	0.0832	0.0871	0.0910	0.0948	0.0987	0.1026	0.1064	0.1103	0.1141
0.3	0.1179	0.1217	0.1255	0.1293	0.1331	0.1368	0.1406	0.1443	0.1480	0.1517
0.4	0.1554	0.1591	0.1628	0.1664	0.1700	0.1736	0.1772	0.1808	0.1844	0.1879
0.5	0.1915	0.1950	0.1985	0.2019	0.2054	0.2088	0.2123	0.2157	0.2190	0.2224
0.6	0.2257	0.2291	0.2324	0.2357	0.2389	0.2422	0.2454	0.2486	0.2517	0.2549
0.7	0.2580	0.2611	0.2642	0.2673	0.2704	0.2734	0.2764	0.2794	0.2823	0.2852
0.8	0.2881	0.2910	0.2939	0.2967	0.2995	0.3023	0.3051	0.3078	0.3106	0.3133
0.9	0.3159	0.3186	0.3212	0.3238	0.3264	0.3289	0.3315	0.3340	0.3365	0.3389
1.0	0.3413	0.3438	0.3461	0.3485	0.3508	0.3531	0.3554	0.3577	0.3599	0.3621
1.1	0.3643	0.3665	0.3686	0.3708	0.3729	0.3749	0.3770	0.3790	0.3810	0.3830
1.2	0.3849	0.3869	0.3888	0.3907	0.3925	0.3944	0.3962	0.3980	0.3997	0.4015
1.3	0.4032	0.4049	0.4066	0.4082	0.4099	0.4115	0.4131	0.4147	0.4162	0.4177
1.4	0.4192	0.4207	0.4222	0.4236	0.4251	0.4265	0.4279	0.4292	0.4306	0.4319
1.5	0.4332	0.4345	0.4357	0.4370	0.4382	0.4394	0.4406	0.4418	0.4429	0.4441
1.6	0.4452	0.4463	0.4474	0.4484	0.4495	0.4505	0.4515	0.4525	0.4535	0.4545
1.7	0.4554	0.4564	0.4573	0.4582	0.4591	0.4599	0.4608	0.4616	0.4625	0.4633
1.8	0.4641	0.4649	0.4656	0.4664	0.4671	0.4678	0.4686	0.4693	0.4699	0.4706
1.9	0.4713	0.4719	0.4726	0.4732	0.4738	0.4744	0.4750	0.4756	0.4761	0.4767
2.0	0.4772	0.4778	0.4783	0.4788	0.4793	0.4798	0.4803	0.4808	0.4812	0.4817
2.1	0.4821	0.4826	0.4830	0.4834	0.4838	0.4842	0.4846	0.4850	0.4854	0.4857
2.2	0.4861	0.4864	0.4868	0.4871	0.4875	0.4878	0.4881	0.4884	0.4887	0.4890
2.3	0.4893	0.4896	0.4898	0.4901	0.4904	0.4906	0.4909	0.4911	0.4913	0.4916
2.4	0.4918	0.4920	0.4922	0.4925	0.4927	0.4929	0.4931	0.4932	0.4934	0.4936
2.5	0.4938	0.4940	0.4941	0.4943	0.4945	0.4946	0.4948	0.4949	0.4951	0.4952
2.6	0.4953	0.4955	0.4956	0.4957	0.4959	0.4960	0.4961	0.4962	0.4963	0.4964
2.7	0.4965	0.4966	0.4967	0.4968	0.4969	0.4970	0.4971	0.4972	0.4973	0.4974
2.8	0.4974	0.4975	0.4976	0.4977	0.4977	0.4978	0.4979	0.4979	0.4980	0.4981
2.9	0.4981	0.4982	0.4982	0.4983	0.4984	0.4984	0.4985	0.4985	0.4986	0.4986
3.0	0.4987	0.4987	0.4987	0.4988	0.4988	0.4989	0.4989	0.4989	0.4990	0.4990

KAPLAN PUBLISHING

Section 1

SECTION A-TYPE QUESTIONS

Note: All questions carry two marks

SYLLABUS AREA A – THE NATURE, SOURCE AND PURPOSE OF MANAGEMENT INFORMATION

ACCOUNTING FOR MANAGEMENT

1   **Which of the following statements are correct?**

(i)   Strategic information is mainly used by senior management in an organisation.

(ii)   Productivity measurements are examples of tactical information.

(iii)   Operational information is required frequently by its main users.

A   (i) and (ii) only

B   (i) and (iii) only

C   (ii) and (iii) only

D   (i), (ii) and (iii)

2   Reginald is the manager of production department M in a factory which has ten other production departments.

He receives monthly information that compares planned and actual expenditure for department M. After department M, all production goes into other factory departments to be completed prior to being despatched to customers. Decisions involving capital expenditure in department M are not taken by Reginald.

Which of the following describes Reginald's role in department M?

A   A cost centre manager

B   An investment centre manager

C   A revenue centre manager

D   A profit centre manager

3   Which of the following statements is NOT correct?

A   Cost accounting can be used for inventory valuation to meet the requirements of internal reporting only.

B   Management accounting provides appropriate information for decision making, planning, control and performance evaluation.

C   Routine information can be used for both short-term and long-run decisions.

D   Financial accounting information can be used for internal reporting purposes.

4   The following statements relate to financial accounting or to cost and management accounting:

(i)   Financial accounts are historical records.

(ii)   Cost accounting is part of financial accounting and establishes costs incurred by an organisation.

(iii)   Management accounting is used to aid planning, control and decision making.

Which of the statements are correct?

A   (i) and (ii) only

B   (i) and (iii) only

C   (ii) and (iii) only

D   (i), (ii) and (iii)

5   Which of the following statements is correct?

A   Qualitative data is generally non-numerical information

B   Information can only be extracted from external sources

C   Operational information gives details of long-term plans only

D   Quantitative data is always accurate

6   The manager of a profit centre is responsible for which of the following?

(i)   Revenues of the centre

(ii)   Costs of the centre

(iii)   Assets employed in the centre

A   (i) only

B   (ii) only

C   (i) and (ii) only

D   (i), (ii) and (iii)

7   **Which of the following would be best described as a short-term tactical plan?**

A   Reviewing cost variances and investigate as appropriate

B   Comparing actual market share to budget

C   Lowering the selling price by 15%

D   Monitoring actual sales to budget

8   **Which of the following relates to management accounts and which to financial accounts?**

	Management accounts	*Financial accounts*
Prepared yearly		
For internal use		
Contains future information		

9   The following statements refer to strategic planning:

(i)   It is concerned with quantifiable and qualitative matters.

(ii)   It is mainly undertaken by middle management in an organisation.

(iii)   It is concerned predominantly with the long term.

Which of the statements are correct?

A   (i) and (ii) only

B   (i) and (iii) only

C   (ii) and (iii) only

D   (i), (ii) and (iii)

10   The following statements relate to responsibility centres:

(i)   Return on capital employed is a suitable measure of performance in both profit and investment centres.

(ii)   Cost centres are found in manufacturing organisations but not in service organisations.

(iii)   The manager of a revenue centre is responsible for both sales and costs in a part of an organisation.

Which of the statements are incorrect?

A   (i) and (ii)

B   (ii) and (iii)

C   (i) and (iii)

D   All of them

11 **Indicate whether each of the following are ways that the management accountant helps the management of an organisation.**

	YES	NO
Control		
Plan		
Co-ordinate		
Make decisions		
Motivate		

12 A paint manufacturer has a number of departments. Each department is located in a separate building on the same factory site. In the mixing department the basic raw materials are mixed together in very large vessels. These are then moved on to the colour adding department where paints of different colours are created in these vessels. In the next department – the pouring department – the paint is poured from these vessels into litre sized tins. The tins then go on to the labelling department prior to going on to the finished goods department.

The following statements relate to the paint manufacturer:

(i)   The mixing department is a cost centre.

(ii)   A suitable cost unit for the colour adding department is a litre tin of paint.

(iii)   The pouring department is a profit centre.

Which statement or statements is/are correct?

A   (i) only

B   (i) and (ii) only

C   (i) and (iii) only

D   (ii) and (iii) only

SOURCES OF DATA

13 The following statements refer to qualities of good information:

(i)   It should be communicated to the right person.

(ii)   It should always be completely accurate before it is used.

(iii)   It should be understandable by the recipient.

Which of the above statements are correct?

A   (i) and (ii) only

B   (i) and (iii) only

C   (ii) and (iii) only

D   (i), (ii) and (iii)

14   **Which of the following describes secondary data?**

A   data that does not provide any information

B   data collected for another purpose

C   data collected specifically for the purpose of the survey being undertaken

D   data collected by post or telephone, not by personal interview

15   **Which of the following are primary sources of data and which are secondary sources of data?**

	Primary	Secondary
Data collected outside a polling station regarding voters choices		
An internet search for the cheapest fuel available in the area		
Government statistics on the levels of unemployment		
Data collected by observation on the number of cars flowing through a junction during peak travel hours		

16   When gathering information you would use both internal sources of information and external sources of information.

Which of the following are examples of external information?

(i)   Trade references.

(ii)   Sales representatives' knowledge.

(iii)   A credit agency report

(iv)   Bank references.

Options:

A   (ii) only

B   (ii), (iii) and (iv) only

C   All of the above

D   (i), (iii) and (iv) only

17   When gathering information on a potential client you can use both internal sources of information and external sources of information.

Which TWO of the following would be classified as internally generated information?

A   Supplier references

B   Credit reference agency reports

C   Sales information

D   Ratio calculations

18   **Which of the following descriptions only contains essential features of useful management information?**

   A   Accurate, understandable, presented in report format

   B   Timely, reliable, supported by calculations

   C   Regular, complete, communicated in writing

   D   Understandable, accurate, relevant for its purpose

19   **Which of the following describes 'Information'?**

   A   data that consists of facts and statistics before they have been processed

   B   data that consists of numbers, letters, symbols, events and transactions which have been recorded but not yet processed into a form that is suitable for making decisions

   C   facts that have been summarised but not yet processed into a form that is suitable for making decisions

   D   data that has been processed in such a way that it has a meaning to the person who receives it, who may then use it to improve the quality of decision making

20   **Which one of the following statements is correct?**

   A   Data is held on computer in digital form whereas information is in a form that is readable to human beings

   B   Information is obtained by processing data

   C   Data and information mean the same thing

   D   Data consists of numerical or statistical items of information

21   **Which of the following is an example of external information that could be used in a management accounting system?**

   A   Consumer price index statistics

   B   Price list for the products sold by the business

   C   Production volume achieved by the production department

   D   Discounts given to customers

22   **Which of the following would be classified as data?**

   A   Number of purchase requisitions

   B   Analysis of wages into direct and indirect costs

   C   Table showing variances from budget

   D   Graph showing the number of labour hours worked

23   **Which of the following are primary data?**

   (i)   Information on timesheets used for making up wages

   (ii)   Information from a government publication concerning forecast inflation rates used for budgeting

   (iii)   Information from a trade publication used to choose a supplier of raw materials

   A   (i) and (ii)

   B   (i) and (iii)

   C   (i) only

   D   (i), (ii) and (iii)

24   **Which one of the following is an example of internal information for the wages department of a large company?**

   A   A Code of Practice issued by the Institute of Directors

   B   A new national minimum wage

   C   Changes to tax coding arrangements issued by the tax authorities

   D   The company's employees' schedule of hours worked

25   **Identify which of the following statements about Big Data are true or false?**

	True	False
Big Data management involves using sophisticated systems to gather, store and analyse large volumes of data		
Data can be a variety of structured and unstructured formats.		
Big data does not include traditional data from internal sources such as sales history, preferences, order frequency and pricing information.		
Big Data does include information from external sources such as websites, trade publications and social networks.		

26   **Which TWO of the following are advantages of big data analysis?**

   A   Big data analysis allows companies to gain a variety of insights into customer behaviour

   B   Big data analysis can help to more accurately predict customer demand

   C   Demand forecasts based on big data analysis can be in terms of predicted volume demands but not the type of products required

   D   Companies cannot use the information to understand which products and features are most popular with customers.

27   Big data can be difficult to manage for a variety of reasons. These can be summarised using the 3 V's.

Which of the following correctly describes velocity?

A   The speed at which data is generated

B   The quantity of the data that is generated

C   The range of data that is generated

D   The accuracy of the data that is generated

28   **Which THREE of the following statements relating to Big Data are true?**

A   Big Data refers to any financial data over $1 billion

B   The defining characteristics of Big Data are Velocity, Volume and Variety

C   Managing Big Data effectively can lead to increased competitive advantage

D   Big Data contains both financial and non-financial data

29   Big data can be difficult to manage for a variety of reasons. These can be summarised using the 3 V's.

Which of the following correctly describes volume?

A   The speed at which data is generated

B   The quantity of the data that is generated

C   The range of data that is generated

D   The accuracy of the data that is generated

30   **Which THREE of the following are typical problems that organisations may face when dealing with Big Data?**

A   The increasing use of electronic devices within society at large

B   A lack of skills in the labour pool relating to the handling of Big Data

C   Legal and privacy issues if data is held about individuals

D   Measurement of metrics that have no use to the organisation

31   Big data can be difficult to manage for a variety of reasons. These can be summarised using the 3 V's.

Which of the following correctly describes variety?

A   The speed at which data is generated

B   The quantity of the data that is generated

C   The range of data that is generated

D   The accuracy of the data that is generated

PRESENTING INFORMATION

32 The following table shows that the typical salary of part qualified accountants in five different regions of England.

Area	Typical salary $
South-east	21,500
Midlands	20,800
North-east	18,200
North-west	17,500
South-west	16,700

Which diagram would be the best one to draw to highlight the differences between areas?

A   a pie diagram

B   a multiple bar chart

C   a percentage component bar chart

D   a simple bar chart

33 **A line graph is being produced to show the cost of advertising and sales revenue for a business. Which values would be shown on which axis?**

A   Both on the y-axis

B   Both on the x-axis

C   Cost of advertising on the x-axis and sales revenue on the y-axis

D   Sales revenue on the x-axis and cost of advertising on the y-axis

34 A pie chart is being produced to represent the sales from different regional offices of a business:

	$000
North	125
North West	180
East	241
South	691
South East	147
Total	1,384

What would be the angle of the East divisions section on the pie chart (to the nearest whole degree)?   ☐ °

---

35   The overhead cost of a business has been allocated and apportioned into the different cost centres. A pie chart has been used to present this information. The assembly department is represented by a section that has an angle of 45°. The total overhead cost is $800,000.

What is the value of the overhead that has been allocated and apportioned to assembly?

A $360,000

B $100,000

C $120,000

D $640,000

36   **XYZ produces three main products. Which would be the most appropriate chart or diagram for showing total revenue analysed into product revenue month by month?**

A   Scatter graph

B   Line graph

C   Pie chart

D   Component bar chart

37   The pie chart shows the sales volumes of 4 different products.

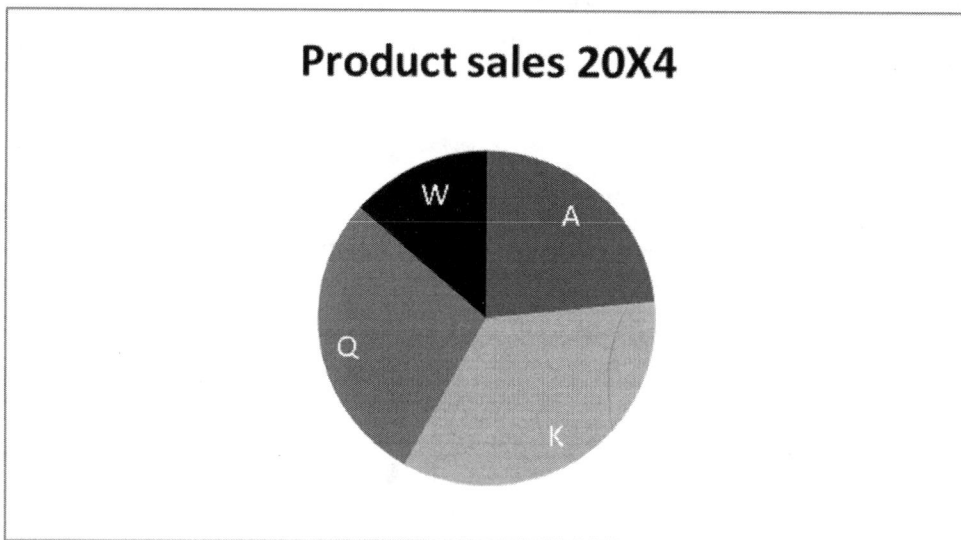

Product sales 20X4

If the products are ranked from largest sales volume to smallest sales volume what would be the correct order for the products?

A   K, Q, A, W

B   Q, K, A, W

C   K, A, Q, W

D   K, Q, W, A

38 **Which member of the sales team had the highest sales in February?**

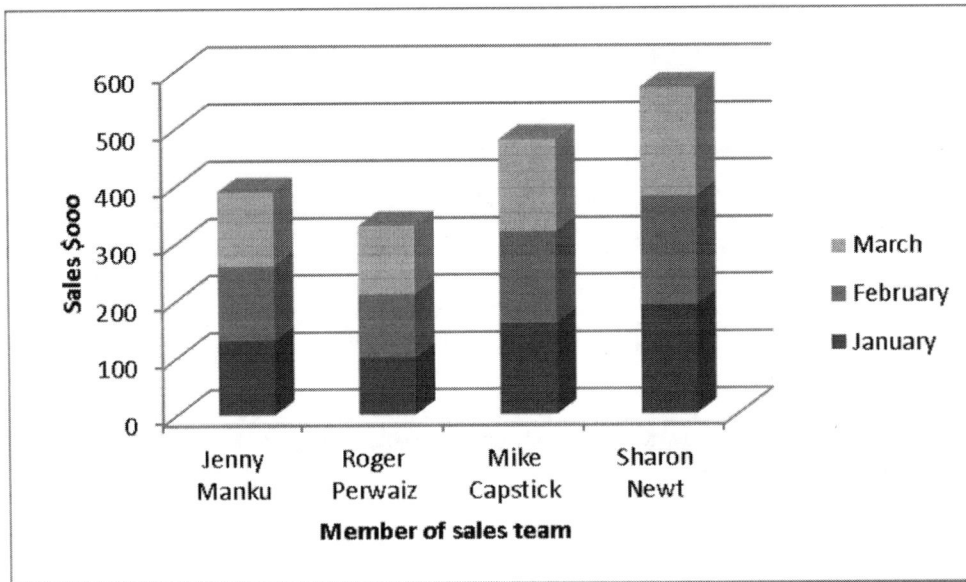

A   Jenny Manku

B   Roger Perwaiz

C   Mike Capstick

D   Sharon Newt

39 **Referring to the graph which statements are true and which are false?**

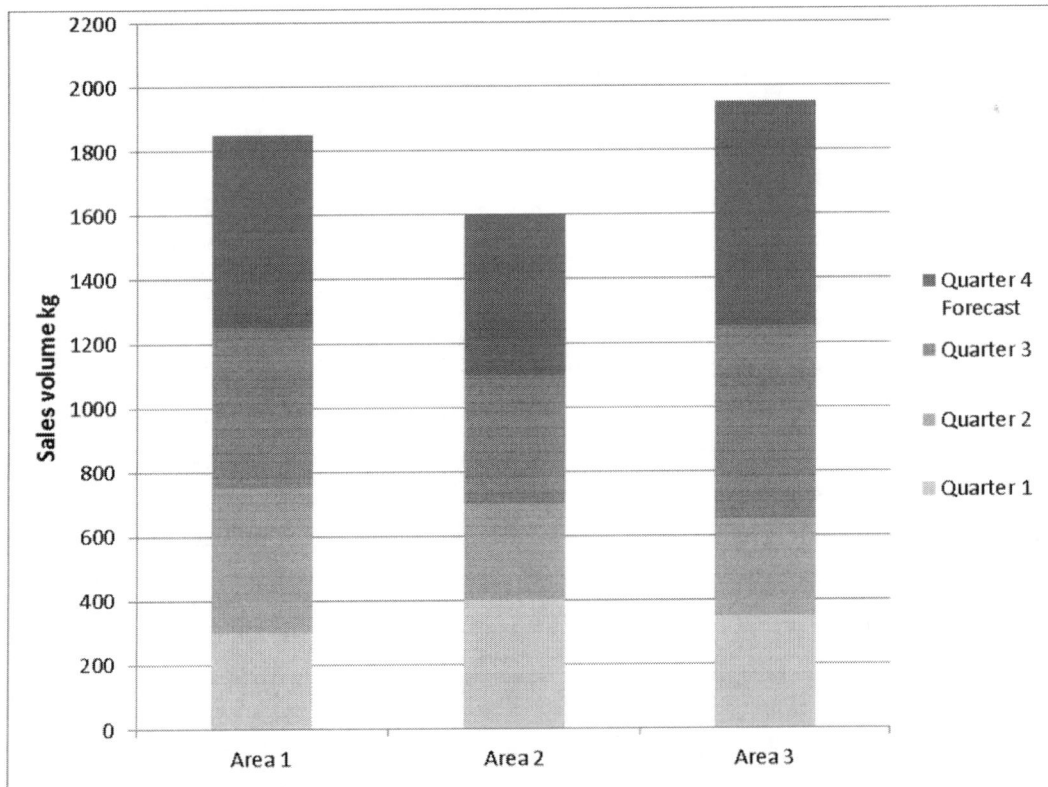

	True	False
Area 3 shows the best performance in Q3		
Area 2 sales are consistent quarter on quarter		
Q4 has the largest volume of sales across all areas		
Area 1 shows the best performance in Q2		

40 A farmer has land extending to 100 acres which comprises 43% wheat, 20% barley, 16% grass, 12% oats and 9% fallow.

If these figures were drawn in a pie chart, calculate the angle of the following crops (to the nearest whole number):

(a) Wheat

(b) Oats

COST CLASSIFICATION

41 The following diagram represents the behaviour of one element of cost:

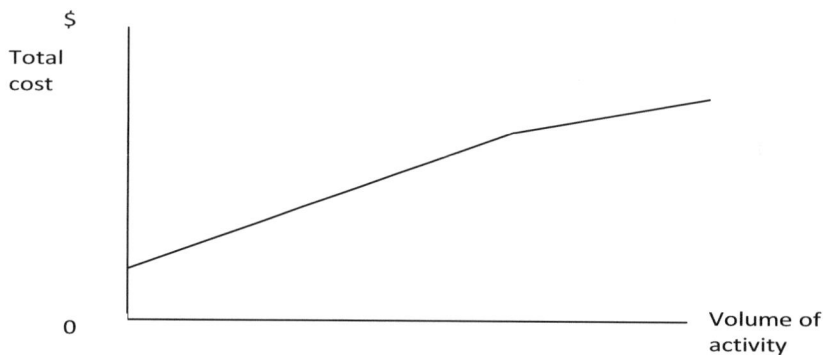

Which one of the following descriptions is consistent with the above diagram?

A Annual total cost of factory power where the supplier sets a tariff based on a fixed charge plus a constant unit cost for consumption which is subject to a maximum annual charge.

B Total annual direct material cost where the supplier charges a constant amount per unit which then reduces to a lower amount per unit after a certain level of purchases.

C Total annual direct material cost where the supplier charges a constant amount per unit but when purchases exceed a certain level a lower amount per unit applies to all purchases in the year.

D Annual total cost of telephone services where the supplier makes a fixed charge and then a constant unit rate for calls up to a certain level. This rate then reduces for all calls above this level.

42 An organisation has the following total costs at three activity levels:

Activity level (units)	8,000	12,000	15,000
Total cost	$204,000	$250,000	$274,000

Variable cost per unit is constant within this activity range and there is a step up of 10% in the total fixed costs when the activity level exceeds 11,000 units.

What is the total cost at an activity level of 10,000 units?

A $220,000

B $224,000

C $227,000

D $234,000

43 A firm has to pay a $0.50 per unit royalty to the inventor of a device which it manufactures and sells.

How would the royalty charge be classified in the firm's accounts?

A selling expense

B direct expense

C production overhead

D administrative overhead

44 Pliant plc produces cars and motorbikes. The company is split into four different divisions:

Car sales division – this department's manager has been given responsibility for selling the cars, as well as keeping control of the division's costs.

Motorbike sales division – this department's manager has been given responsibility for selling the motorbikes as well as controlling divisional costs. In addition, he has been told to plan what assets he should purchase for the coming year.

Manufacturing division – this division makes the cars and bikes and passes them to the finishing division. The divisional manager is only responsible for controlling the division's costs.

Finishing division – this division tests the cars and cleans them ready to be sold. They transfer the goods to the sales divisions and charge the sales divisions a set price, which is set by the finishing division's manager. The manager is also responsible for managing the division's costs as well as the investment in divisional assets.

Are these centres being operated as a cost, profit or investment centre?

Division	Cost centre	Profit centre	Investment centre
Car sales			
Motorbike sales			
Manufacturing			
Finishing			

45 **Which of the following can be included when valuing inventory?**

(i)   Direct material

(ii)   Direct labour

(iii)   Administration costs

(iv)   Production overheads

A   (i) and (ii) only

B   (i), (ii) and (iv)

C   (I), (ii) and (iii)

D   all of them

46 **Which of the following is usually classed as a step cost?**

A   Supervisor's wages

B   Raw materials

C   Rates

D   Telephone

47 **Which of the following is NOT a cost object?**

A   A cost centre

B   A customer

C   A manager

D   A product

48 **Which of the following describes depreciation of fixtures?**

A   Not a cash cost so is ignored in the cost accounts

B   Part of overheads

C   Part of prime cost

D   Is a cash outflow

49 **Which of the following costs would NOT be classified as a production overhead cost in a food processing company?**

A   The cost of renting the factory building

B   The salary of the factory manager

C   The depreciation of equipment located in the materials store

D   The cost of ingredients

50   **Which TWO of the following are included in the prime cost of a product?**

A   Direct material

B   Direct labour

C   Administration costs

D   Production overheads

51   There is to be an increase next year in the rent from $12,000 to $14,000 for a warehouse used to store finished goods ready for sale.

What will be the impact of this increase on the value of inventory manufactured and held in the warehouse?

A   an increase of $14,000

B   a decrease of $14,000

C   no change

D   an increase of $2,000

52   **Gilbert plc is a furniture manufacturer. How would he classify the following costs?**

Cost	Fixed	Variable	Semi-variable
Director's salary			
Wood			
Rent of factory			
Phone bill – includes a line rental			
Factory workers wage			

53   The diagram represents the behaviour of a cost item as the level of output changes:

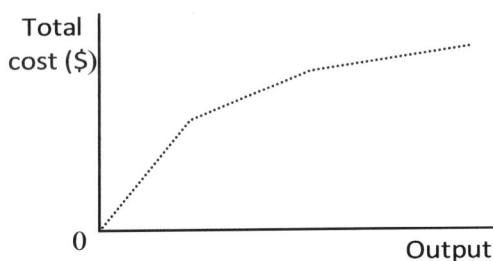

Which ONE of the following situations is described by the graph?

A   Discounts are received on additional purchases of material when certain quantities are purchased

B   Employees are paid a guaranteed weekly wage, together with bonuses for higher levels of production

C   A licence is purchased from the government that allows unlimited production

D   Additional space is rented to cope with the need to increase production

54   Bytes Limited operates an IT consultancy business and uses a coding system for its elements of cost (materials, labour or overheads) and then further classifies each element by nature (direct or indirect cost):

Element of cost	Code	Nature of cost	Code
Materials	A	Direct	100
		Indirect	200
Labour	B	Direct	100
		Indirect	200
Overheads	C	Direct	100
		Indirect	200

What would the codes be for the following costs?

Cost	Code
Salary of trainee IT consultant	
Planning costs to renew lease of the office	
Wages of the office manager	
Cleaning materials used by cleaner	

55   **How would a clothes retailer classify the following costs?**

Cost	Materials	Labour	Expenses
Designer skirts			
Heating costs			
Depreciation of fixtures and fittings			
Cashier staff salaries			

56   **Which of the following would be classified as direct labour?**

A   Personnel manager in a company servicing cars

B   Bricklayer in a construction company

C   General manager in a DIY shop

D   Maintenance manager in a company producing cameras

57   **Which of the following describes cost centres?**

A   units of product or service for which costs are ascertained

B   amounts of expenditure attributable to various activities

C   functions or locations for which costs are ascertained

D   a section of an organisation for which budgets are prepared and control exercised

58   The following data relate to two output levels of a department:

Machine hours	17,000	18,500
Overheads	$246,500	$251,750

What is the amount of fixed overheads?

$$\boxed{\$ \qquad}$$

59   A kitchen fitting company receives an invoice for sub-contractors who were used to connect the gas supply to a cooker installed in a new kitchen.

How would this invoice be classified?

A   Direct expenses

B   Indirect expenses

C   Direct labour

D   Indirect labour

60   A manufacturing company has four types of cost (identified as T1, T2, T3 and T4).

The total cost for each type at two different production levels is:

Cost type	Total cost for 125 units	Total cost for 180 units
	$	$
T1	1,000	1,260
T2	1,750	2,520
T3	2,475	2,826
T4	3,225	4,644

Which two cost types would be classified as being semi-variable?

A   T1 and T3

B   T1 and T4

C   T2 and T3

D   T2 and T4

61   **P Harrington is a golf ball manufacturer. Classify the following costs by nature (direct or indirect) in the table below.**

Cost	Direct	Indirect
Machine operators wages		
Supervisors wages		
Resin for golf balls		
Salesmen's salaries		

62 The following data relate to the overhead expenditure of contract cleaners at two activity levels:

Square metres cleaned	12,750	15,100
Overheads	$73,950	$83,585

Using the high-low method, what is the estimate of the overhead cost if 16,200 square metres are to be cleaned?

A $88,095

B $89,674

C $93,960

D $98,095

63 A company manufactures and sells toys and incurs the following three costs:

(i)   Rental of the finished goods warehouse

(ii)   Depreciation of its own fleet of delivery vehicles

(iii) Commission paid to sales staff.

Which of these are classified as distribution costs?

A   (i) and (ii) only

B   (ii) and (iii) only

C   (ii) and (iii) only

D   (i), (ii) and (iii)

64 A company incurs the following costs at various activity levels:

Total cost	Activity level
$	Units
250,000	5,000
312,500	7,500
400,000	10,000

Using the high-low method what is the variable cost per unit?

A $25

B $30

C $35

D $40

65   An organisation manufactures a single product. The total cost of making 4,000 units is $20,000 and the total cost of making 20,000 units is $40,000. Within this range of activity the total fixed costs remain unchanged.

What is the variable cost per unit of the product?

A $0.80

B $1.20

C $1.25

D $2.00

66   The total materials cost of a company is such that when total purchases exceed 15,000 units in any period, then all units purchased, including the first 15,000, are invoiced at a lower cost per unit.

Which of the following graphs is consistent with the behaviour of the total materials cost in a period?

A

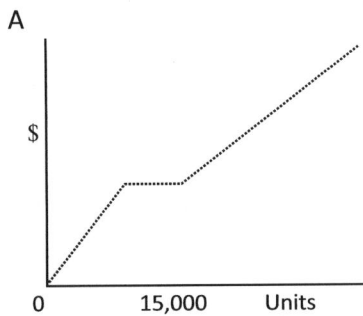

B

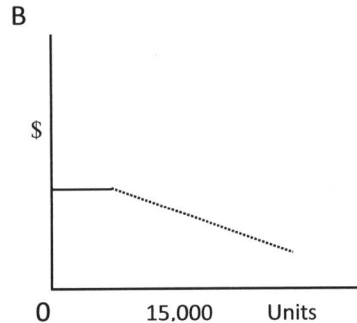

C

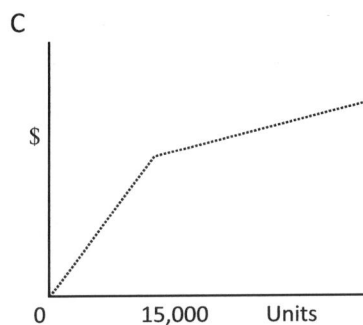

D

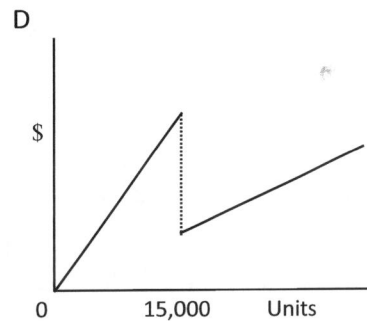

67   George plc makes stationery. How would he classify the following costs?

Cost	Production	Administration	Distribution
Purchases of plastic to make pens			
Managing director's bonus			
Depreciation of factory machinery			
Salaries of factory workers			
Insurance of sales team cars			

68 A supplier of telephone services charges a fixed line rental per period. The first 10 hours of telephone calls by the customer are free, after that all calls are charged at a constant rate per minute up to a maximum, thereafter all calls in the period are again free.

Which of the following graphs depicts the total cost to the customer of the telephone services in a period?

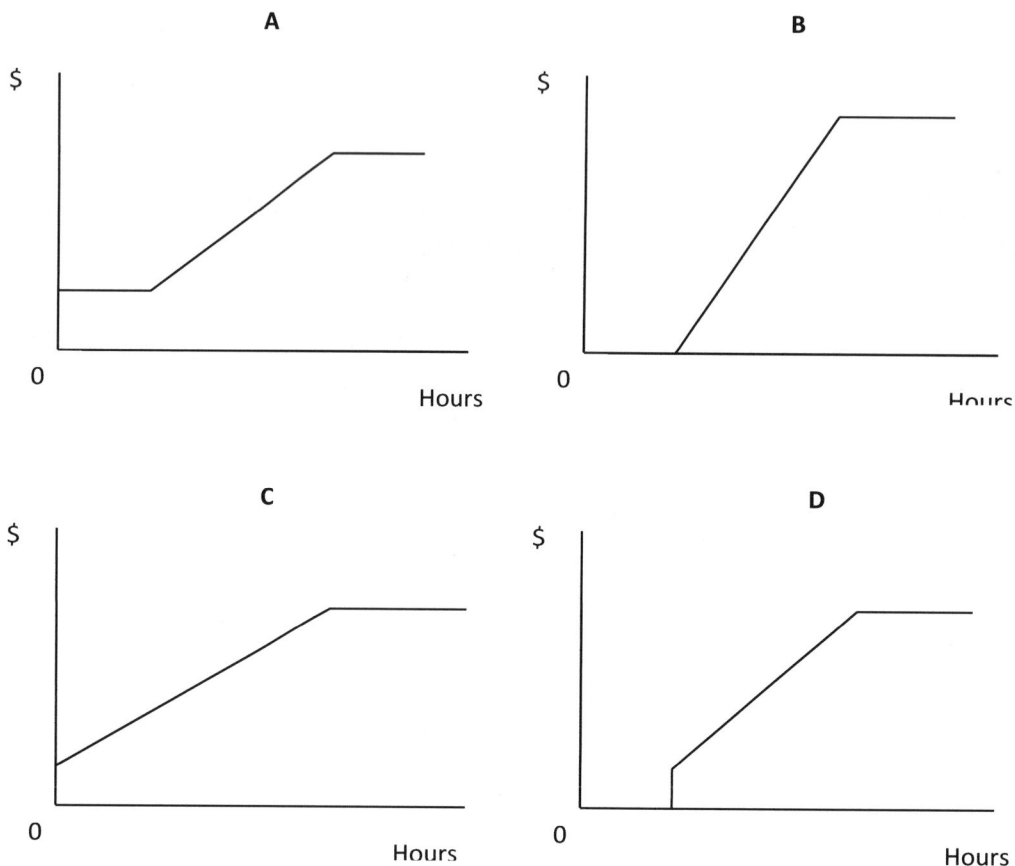

A

$

0

Hours

B

$

0

Hours

C

$

0

Hours

D

$

0

Hours

69 The following production and total cost information relates to a single product organisation for the last three months:

Month	Production units	Total cost $
1	1,200	66,600
2	900	58,200
3	1,400	68,200

The variable cost per unit is constant up to a production level of 2,000 units per month but a step up of $6,000 in the monthly total fixed cost occurs when production reaches 1,100 units per month.

What is the total cost for a month when 1,000 units are produced?

A $54,200

B $55,000

C $59,000

D $60,200

70   **Camberwell runs a construction company. Classify the following costs by nature (direct or indirect) in the table below.**

Cost	Direct	Indirect
Bricks		
Plant hire for long term contract		
Builders' wages		
Accountants' wages		

SYLLABUS AREA B – DATA ANALYSIS AND STATISTICAL TECHNIQUES

SAMPLING METHODS

71   **Which of the following statements describes the essence of systematic sampling?**

A   each element of the population has an equal chance of being chosen

B   members of various strata are selected by the interviewers up to predetermined limits

C   every nth member of the population is selected

D   every element of one definable sub-section of the population is selected

72   A firm which bottles shampoo selects some filled bottles for examination. The procedure used is to select a random starting point x (xth bottle filled) and every bottle at an interval of y is then chosen for examination.

What is this type of sampling known as?

A   Multi-stage

B   Random

C   Systematic

D   Stratified

73   The following statements are often made about 'simple random sampling'.

(i)   It ensures a representative sample.

(ii)   It eliminates selection bias.

Which of the following is always true?

A   (i) only

B   (ii) only

C   Both (i) and (ii)

D   Neither (i) nor (ii)

74   An accountant has to check a sample of invoices. The invoices are divided into three groups, by value as follows: 'under £100', '£100 – £500' and 'over £500'. Samples are then selected randomly from each group.

Which ONE of the following sampling methods is involved?

A   Cluster

B   Multi-stage

C   Quota

D   Stratified

75 **A sample of 10% of ACCA students is required. Which ONE of the following methods will provide the best simple random sample?**

A   Select every tenth ACCA student to arrive at their college/institute on one specific day.

B   Select randomly, using random number tables, one in ten of every ACCA class.

C   Select 10% of colleges/institutions providing ACCA courses, then from these choose all students who are registered with ACCA.

D   Select 10% of all students registered with ACCA, giving each a chance of 0.1 of being picked.

FORECASTING TECHNIQUES

76 The following information for advertising and sales revenue has been established over the past six months:

Month	Sales revenue	Advertising expenditure
1	155,000	3,000
2	125,000	2,500
3	200,000	6,000
4	175,000	5,500
5	150,000	4,500
6	225,000	6,500

Using the high-low method, which of the following is the correct equation for linking advertising and sales revenue from the above data?

A   Sales revenue = 62,500 + (25 × advertising expenditure)

B   Advertising expenditure = −2,500 + (0.04 × sales revenue)

C   Sales revenue = 95,000 + (20 × advertising expenditure)

D   Advertising expenditure = −4,750 + (0.05 × sales revenue)

77 **A company's weekly costs ($C) were plotted against production level (P) for the last 50 weeks and a regression line calculated to be C = 1,000 +250P. Which statement about the breakdown of weekly costs is true?**

A   Weekly fixed costs are $1,000, variable costs per unit are $5

B   Weekly fixed costs are $250, variable costs per unit are $1000

C   Weekly fixed costs are $1,000, variable costs per unit are $250

D   Weekly fixed costs are $20, variable costs per unit are $5

78 If a forecasting model based on total cost = fixed cost + variable costs is graphed, the equation is C = F+Vx and the intercept is $7,788. Total costs are $14,520 and x is 3,300.

What is the value of the slope, to two decimal places?

[   ]

79 The correlation coefficient (r) for measuring the connection between two variables (x and y) has been calculated as 0.6.

How much of the variation in the dependent variable (y) is explained by the variation in the independent variable (x)?

A   36%

B   40%

C   60%

D   64%

80 A company uses regression analysis to establish its selling overhead costs for budgeting purposes. The data used for the analysis is as follows:

Month	Number of salesmen	Sales overhead costs $000
1	3	35,100
2	6	46,400
3	4	27,000
4	3	33,500
5	5	41,000
	───	───
	21	183,000
	───	───

The gradient of the regression line is 4,200. Using regression analysis, what would be the budgeted sales overhead costs for the month, in $000, if there are 2 salesmen employed?

A   27,360

B   39,960

C   41,000

D   56,760

81 **Which of the following are correct with regard to regression analysis?**

(i)   In regression analysis the n stands for the number of pairs of data.

(ii) Σx^2 is not the same calculation as $(\Sigma x)^2$

(iii) Σxy is calculated by multiplying the total value of x and the total value of y

A   (i) and (ii) only

B   (i) and (iii) only

C   (ii) and (iii) only

D   (i), (ii) and (iii)

82   Regression analysis is being used to find the line of best fit (y = a + bx) from eleven pairs of data. The calculations have produced the following information:

$\Sigma x = 440$, $\Sigma y = 330$, $\Sigma x^2 = 17,986$, $\Sigma y^2 = 10,366$ and $\Sigma xy = 13,467$

What is the value of 'b' in the equation for the line of best fit (to 2 decimal places)?

83   An organisation is using linear regression analysis to establish an equation that shows a relationship between advertising expenditure and sales revenue. It will then use the equation to predict sales revenue for given levels of advertising expenditure. Data for the last five periods are as follows:

Period number	Advertising Expenditure $	Sales revenue $
1	17,000	108,000
2	19,000	116,000
3	24,000	141,000
4	22,000	123,000
5	18,000	112,000

What are the values of 'Σx', 'Σy' and 'n' that need to be inserted into the appropriate formula?

	Σx	Σy	n
A	$600,000	$100,000	5
B	$100,000	$600,000	5
C	$600,000	$100,000	10
D	$100,000	$600,000	10

84   The coefficient of determination (r^2) has been calculated as 60%.

What does this mean?

A   60% of the variation in the dependent variable (y) is explained by the variation in the independent variable (x)

B   40% of the variation in the dependent variable (y) is explained by the variation in the independent variable (x)

C   60% of the variation in the dependent variable (x) is explained by the variation in the independent variable (y)

D   40% of the variation in the dependent variable (x) is explained by the variation in the independent variable (y)

85 A company has recorded its total cost for different levels of activity over the last five months as follows:

Month	Activity level (units)	Total cost ($)
7	300	17,500
8	360	19,500
9	400	20,500
10	320	18,500
11	280	17,000

The equation for total cost is being calculated using regression analysis on the above data. The equation for total cost is of the general form 'y = a + bx' and the value of 'b' has been calculated correctly as 29.53.

What is the value of 'a' (to the nearest $) in the total cost equation?

A 7,338

B 8,796

C 10,430

D 10,995

86 Which of the following correlation coefficients indicates the weakest relationship between two variables?

A + 1.0

B + 0.4

C − 0.6

D − 1.0

87 Regression analysis is being used to find the line of best fit (y = a + bx) from five pairs of data. The calculations have produced the following information:

$\Sigma x = 129$ $\qquad$ $\Sigma y = 890$ $\qquad$ $\Sigma xy = 23,091$ $\qquad$ $\Sigma x^2 = 3,433$ $\qquad$ $\Sigma y^2 = 29,929$

What is the value of 'a' in the equation for the line of best fit (to the nearest whole number)?

A 146

B 152

C 210

D 245

88   L Co wants to be able to predict their overhead costs with more accuracy. The company accountant has analysed costs for the past six months:

Note: perform all calculations to the nearest $

	Production level (units)	Overhead costs ($)
January	10	3,352
February	10.5	3,479
March	12	3,860
April	9	3,098
May	9.5	3,225
June	10.25	3,416

Further analysis has revealed:

$\Sigma x = 61.25$ $\Sigma y = 20,430$ $\Sigma xy = 209,903$ $\Sigma x^2 = 630.56$

Use regression analysis, what is the variable cost per unit?

$ ☐

89   **Which of the following is a feasible value for a correlation coefficient?**

A   +1.2

B   0

C   −1.2

D   −2.0

90   **Which graph shows best the relationship between production levels and overhead costs for L Co?**

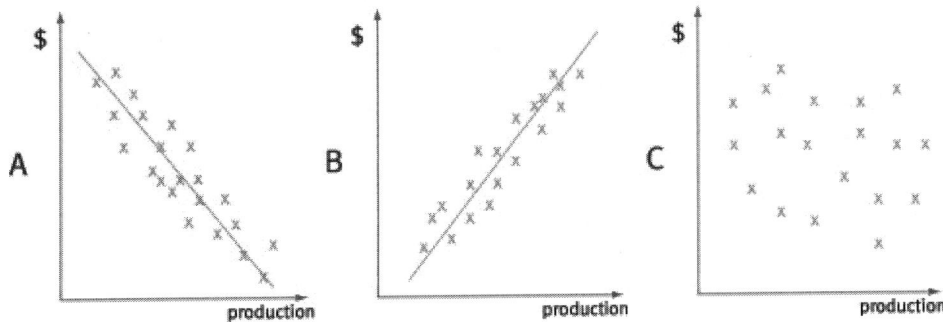

91 **What is the correct order for the stages of the product life cycle?**

(i)   Growth

(ii)   Decline

(iii)   Maturity

(iv)   Development

(v)   Introduction

A   (i), (v), (iii), (iv), (ii)

B   (v), (iv), (i), (iii), (ii)

C   (iv), (v), (i), (iii), (ii)

D   (iv), (i), (iv), (iii), (ii)

92 An inflation index and index numbers of a company's sales ($) for the last year are given below.

Quarter:	1	2	3	4
Sales ($) index:	109	120	132	145
Inflation index:	100	110	121	133

How are the 'Real' sales performing, i.e. adjusted for inflation?

A   approximately constant and keeping up with inflation

B   growing steadily and not keeping up with inflation

C   growing steadily and keeping ahead of inflation

D   falling steadily and not keeping up with inflation

93 Four years ago material X cost $5 per kg and the price index most appropriate to the cost of material X stood at 150. The same index now stands at 430.

What is the best estimate of the current cost of material X per kg?

A $1.74

B $9.33

C $14.33

D $21.50

94 Further analysis has shown that there is a price index applicable to the overhead costs:

	Production level (units)	Overhead costs ($)	Index
January	10	3,352	100
February	10.5	3,479	101
March	12	3,860	102
April	9	3,098	104
May	9.5	3,225	105
June	10.25	3,416	106

Using high low analysis, what is the variable cost per unit in June's prices?

$ [   ]

The following data are to be used for the next TWO questions

The managers of the catering division of a hospital wish to develop an index number series for measuring changes in food prices. As an experiment, they have chosen four items in general use which are summarised below:

	Prices per unit		Quantities	
	20X1	20X2	20X1	20X2
Flour (kgs)	0.25	0.30	8,000	10,000
Eggs (boxes)	1.00	1.25	4,000	5,000
Milk (litres)	0.30	0.35	10,000	10,000
Potatoes (kgs)	0.05	0.06	6,000	10,000

---

95 Calculate a weighted price index for 20X2 for these four products (with 20X1 as the base year) using the 20X1 sales quantities as weights.

A   118.3

B   119.6

C   119.9

D   129.9

96 Calculate a weighted quantity index for 20X2 for these four products (with 20X1 as the base year) using the 20X1 sales revenue as weights.

A   118.3

B   119.6

C   119.9

D   129.9

The following data are to be used for the next TWO questions

A company is preparing its forecast sales information for the end of the current year. The actual sales information for the first nine months of the current year (20X1) is below:

	Sales volume (units)
January	172,100
February	149,600
March	165,800
April	182,600
May	160,100
June	197,100
July	174,600
August	190,800
September	207,600

97 The sales volume trend is to be identified using a 5-point moving average.

What is the monthly trend?

A 50 units

B 500 units

C 5,000 units

D 50,000 units

98 **What is the expected sales volume including seasonal variation for December 20X1?**

A 206,040 units

B 211,040 units

C 222,480 units

D 199,600 units

99 **Which of the following are components of a time series analysis?**

(i) Trend

(ii) Seasonal variation

(iii) Cyclical variation

A (i) and (ii) only

B (i) and (iii) only

C (ii) and (iii) only

D (i), (ii) and (iii)

100 Two years ago the price index appropriate to the cost of material X had a value of 120. It now has a value of 160.

If material X costs $2,000 per kg today, what would its cost per kg have been two years ago?

A $1,500

B $1,667

C $2,667

D $3,200

101 A time series model of sales volume has the following trend and additive seasonal variation.

Trend

Y = 5,000 + 4,000 X.

Where Y = quarterly sales volume in units.

X = the quarter number (Where the first quarter of 2009 = quarter 17, the second quarter of 2009 = quarter 18 etc).

Seasonal variation

Quarter	Seasonal variation (units)
First	+3,000
Second	+1,000
Third	−1,500
Fourth	−2,500

What would be the time series forecast of sales units for the third quarter of 2010?

A   79,500

B   95,500

C   97,000

D   98,500

102 **Within time series analysis, which TWO of the following are concerned with long term movements/fluctuations in variables?**

A   Seasonal variations

B   Cyclical variations

C   Random variations

D   The trend

The following data are to be used for the next TWO questions

A company is preparing its annual budget and is estimating the cost of production. The company has the identified the following trend for the production of its product:

$y = a + bx$ where

y = number of units produced in a month

a = 3,000 units

b = 150 units

x = the month number (January 20X1 is month 1, February 20X1 is month 2, etc).

For the first 6 months of 20X1 the actual production, which was affected by seasonal variations, was as follows:

	Units produced
January	3,000
February	3,250
March	3,500
April	3,750
May	3,825
June	3,825

103 **What is the seasonal variation for March 20X1?**

 A   +50

 B   −50

 C   +75

 D   −75

104 **What is the expected production for March 20X2 after adjusting for the seasonal variation using the additive model?**

 A   5,250 units

 B   5,200 units

 C   5,300 units

 D   5,150 units

105 **The product life cycle model has 5 stages – for how many of the stages is it thought that a loss could be made?**

 A   1

 B   2

 C   3

 D   4

The following data are to be used for the next TWO questions

A company buys and uses five different materials. Details of the prices and quantities used for 20X1 and 20X2 are as follows:

Material	20X1 Quantity (000)	20X1 Unit price $	20X2 Quantity (000)	20X2 Unit price $
F	21	11	25	12
G	56	22	52	26
H	62	18	79	18
I	29	20	35	22
J	31	22	36	23

106 What is the weighted price index for 20X1 for these five products (with 20X2 as the base year) using the 20X2 sales quantities as weights?

    A   107.4

    B   89.3

    C   93.7

    D   108.2

107 What is the weighted quantity index for 20X1 for these four products (with 20X2 as the base year) using the 20X2 sales revenue as weights?

    A   107.4

    B   89.3

    C   93.7

    D   108.2

SUMMARISING AND ANALYSING DATA

The next two questions use the following data:

Some details from a frequency distribution of time taken in seconds to produce a particular product are given:

Time taken (mid-point)	f	fx	fx^2
107.5	2	215.00	23,112.50
112.5	5	562.50	63,281.25
117.5	4	470.00	55,225.00
122.5	8	980.00	120,050.00
127.5	10	1,275.00	162,562.50
132.5	5	662.50	87,781.25
137.5	4	550.00	75,625.00
142.5	2	285.00	40,612.50

108 **What is the mean of this frequency distribution?**

109 **What is the standard deviation of this frequency distribution?**

110 The mean weight of 10 parcels is 20KG. The individual weights in kilograms are:

15, x, 22, 14, 21, 15, 20, x, 18 and 27

What is the value of x?

111 **What are the correct words to complete the sentences?**

- The mean/median/mode is the value which appears with the highest frequency

- The mean/median/mode is calculated by adding all of the values and dividing the total by the number of values

- The mean/median/mode is the middle of a set of values

112 The following shows the number of orders placed by customers in the last period.

Number of orders	Frequency
1	3
2	5
3	10
4	14
5	8

What is the standard deviation of the above data?

THREE questions are based on the following data:

A sample of 12 packets of crisps taken from a box had the following weights in grams:

504, 506, 501, 505, 507, 506, 504, 508, 503, 505, 502, 504.

113   What is the mean weight?

    A   502.3

    B   503.4

    C   504.6

    D   505.7

114   What is the median weight?

    A   504.0

    B   504.5

    C   505.0

    D   505.5

115   What is the modal weight?

    A   504

    B   505

    C   506

    D   507

116   CDE runs a race track. The following numbers in seconds show the lap times of 40 drivers

126	120	122	105	129	119	131	138	130	112
125	127	113	112	130	122	134	136	142	106
128	126	117	114	120	123	127	140	135	122
124	127	114	111	116	131	128	138	116	127

CDE wishes to group the data into eight classes. The analysis has been started below but some figures are missing.

Complete the table below.

Time		Frequency
105 >	110	2
110 >	115	
115 >	120	4
120 >		7
125 >	130	
130 >	135	5
135 >		4
140 >	145	2

117 Consider the three averaging methods:

- Mean

- Median

- Mode

Match the following disadvantages with the method to which it relates:

A   Data has to be arranged in order of size which is time consuming

B   It may give undue weight or be influenced by extreme values

C   Data has to be arranged to ascertain which figure appears the most often

118 **Which TWO of the following are NOT features of a normal distribution?**

A   It is symmetrical

B   It is bell-shaped

C   The area under the curve is equal to 0.5

D   The mean is equal to the mode

E   The mean is above the median

119 **If the three possible outcomes of a decision are profits of $10, $50 or $80 with probabilities of 0.3, 0.3 and 0.4 respectively, what is the expected profit?**

A $40

B $44

C $47

D $50

120 A local council is considering purchasing a snow plough which could cost $20,000 per annum. This would save on outside contractors but the amount would depend on the severity of the winter weather

Weather	Annual savings	Probability
Severe	$40,000	0.2
Average	$20,000	0.5
Mild	$10,000	0.3

Based on the above figures, what is the cost or saving for the council if they bought their own plough?

$	saving/cost

121   **A new product is expected to generate the following profits or losses:**

Level of demand   Profit/Loss   Probability
High $100,000   0.1
Medium $50,000   0.5
Low $20,000 loss   0.4

What is the expected profit or loss from the new product?

$	profit/loss

The next TWO questions are based on the following data:

A group of workers have a weekly wage which is normally distributed with a mean of $360 per week and a standard deviation of $15.

122   **What is the probability that a worker earns less than $330?**

A   1.3%

B   2.3%

C   3.1%

D   4.6%

123   **What is the probability that a worker earns between $370 and $400?**

A   1%

B   15%

C   20%

D   25%

124   A baker produces four flavours of their best-selling cupcake (chocolate, vanilla, lemon and strawberry) in equal quantities. For quality checking purposes, one cake is selected from each batch of 100 cakes produced.

What is the probability that the cake selected is chocolate flavoured? | | % |

125   A company has compiled data on the number of items purchased by a customer in his last 7 orders:

10, 22, 3, 6, 17, 14, 19

Which TWO of the following statements are correct?

A   The arithmetic mean is 13

B   The median is 6

C   The arithmetic mean is 15

D   The median is 14

E   The arithmetic mean value is higher than the median value

126 X Company can choose from five mutually exclusive projects. The projects will each last for one year only and their net cash inflows will be determined by the prevailing market conditions. The forecast annual cash inflows and their associated probabilities are shown below.

Market conditions	Poor	Good	Excellent
Probability	0.20	0.50	0.30
	$000	$000	$000
Project L	500	470	550
Project M	400	550	570
Project N	450	400	475
Project O	360	400	420
Project P	600	500	425

Based on the expected value of the net cash inflows, which project should be undertaken?

A   L

B   M

C   N

D   P

127 Which of the following are disadvantages of using an expected value technique?

	Disadvantage of EVs?
Expected values only provides the most likely result	
It ignores attitudes to risk	
Only two possible outcomes can be considered	
Probabilities are subjective	
The answer provided may not exist	

128 A production manager has determined that when the equipment is working properly, the mean weight of items coming off a production line is 800g. The standard deviation is 12g

An item has just been taken from the production line at random and weighs 823g.

What is the percentage chance (to two decimal places) that an item would weigh 823g or more when the equipment is working properly?

%

129 A company has a normally distributed sales pattern for one of its products, with a mean of $110. The probability of a sale worth more than $120 is 0.0119

Using normal distribution tables, what is the standard deviation, to two decimal places, associated with sales?

A $4.41

B $4.42

C $4.43

D $4.44

130 The weights of a certain mass produced item are known, over a long period of time, to be normally distributed with a mean of 8kg and a standard deviation of 0.02kg.

If items whose weights lie outside the range 7.985 – 8.035kg are deemed to be faulty, what percentage of products will be faulty (to two decimal places)?

| % |

131 XYZ manufactures chemicals used in industry. It sells its chemical XX in 500 litre containers. The containers are filled automatically by specially designed equipment. Though testing a sample of filled containers it is found that the quantities follow a normal distribution and have a mean of 500 litres. Recent tests showed that 7% of containers contained more than 510 litres.

What is the standard deviation of the distribution?

A   6.76

B   10.52

C   14.80

D   35.41

132 A soft drink manufacturer bottles its products in 500 ml bottles. A review of one of the bottling machines showed that the mean amount in each bottle is 498ml, with a standard deviation of 0.9ml.

Adopting a normal distribution, what percentage of containers will contain more than the notional contents of 500ml (to 2 decimal places)?

| % |

133 A business has analysed its customer collection data and has found that a customer takes 37 days to pay on average with a standard deviation of 4 days.

Assuming the data follows a normal distribution, what is the probability that a customer will take longer than 47 days to pay (to 2 decimal places)?

| % |

SPREADSHEETS

134 **Which TWO of the following statements are true in relation to spreadsheets?**

A   A spreadsheet consists of records and files.

B   Most spreadsheets have a facility to allow data within them to be displayed graphically.

C   A spreadsheet could be used to prepare a budgeted statement of profit or loss.

D   A spreadsheet is the most suitable software for storing large volumes of data.

135 John has produced the following spreadsheet to calculate the correlation coefficient between average daily fruit and vegetable intake (measured in normal portions) and success in exams (number of passes above C grade).

	A	B	C	D	E	F
1	**Correlation**					
2		Vitamins	Exam			
3		**x**	**y**	**xy**	x^2	y^2
4		0	6			
5		1	5			
6		2	4			
7		3	4			
8		4	6			
9		5	7			
10		6	7			
11	**Totals**					
12						
13	**Correlation coefficient**		=			
14						
15						

What should the formula in cell D13 be?

A   (6*D11-B11*C11)/((6*E11-B11^2)*(6*F11-C11^2))^0.5

B   (7*D11-B11*C11)/((7*E11-B11^2)*(7*F11-C11^2))

C   (7*D11-B11*C11)/((7*E11-B11^2)*(7*F11-C11^2))^0.5

D   (6*D11-B11*C11)/((6*E11-B11^2)*(6*F11-C11^2))

136 **Which of the following are advantages of spreadsheet software over manual approaches?**

(i)   Security

(ii)   Speed

(iii)   Accuracy

(iv)   Legibility

A   All of them

B   (ii), (iii) and (iv)

C   (ii) and (iv)

D   (i) and (iv)

137 A company manufactures a single product. In a computer spreadsheet the cells F1 to F12 contain the budgeted monthly sales units for the 12 months of next year in sequence with January sales in cell F1 and finishing with December sales in F12. The company policy is for the closing inventory of finished goods each month to be 10% of the budgeted sales units for the following month.

Which of the following formulae will generate the budgeted production (in units) for March next year?

A   = [F3 +(0.1*F4)]

B   = [F3 − (0.1*F4)]

C   = [(1.1*F3) − (0.1*F4)]

D   = [(0.9*F3) + (0.1*F4)]

138 **Which of the following is not one of the main aspects of formatting cells?**

A   Wrapping text

B   Using graphics

C   Setting number specification, e.g. working to 2 decimal places

D   Changing the font, size or colour of text

SYLLABUS AREA C – COST ACCOUNTING TECHNIQUES

ACCOUNTING FOR MATERIALS

139 A manufacturing company uses 28,000 components at an even rate during the year. Each order placed with the supplier of the components is for 1,500 components, which is the economic order quantity. The company holds a buffer inventory of 700 components. The annual cost of holding one component in inventory is $3.

What is the total annual cost of holding inventory of the component?

$\boxed{\$}$

140 The following represent the materials transactions for a company for the month of December 20X6:

	$000s
Materials purchases	176
Issued to production	165
Materials written off	4
Returned to stores	9
Returned to suppliers	8

The material inventory at 1 December 20X6 was $15,000.

What is the closing balance on the materials inventory account at 31 December 20X6?

A $5,000

B $16,000

C $23,000

D $31,000

141 **Which of the following statements is correct?**

A   A stores ledger account will be updated from a goods received note only

B   A stores requisition will only detail the type of product required by a customer

C   The term 'lead time' is best used to describe the time between receiving an order and paying for it

D   To make an issue from stores authorisation should be required

142 **What is the correct description of perpetual inventory?**

A   The counting and valuing of selected items on a rotating basis

B   The recording, as they occur, of receipts, issues and the resulting balances of individual items of inventory

C   The recording of inventory that is constantly changing

D   The counting and valuing inventory on a regular (e.g. weekly) basis

143 **What would be the double entry for an issue of indirect production materials?**

A	Dr Materials control account		Cr Finished goods control account
B	Dr Production overhead control a/c		Cr Materials control account
C	Dr Work-in-progress control account		Cr Production overhead control a/c
D	Dr Work-in-progress control account		Cr Materials control account

144 **Which of the following documents would be completed in each situation?**

	Material Requisition	Purchase Requisition	Goods received note	Goods returned note
Material returned to stores from production				
Form completed by the stores department detailing inventory requirements				
Materials returned to supplier				
Form completed by stores on receipt of goods				
Form completed by production detailing inventory requirements.				

145 **Which of the following will be completed by a production department requiring new materials to be obtained from suppliers?**

A   A purchase order

B   A delivery note

C   A goods requisition note

D   A goods received note

146 **The following represent transactions on the material account for a company for the month of March 20X8:**

	$000s
Issued to production	144
Returned to stores	5

The material inventory at 1 March 20X8 was $23,000 and at 31 March 20X8 was $15,000.

How much material was purchased in March 20X8?

$

147   Which of the following procedures are carried out to minimise losses from inventory?

(i)   use of standard costs for purchases

(ii)   restricted access to stores

(iii)   regular stocktaking

A   (i) and (ii)

B   (ii) and (iii)

C   (ii) only

D   All of them

148   Appleby buys and sells inventory during the month of August as follows:

Opening inventory		100 units	$2.52/unit
4 August	Sales	20 units	
8 August	Purchases	140 units	$2.56/unit
10 August	Sales	90 units	
18 August	Purchases	200 units	$2.78/unit
20 August	Sales	180 units	

The periodic weighted average for the month is calculated as follows:

Total value of inventory (opening inventory plus purchase costs during the month) divided by total units (opening inventory plus purchase costs during the month).

Which of the following statements is true?

A   Closing inventory is $19.50 higher when using the FIFO method instead of the periodic weighted average.

B   Closing inventory is $19.50 lower when using the FIFO method instead of the periodic weighted average.

C   Closing inventory is $17.50 higher when using the FIFO method instead of the periodic weighted average.

D   Closing inventory is $17.50 lower when using the FIFO method instead of the periodic weighted average.

149   In the year ended 31 August 20X4, Aplus' records show closing inventory of 1,000 units compared to 950 units of opening inventory. Which of the following statements is true assuming that prices have fallen throughout the year?

A   Closing inventory and profit are higher using FIFO rather than AVCO

B   Closing inventory and profit are lower using FIFO rather than AVCO

C   Closing inventory is higher and profit lower using FIFO rather than AVCO

D   Closing inventory is lower and profit higher using FIFO rather than AVCO

150 Inventory movements for product X during the last quarter were as follows:

January	Purchases	10 items at $19.80 each
February	Sales	10 items at $30 each
March	Purchases	20 items at $24.50
	Sales	5 items at $30 each

Opening inventory at 1 January was 6 items valued at $15 each.

What would the gross profit be for the quarter using the weighted average cost method?

A $135.75

B $155.00

C $174.00

D $483.00

151 Your firm values inventory using the weighted average cost method. At 1 October 20X8, there were 60 units in inventory valued at $12 each. On 8 October, 40 units were purchased for $15 each, and a further 50 units were purchased for $18 each on 14 October. On 21 October, 75 units were sold for $1,200.

What was the value of closing inventory at 31 October 20X8?

$ [   ]

152 An organisation's inventory at 1 July is 15 units at $3.00 each. The following movements occur:

3 July 20X4	5 units sold at $3.30 each
8 July 20X4	10 units bought at $3.50 each
12 July 20X4	8 units sold at $4.00 each

What would be the closing inventory valuation at 31 July using the FIFO method of inventory valuation?

A $31.50

B $36.00

C $39.00

D $41.00

153 **In times of rising prices, the valuation of inventory using the First In First Out method, as opposed to the Weighted Average Cost method, will result in which ONE of the following combinations?**

	Cost of sales	Profit	Closing inventory
A	Lower	Higher	Higher
B	Lower	Higher	Lower
C	Higher	Lower	Higher
D	Higher	Higher	Lower

154 A company determines its order quantity for a component using the Economic Order Quantity (EOQ) model.

What would be the effects on the EOQ and the total annual ordering cost of an increase in the annual cost of holding one unit of the component in inventory?

	EOQ	Total annual ordering cost
A	Lower	Higher
B	Higher	Lower
C	Lower	No effect
D	Higher	No effect

155 A company uses the Economic Order Quantity (EOQ) model to establish reorder quantities. The following information relates to the forthcoming period:

Order costs = $25 per order

Holding costs = 10% of purchase price

Annual demand = 20,000 units

Purchase price = $40 per unit

EOQ = 500 units

No safety inventory is held.

What are the total annual costs of inventory (i.e. the total purchase cost plus total order cost plus total holding cost)?

A $22,000

B $33,500

C $802,000

D $803,000

156 Data relating to a particular stores item are as follows:

Average daily usage	400 units
Maximum daily usage	520 units
Minimum daily usage	180 units
Lead time for replenishment of inventory	10 to 15 days
Reorder quantity	8,000 units

What is the reorder level (in units) that avoids inventory stockouts?

units

157   A large store selling office furniture stocks a popular chair for which the following information is available:

Annual demand: 4,000 chairs
Maximum inventory: 75 chairs
Minimum inventory: 20 chairs
Lead time: 5 days
Re-order quantity: 100 chairs

What is the average inventory level?

A   75 chairs

B   70 chairs

C   55 chairs

D   47 chairs

158   **What is the economic batch quantity used to establish?**

A   Optimal reorder quantity

B   Optimal reorder level

C   Maximum inventory levels

D   Optimal quantity to be manufactured

159   **Which method of inventory valuation is being described?**

Characteristic	FIFO	LIFO	AVCO
Potentially out of date valuation on issues.			
The valuation of inventory rarely reflects the actual purchase price of the material.			
Potentially out of date closing inventory valuation.			
This inventory valuation method is particularly suited to inventory that consist of liquid materials e.g. oil.			
This inventory valuation method is particularly suited to inventory that has a short shelf life e.g. dairy products.			
This inventory valuation method is suited to a wheat farmer who has large silos of grain. Grain is added to and taken from the top of these silos.			
In times of rising prices this method will give higher profits.			
In times of rising prices this method will give lower profits.			
In times of rising prices this method gives a middle level of profits compared to the other two.			
Issues are valued at the most recent purchase cost.			
Inventory is valued at the average of the cost of purchases.			
Inventory is valued at the most recent purchase cost.			

160 A company manufactures a product in batches and then holds the items produced in finished goods inventory until they are sold. It is capable of replenishing the product at the rate of 100,000 units/year, but annual sales demand is just 40,000 units. The cost of setting up a batch production run is $1,500 and the cost of holding a unit of the product in inventory is $25/year.

What is the economic batch quantity for manufacturing this product?

A   2,191 units

B   2,828 units

C   4,472 units

D   10,954 units

161 **Which TWO of the following are included in the cost of holding inventory?**

A   The cost of insurance

B   The delivery costs

C   Rental payments on storage space

D   The cost of placing an order

162 A manufacturing company uses 25,000 components at an even rate during a year. Each order placed with the supplier of the components is for 2,000 components, which is the economic order quantity. The company holds a buffer inventory of 500 components. The annual cost of holding one component in inventory is $2.

What is the total annual cost of holding inventory of the component?

A $2,000

B $2,500

C $3,000

D $4,000

163 The purchase price of an inventory item is $42 per unit. In each three-month period the usage of the item is 2,000 units. The annual holding costs associated with one unit is 5% of its purchase price. The EOQ is 185 units.

What is the cost of placing an order (to 2 decimal places)?

$ [   ]

164 **Are the following statements true or false?**

Statement	True	False
In periods of rising prices, FIFO gives a higher valuation of closing inventory than LIFO or AVCO.		
In periods of falling prices, LIFO gives a higher valuation of issues of inventory than FIFO or AVCO.		
AVCO would normally be expected to produce a valuation of closing inventory somewhere between valuations FIFO and LIFO.		
FIFO costs issues of inventory at the most recent purchase price.		
AVCO costs issues of inventory at the oldest purchase price.		
LIFO costs issues of inventory at the oldest purchase price.		
FIFO values closing inventory at the most recent purchase price.		
LIFO values closing inventory at the most recent purchase price.		
AVCO values closing inventory at the latest purchase price.		

The following information applies to the next THREE questions

Point uses the economic order quantity (EOQ) model to establish the reorder quantity for raw material Y. The company holds no buffer inventory. Information relating to raw material Y is as follows:

Annual usage	48,000 units
Purchase price	$80 per unit
Ordering costs	$120 per order
Annual holding costs	10% of the purchase price

165 **What is the EOQ for raw material Y?**

 A   438

 B   800

 C   1,200

 D   3,795

166 **What is the total annual cost of purchasing, ordering and holding inventory of raw material Y?**

 A $3,849,600

 B $3,850,400

 C $3,853,600

 D $3,854,400

167 The supplier has offered Point a discount of 1% on the purchase price if each order placed is for 2,000 units.

What is the total annual saving to Point of accepting this offer?

A $29,280

B $30,080

C $37,200

D $38,000

168 A company uses components at the rate of 600 units per month, which are bought in at a cost of $2.24 each from the supplier. It costs $8.75 each time to place an order, regardless of the quantity ordered. The supplier offers a 5% discount on the purchase price for order quantities of 2,000 items or more. The current EOQ is 750 units. The total holding cost is 10% per annum of the value of inventory held.

What is the change in total cost to the company of moving to an order quantity of 2,000 units?

A $601 additional cost

B $730 additional cost

C $730 saving

D $601 saving

169 A company makes a component for one of its products in-house. It uses an average of 5,000 of these throughout the year. The production rate for these components is 500 per week and the cost of holding one item for the year is $1.50. The factory is open for 50 weeks per year. The company has calculated that the economic batch quantity is 2,000.

What is the production setup cost per batch?

A $213

B $240

C $480

D $960

170 **Which of the following is in the correct chronological sequence for sales documents?**

A   Enquiry – Order – Invoice – Payment

B   Order – Enquiry – Invoice – Payment

C   Enquiry – Order – Payment – Invoice

D   Enquiry – Invoice – Order – Payment

171 Which of the following is in the correct chronological sequence for purchase documents?

A   Purchase order – Invoice – Goods received note – Delivery note

B   Delivery note – Goods received note – Purchase order – Invoice

C   Purchase order – Delivery note – Goods received note – Invoice

D   Goods received note – Delivery note – Purchase order – Invoice

172 Which of the following describes a purchase order?

A   Issued by the purchasing department, sent to the supplier requesting materials

B   Issued by the stores department, sent to the purchasing department requesting materials

C   Received together with the materials and compared to the materials received

D   Issued by the production department, sent to the stores department requesting materials

173 Which TWO of the following statements describe the information a Goods Received Note (GRN) provides?

A   Information used to update inventory records

B   Information to check that the correct price has been recorded on the supplier's invoice

C   Information to check that the correct quantity of goods has been recorded on the supplier's invoice

D   Information to record any unused materials which are returned to stores

174 When charging direct material cost to a job or process, the details would be taken from which document?

A   Purchase requisition

B   Material requisition

C   Goods received note

D   Purchase order

175 Which TWO of these documents are matched with the goods received note in the buying process?

A   Invoice from supplier

B   Purchase order

C   purchase requisition

D   Stores requisition

176 The following relate to the management of raw materials:

(i) Holding costs per unit of inventory would increase

(ii) The economic order quantity would decrease

(iii) Average inventory levels would increase

(iv) Total ordering costs would decrease

Which of the above would result from the introduction of buffer (safety) inventory?

A (iii) only

B (ii) and (iii) only

C (ii), (iii) and (iv) only

D (i), (ii), (iii) and (iv)

177 **Which of the following is least relevant to the simple economic order quantity model for inventory?**

A Safety inventory

B Annual demand

C Holding costs

D Ordering costs

178 The following documents are used in accounting for raw materials:

(i) goods received note

(ii) materials returned note

(iii) materials requisition note

(iv) delivery note

Which of the documents may be used to record raw materials sent back to stores from production?

A (i) and (ii)

B (i) and (iv)

C (ii) only

D (ii) and (iii)

179 **Which of the following documents should be checked before a purchase invoice is paid, to confirm that the price and quantities are correct?**

	Price check	Quantity check
A	Purchase order	Purchase order
B	Goods received note	Delivery note
C	Purchase invoice	Goods received note
D	Purchase order	Goods received note

ACCOUNTING FOR LABOUR

180 The following statements relate to labour costs:

There would be an increase in the total cost for labour as a result of:

(i)   additional labour being employed on a temporary basis

(ii)   a department with spare capacity being made to work more hours

(iii)   a department which is at full capacity switching from the production of one product to another.

Which of the above is/are correct?

A   (i) only

B   (ii) only

C   (iii) only

D   (i) and (iii) only

181 A manufacturing firm is very busy and overtime is being worked.

What would the amount of overtime premium contained in direct wages normally be classed as?

A   part of prime cost

B   factory overheads

C   direct labour costs

D   administrative overheads

182 KL currently pays its direct production workers on a time basis at a rate of $6.50 per hour. In an effort to improve productivity, the company is introducing a bonus based on (time taken/time allowed) × time saved × rate per hour. The standard time allowed for a worker in the Assembly Department to perform this particular operation once has been agreed at 37.5 minutes.

In the first week of the scheme's operation, one employee worked for a total of 44 hours and performed 94 operations.

What are the gross wages for this employee based on a time rate of $6.50 per hour plus the productivity bonus based on (time taken/time allowed) × time saved × rate per hour, to 2 decimal places?

A $214.20

B $357.80

C $381.88

D $977.60

183 How would the cost be recorded in the cost ledger if the direct labour costs in a manufacturing company are $95,000?

A   Debit Work-in-progress $95,000, Credit Wages and salaries $95,000

B   Debit Wages and salaries $95,000, Credit Bank $95,000

C   Debit Wages and salaries $95,000, Credit Work-in-progress $95,000

D   Debit Bank $95,000, Credit Wages and salaries $95,000

184 How would the following labour costs be classified?

Cost	Direct	Indirect
Basic pay for production workers		
Supervisors wages		
Bonus for salesman		
Production workers overtime premium due to general pressures.		
Holiday pay for production workers		
Sick pay for supervisors		
Time spent by production workers cleaning the machinery		

185 Budgeted production in a factory for next period is 4,800 units. Each unit requires five labour hours to make. Labour is paid $10 per hour. Idle time represents 20% of the total labour time.

What is the budgeted total labour cost for the next period?

$

186 The following statements refer to situations occurring in Process Q of an organisation which operates a series of consecutive processes:

(i)   Direct labour is working at below the agreed productivity level.

(ii)   A machine breakdown has occurred.

(iii) Direct labour is waiting for work to be completed in a previous process.

Which of these situations could give rise to idle time?

A   (i) and (ii) only

B   (i) and (iii) only

C   (ii) and (iii) only

D   (i), (ii) and (iii)

187 A direct labour employee works a standard 37 hour week and is paid a basic rate of $15 per hour. Overtime is paid at time and a half. In a week when 40 hours were worked and a bonus of $20 was paid, what was the direct labour cost?

    A $555

    B $600

    C $622.50

    D $642.50

188 At 1 January a company employed 5,250 employees. Due to expansion the number of employees increased to 5,680 by 31 December. During the year 360 staff left the company and were replaced. What was the labour turnover rate?

    A   6.3%

    B   6.6%

    C   6.9%

    D   360 staff

The following information applies to the next THREE questions

A company records the following information concerning a product:

Standard time allowed per unit	16 minutes
Actual output in period	720 units
Actual hours worked	180
Budgeted hours	185

189 **What is the labour efficiency ratio?**

    A   93.75%

    B   97.3%

    C   102.5%

    D   106.7%

190 **What is the labour capacity ratio?**

    A   102.8%

    B   99.4%

    C   98.6%

    D   97.3%

191 **What is the production volume ratio?**

    A   97.3%

    B   102.5%

    C   103.8%

    D   106.7%

192   What is the hourly payment method being described?

Payment method	Basic rate	Overtime premium	Overtime payment
This is the amount paid above the basic rate for hours worked in excess of the normal hours.			
This is the total amount paid per hour for hours worked in excess of the normal hours.			
This is the amount paid per hour for normal hours worked.			

193   H&H operates an incentive scheme based on differential piecework. Employees are paid on the following basis:

Weekly output up to:	600 units	–	$0.40 per unit
	601–650 units	–	$0.50 per unit
	650 units +	–	$0.75 per unit

Only the additional units qualify for the higher rates.

In Week 17, an employee produced 660 units.

What would be the gross pay for the week?

A $260.40

B $272.50

C $325.75

D $488.25

194   Which of the following methods of remuneration is not an incentive-based scheme?

A   Straight piecework

B   Day rate

C   Group bonus

D   Differential piecework

195   A differential piecework scheme has a basic rate of $0.50 per unit. Output in addition to 500 units is paid at higher rates. The premiums over and above the basic rate, which apply only to additional units over the previous threshold, are:

Output (units)	Premium (per unit)
501–600	$0.05
above 600	$0.10

What is the total amount paid if output is 620 units?

A $317

B $318

C $322

D $372

SECTION A-TYPE QUESTIONS : **SECTION 1**

196 **Which remuneration method is being described?**

Payment method	Time-rate	Piecework	Piece-rate plus bonus
Labour is paid based solely on the production achieved.			
Labour is paid extra if an agreed level of output is exceeded.			
Labour is paid according to hours worked.			

197 **Which TWO of the following labour records may be used to allocate costs to the various cost units in a factory?**

    A   Employee record card

    B   Attendance record card

    C   Timesheet

    D   Job card

198 A business employs two grades of labour in its production department. Grade A workers are considered direct labour employees, and are paid $10 per hour. Grade B workers are considered indirect labour employees, and are paid $6 per hour.

In the week just ended, Grade A labour worked 30 hours of overtime, 10 hours on a specific customer order at the customer's request, and the other 20 hours as general overtime. Grade B labour worked 45 hours of overtime, as general overtime. Overtime is paid at time-and-one-half.

What would be the total amount of pay for overtime worked in the week that is considered to be a direct labour cost?

    A $50

    B $150

    C $285

    D $350

199 An employee is paid on a piecework basis. The scheme is as follows:

1 – 200 units per day	$0.15 per unit
201 – 500 units per day	$0.20 per unit
> 500 units per day	$0.25 per unit

Only the additional units qualify for the higher rates. Rejected units do not qualify for payment. An employee produced 512 units in a day of which 17 were rejected as faulty.

What wage is paid to the employee?

    A $128

    B $103

    C $99

    D $89

200   H&H employed on average 55 employees during the year. There had been 8 leavers all of whom were replaced.

What was the company's labour turnover ratio?

A   7.30%

B   8.50%

C   14.55%

D   17.00%

ACCOUNTING FOR OVERHEADS

201   A factory consists of two production cost centres (G and H) and two service cost centres (J and K). The total overheads allocated and apportioned to each centre are as follows:

G	H	J	K
$40,000	$50,000	$30,000	$18,000

The work done by the service cost centres can be represented as follows:

	G	H	J	K
Percentage of service cost centre J to	30%	70%	–	–
Percentage of service cost centre K to	50%	40%	10%	–

The company apportions service cost centre costs to production cost centres using a method that fully recognises any work done by one service cost centre for another.

What are the total overheads for production cost centre G after the reapportionment of all service cost centre costs?

$ [   ]

202   **What is an overhead absorption rate used for?**

A   share out common costs over benefiting cost centres

B   find the total overheads for a cost centre

C   charge overheads to products

D   control overheads

203 A factory consists of two production cost centres (P and Q) and two service cost centres (X and Y). The total allocated and apportioned overhead for each is as follows:

P	Q	X	Y
$95,000	$82,000	$46,000	$30,000

It has been estimated that each service cost centre does work for the other cost centres in the following proportions:

	P	Q	X	Y
Percentage of service cost centre X to	40	40	–	20
Percentage of service cost centre Y to	30	60	10	–

After the reapportionment of service cost centre costs has been carried out using a method that fully recognises the reciprocal service arrangements in the factory, what is the total overhead for production cost centre P?

A $122,400

B $124,716

C $126,000

D $127,000

204 A cost centre has an overhead absorption rate of $4.25 per machine hour, based on a budgeted activity level of 12,400 machine hours.

In the period covered by the budget, actual machine hours worked were 2% more than the budgeted hours and the actual overhead expenditure incurred in the cost centre was $56,389.

What was the total over or under absorption of overheads in the cost centre for the period?

A $1,054 over absorbed

B $2,635 under absorbed

C $3,689 over absorbed

D $3,689 under absorbed

205 **Which of the following situations would cause overheads to be over-absorbed?**

A   when absorbed overheads exceed actual overheads

B   when absorbed overheads exceed budgeted overheads

C   when actual overheads exceed budgeted overheads

D   when budgeted overheads exceed absorbed overheads

206 The management accountant's report shows that fixed production overheads were over-absorbed in the last accounting period.

What is the combination that is certain to lead to this situation?

A   production volume is lower than budget and actual expenditure is higher than budget

B   production volume is higher than budget and actual expenditure is higher than budget

C   production volume and actual cost are as budgeted

D   production volume is higher than budget and actual expenditure is lower than budget

207 **What would the accounting entries be for $10,000 of over-absorbed overheads?**

A   Dr   Work-in-progress control account   Cr   Overhead control account

B   Dr   Statement of profit or loss   Cr   Work-in-progress control account

C   Dr   Statement of profit or loss   Cr   Overhead control account

D   Dr   Overhead control account   Cr   Statement of profit or loss

208 During a period $50,000 were incurred for indirect labour.

What would the double entry be in a typical cost ledger?

A   Dr   Wages control   Cr   Overhead control

B   Dr   WIP control   Cr   Wages control

C   Dr   Overhead control   Cr   Wages control

D   Dr   Wages control   Cr   WIP control

209 Iddon makes two products, Pye and Tan, in a factory divided into two production departments, machining and assembly. In order to find a fixed overhead cost per unit, the following budgeted data are relevant.

	Machining	Assembly
Direct and allocated fixed costs	$120,000	$72,000
Labour hours per unit		
Pye	0.50 hour	0.20 hour
Tan	1.00 hour	0.25 hour

Budgeted production is 4,000 units of each product (8,000 units in all) and fixed overheads are to be absorbed by reference to labour hours.

What is the budgeted fixed overhead cost of a unit of Pye (to 2 decimal places)?

$ [   ]

210 **What is cost apportionment?**

A   The charging of discrete identifiable items of cost to cost centres or cost units

B   The collection of costs attributable to cost centres and cost units using the costing methods, principles and techniques prescribed for a particular business entity

C   The process of establishing the costs of cost centres or cost units

D   The division of costs amongst two or more cost centres in proportion to the estimated benefit received, using a proxy, e.g. square metres

211 A law firm recovers overheads on chargeable consulting hours. Budgeted overheads were $615,000 and actual consulting hours were 32,150. Overheads were under-recovered by $35,000. Actual overheads were $694,075.

What is the budgeted overhead absorption rate per hour (to 2 decimal places)?

A $20.21

B $20.50

C $21.59

D $22.68

212 A finishing department absorbs production overheads using a direct labour hour basis. Budgeted production overheads for the year just ended were $268,800 for the department, and actual production overhead costs were $245,600.

If actual labour hours worked were 45,000 and production overheads were over-absorbed by $6,400, what was the overhead absorption rate per labour hour?

A $5.32

B $5.60

C $5.83

D $6.12

213 A firm absorbs overheads on labour hours. In one period 11,500 hours were worked, actual overheads were $138,000 and there was $23,000 over-absorption.

What was the overhead absorption rate per hour (to 2 decimal places)?

$ [   ]

214 A factory has two production departments, X and Y, and two service departments C and D.

The following information costs relates to the overhead costs in each department.

	Manufacturing departments		Service departments	
	X	Y	C	D
Overhead costs	$5,000	$7,500	$3,200	$4,600
Proportion of usage of services of C	50%	40%	–	10%
Proportion of usage of services of D	20%	60%	20%	–

Using the reciprocal method of apportioning service department costs what is the total overhead cost allocated to department X?

A $5,000

B $7,520

C $8,106

D $12,195

215 The following budgeted and actual results relate to production activity and overhead costs in WX.

	Budget	Actual
Production overhead costs		
Fixed	$36,000	$39,000
Variable	$9,000	$12,000
Direct labour hours worked	18,000 hours	20,000 hours

An absorption costing system is used and production overhead costs are absorbed into output costs on a direct labour hour basis.

What is the total production overhead (both fixed and variable) during the period?

A   over-absorbed by $1,000

B   under-absorbed by $1,000

C   under-absorbed by $5,000

D   under-absorbed by $6,000

216 Lerna produces hydras in three production departments and needs to apportion budgeted monthly fixed costs between those departments. Budgeted costs are as follows:

	$
Rent	2,000
Rates	1,000
Plant insurance	1,000
Plant depreciation	10,000
Supervisor's salary	7,000
	———
	21,000
	———

The following additional information is available.

	Department A	Department B	Department C
Area (square feet)	3,800	3,500	700
Value of machinery ($000)	210	110	80
Number of employees	34	16	20

What is the total budgeted monthly fixed overhead cost for Department C?

A $1,837.50

B $4,462.50

C $7,000.00

D $10,600.00

217   The following information is available regarding the fixed overhead costs and output of the two production departments of a firm.

Department	S	T
Allocated or apportioned fixed overhead	$60,000	$100,000
Total cost of direct materials used	$120,000	$100,000
Total productive labour hours	5,000	10,000

A particular product has the following variable cost.

				$
Materials				
Department S	3 kg	@	$4 per kg	12
Department T	2 kg	@	$4 per kg	8
Labour				
Department S	½ hour	@	$10 per hour	5
Department T	1½ hours	@	$10 per hour	15
Variable overheads	1 hour	@	$5 per hour	5
				45

What is the fixed overhead cost per unit if fixed overheads are absorbed on the basis of departmental material cost?

A $5.50

B $12.00

C $14.00

D $21.00

ABSORPTION AND MARGINAL COSTING

218 PQR sells one product. The cost card for that product is given below:

	$
Direct materials	4
Direct labour	5
Variable production overhead	3
Fixed production overhead	2
Variable selling cost	3

The selling price per unit is $20. Budgeted fixed overheads are based on budgeted production of 1,000 units. Opening inventory was 200 units and closing inventory was 150 units. Sales during the period were 800 units and actual fixed overheads incurred were $1,500.

What was the total contribution earned during the period?

A $2,000

B $2,500

C $4,000

D $2,500

219 E operates a marginal costing system. For the forthcoming year, variable costs are budgeted to be 60% of sales value and fixed costs are budgeted to be 10% of sales value.

If E were to increase the selling price by 10% and all other costs and production and sales volumes were to remain the same what would be the effect on E's contribution?

A   a decrease of 2%

B   an increase of 5%

C   an increase of 10%

D   an increase of 25%

220 Last month a manufacturing company's profit was $2,000, calculated using absorption costing principles. If marginal costing principles had been used, a loss of $3,000 would have occurred. The company's fixed production cost is $2 per unit. Sales last month were 10,000 units.

What was last month's production (in units)?

units

221 A company produces and sells a single product whose variable cost is $6 per unit.

Fixed costs have been absorbed over the normal level of activity of 200,000 units and have been calculated as $2 per unit.

The current selling price is $10 per unit.

How much profit is made under marginal costing if the company sells 250,000 units?

A $500,000

B $600,000

C $900,000

D $1,000,000

222 A company manufactures and sells a single product. For this month the budgeted fixed production overheads are $48,000, budgeted production is 12,000 units and budgeted sales are 11,720 units.

The company currently uses absorption costing.

If the company used marginal costing principles instead of absorption costing for this month, what would be the effect on the budgeted profit?

A $1,120 higher

B $1,120 lower

C $3,920 higher

D $3,920 lower

223 When opening inventory was 8,500 litres and closing inventory was 6,750 litres, a firm had a profit of $62,100 using marginal costing.

Assuming that the fixed overhead absorption rate was $3 per litre, what would be the profit using absorption costing?

$ [   ]

224 A company has established a marginal costing profit of $72,300. Opening inventory was 300 units and closing inventory is 750 units. The fixed production overhead absorption rate has been calculated as $5/unit.

What was the profit under absorption costing?

A $67,050

B $70,050

C $74,550

D $77,550

225 Which of the following relate to marginal costing and which to absorption costing?

	Marginal costing	Absorption costing
The cost of a product includes an allowance for fixed production costs.		
The cost of a product represents the additional cost of producing an extra unit.		

The following data are for the next TWO questions

The budget for Bright's first month of trading, producing and selling boats was as follows:

	$000
Variable production cost of boats	45
Fixed production costs	30
	——
Production costs of 750 boats	75
Closing inventory of 250 boats	(25)
	——
Production cost of 500 sold	50
Variable selling costs	5
Fixed selling costs	25
	——
	80
Profit	10
	——
Sales revenue	90
	——

The budget has been produced using an absorption costing system.

226 What would the budgeted profit be if a marginal costing system were used?

    A $22,500 lower

    B $10,000 lower

    C $10,000 higher

    D $22,500 higher

227 Assume that at the end of the first month unit variable costs and fixed costs and selling price for the month were in line with the budget and any inventory was valued at the same unit cost as in the above budget.

However, if production was actually 700 and sales 600, what would be the reported profit using absorption costing?

    A $9,000

    B $12,000

    C $14,000

    D $15,000

228 A new company has set up a marginal costing system and has a budgeted contribution for the period of $26,000 based on sales of 13,000 units and production of 15,000 units. This level of production represents the firm's expected long-term level of production. The company's budgeted fixed production costs are $3,000 for the period.

What would the budgeted profit be if the company were to change to an absorption costing system?

A $22,600

B $23,400

C $25,600

D $26,400

229 **Which of these statements are true of marginal costing?**

(i)   The contribution per unit will be constant if the sales volume increases.

(ii)   There is no under- or over-absorption of overheads.

(iii) Marginal costing does not provide useful information for decision making.

A   (i) and (ii) only

B   (ii) and (iii) only

C   (ii) only

D   (i), (ii) and (iii)

230 In a period, a company had opening inventory of 31,000 units of Product G and closing inventory of 34,000 units. Profits based on marginal costing were $850,500 and profits based on absorption costing were $955,500.

If the budgeted fixed costs for the company for the period were $1,837,500, what was the budgeted level of activity?

A   24,300 units

B   27,300 units

C   52,500 units

D   65,000 units

231 In a given period, the production level of an item exactly matches the level of sales.

How would the profit differ if marginal or absorption costing was used?

A   There would not be a difference

B   It would be higher under absorption costing

C   It would be lower under absorption costing

D   It would be higher under marginal costing

232 For a product that has a positive unit contribution, which of the following events would tend to increase total contribution by the greatest amount?

 A   10% decrease in variable cost

 B   10% increase in selling price

 C   10% increase in volume sold

 D   15% decrease in total fixed costs

233 Exp has compiled the following standard cost card for its main product.

	$
Production costs	
Fixed	33.00
Variable	45.10
Selling costs	
Fixed	64.00
Variable	7.20
Profit	14.70
	————
Selling price	164.00
	————

What would the closing inventory be valued at under an absorption costing system (to 2 decimal places)?

$ [   ]

COST ACCOUNTING METHODS

234 A company operates a job costing system. Job 812 requires $60 of direct materials, $40 of direct labour and $20 of direct expenses. Direct labour is paid $8 per hour. Production overheads are absorbed at a rate of $16 per direct labour hour and non-production overheads are absorbed at a rate of 60% of prime cost.

What is the total cost of Job 812?

 A $240

 B $260

 C $272

 D $320

235 Which one of the following statements is incorrect?

 A   Job costs are collected separately, whereas process costs are averages

 B   In job costing the progress of a job can be ascertained from the materials requisition notes and job tickets or time sheet

 C   In process costing information is needed about work passing through a process and work remaining in each process

 D   In process costing, but not job costing, the cost of normal loss will be incorporated into normal product costs

The following data are to be used for the next TWO questions

A firm uses job costing and recovers overheads on a direct labour cost basis.

Three jobs were worked on during a period, the details of which were:

	Job 1	Job 2	Job 3
	$	$	$
Opening work-in-progress	8,500	0	46,000
Material in period	17,150	29,025	0
Labour for period	12,500	23,000	4,500

The overheads for the period were exactly as budgeted, $140,000. Actual labour costs were also the same as budgeted.

Jobs 1 and 2 were the only incomplete jobs at the end of the period.

236 **What was the value of closing work-in-progress?**

   A $81,900

   B $90,175

   C $140,675

   D $214,425

237 Job 3 was completed during the period and consisted of 2,400 identical circuit boards. The firm adds 50% to total production costs to arrive at a selling price.

   What is the selling price of a circuit board?

   A   It cannot be calculated without more information

   B $31.56

   C $41.41

   D $58.33

238 A company uses process costing to value output. During the last month the following information was recorded:

Output:	2,800 kg valued at $7.50/kg
Normal loss:	300 kg which has a scrap value of $3/kg
Abnormal gain:	100 kg

   What was the value of the input?

   $ [   ]

239 ABC manufactures product X in a single process. Normal loss (scrap) in the process is 10% of output and scrapped units can be sold off for $4/unit.

In period 8 there was no opening inventory and no closing inventory. Process costs of direct materials, direct labour and production overheads totalled $184,800. Input to the process in the month was 13,200 units.

What was the cost/unit produced?

A $12.50

B $15.00

C $15.15

D $15.40

240 A company uses process costing to value its output. The following was recorded for the period:

Input materials	2,000 units at $4.50 per unit
Conversion costs	$13,340
Normal loss	5% of input valued at $3 per unit
Abnormal loss	150 units

There were no opening or closing inventories.

What was the valuation of one unit of output (to 2 decimal places)?

$ [   ]

241 A company that operates a process costing system had work-in-progress at the start of last month of 300 units (valued at $1,710) that were 60% complete in respect of all costs.

Last month a total of 2,000 units were completed and transferred to the finished goods warehouse. The cost per equivalent unit for costs arising last month was $10. The company uses the FIFO method of cost allocation.

What was the total value of the 2,000 units transferred to the finished goods warehouse last month?

A $19,910

B $20,000

C $20,510

D $21,710

242 Vare produces various inks at its Normanton factory. Production details for Process 1 are as follows:

Opening work-in-progress, 1 April	400 units	60% complete
Closing work-in-progress, 30 April	600 units	20% complete
Units started	1,000	
Units finished	800	

The degree of completion quoted relates to labour and overhead costs. Three-quarters of the materials are added at the start of the process and the remaining quarter added when the process is 50% complete. The company uses the FIFO method of cost allocation.

What are the equivalent units of production for materials in the period?

A 1,250

B 1,000

C 850

D 680

243 Two products W and X are created from a joint process. Both products can be sold immediately after split-off. There are no opening inventories or work-in-progress. The following information is available for the last period:

Total joint production costs $776,160

Product	Production units	Sales units	Selling price per unit
W	12,000	10,000	$10
X	10,000	8,000	$12

Using the sales value method of apportioning joint production costs, what was the value of the closing inventory of product X for the last period?

$ [   ]

244 In a process where there are no work-in-progress inventories, two joint products (J and K) are created. Information (in units) relating to last month is as follows:

Product	Sales	Opening inventory of finished goods	Closing inventory of finished goods
J	6,000	100	300
K	4,000	400	200

Joint production costs last month were $110,000 and these were apportioned to joint products based on the number of units produced.

What were the joint production costs apportioned to product J for last month?

A $63,800

B $64,000

C $66,000

D $68,200

245 Charleville operates a continuous process producing three products and one by-product. Output from the process for a month was as follows:

Product	Selling price per unit	Units of output from process
1	$18	10,000
2	$25	20,000
3	$20	20,000
4 (by-product)	$2	3,500

Total joint costs were $277,000.

What was the unit cost valuation for product 3 using the sales revenue basis for allocating joint costs assuming that the revenue receivable from the by-product is deducted from the joint costs?

A $4.70

B $4.80

C $5.00

D $5.10

246 A business operates a job costing system and prices its jobs by adding 20% to the total cost of the job. The prime cost of a job was $6,840 and it had used 156 direct labour hours. The fixed production overheads are absorbed on the basis of direct labour hours. The budgeted overhead absorption rate was based upon a budgeted fixed overhead of $300,000 and total budgeted direct labour hours of 60,000.

What should the job be sold for?

A $7,620

B $8,382

C $9,144

D $9,525

247 **If there are abnormal losses in a process how is this recorded in a process account?**

A debit with the scrap value of the abnormal loss units

B debit with the full production cost of the abnormal loss units

C credit with the scrap value of the abnormal loss units

D credit with the full production cost of the abnormal loss units

248 X uses process costing. In Process 3 the normal loss is 4% of total input.

Last period the input from Process 2 was 8,500 kg and additional material of 4,250 kg was added to process 3.

Actual output to finished goods was 12,700 kg.

There was no opening or closing work-in-progress in the period.

What was the abnormal gain or loss in kg for period 3?

A   460 kg gain

B   460 kg loss

C   290 kg gain

D   290 kg loss

249 A chemical process has a normal wastage of 10% of input. In a period, 2,500 kg of material were input and there was an abnormal loss of 75 kg.

What was the quantity of good production?

A   2,175 kg

B   2,250 kg

C   2,325 kg

D   2,675 kg

250 A company operates a job costing system.

Job number 605 requires $300 of direct materials and $400 of direct labour. Direct labour is paid at the rate of $8 per hour. Production overheads are absorbed at a rate of $26 per direct labour hour and non-production overheads are absorbed at a rate of 120% of prime cost.

What is the total cost of job number 605?

A $2,000

B $2,400

C $2,840

D $4,400

251 A factory manufactures model cars. During October work commenced on 110,000 new cars. This was in addition to 20,000 that were 50% complete at the start of the month. At the end of October there were 40,000 cars that were 50% complete.

Costs for October were:

	$000
Brought forward	11,000
Incurred this period	121,000
	$132,000

If this factory chooses the weighted average method of spreading costs, what is the cost per car for October production?

A $1,100

B $1,200

C $1,210

D $1,320

252 In a production process the percentage completion of the work-in-progress (WIP) at the end of a period is found to have been understated.

When this is corrected what will be the effect on the cost per unit and the total value of the WIP?

	Cost per unit	Total value of WIP
A	Decrease	Decrease
B	Decrease	Increase
C	Increase	Decrease
D	Increase	Increase

253 The following information is available for a production process for the last period:

Material input	200 kg at $4 per kg
Labour input	100 hours at $15 per hour
Department overhead	$1,000
Transfer to finished goods	150 kg

Normal loss is 10% of input. Losses are identified when the process is 50% complete.

There is no opening or closing work-in-progress.

What is the total cost of a completed unit?

A $22.00

B $20.48

C $19.59

D $18.33

254 At the start of the month, there were 2,000 units of work-in-progress in a factory. During the month, 12,000 units were started. At the end of the month, 3,000 units were in closing work in progress. The degree of completion of opening work-in-progress was 70% and closing work in progress was 20%.

How many equivalent units of production were achieved during the month if FIFO were used?

EU

255 The following information is available for a production process for the last period:

Material input	200 kg at $6 per kg
Labour and overhead input	$3,500
Transfer to finished goods	190 kg

Normal loss is 15% of input and has a scrap value of $1 per kg.

There is no opening or closing work-in-progress.

What is the value of the finished output for the period (to the nearest $)?

A $4,465

B $4,670

C $5,219

D $5,253

256   **Which of the following are features of process costing?**

(i)   Homogeneous products

(ii)   Customer-driven production

(iii)   Finished goods are valued at an average cost per unit

A   (i) and (iii)

B   (ii) and (iii)

C   (iii) only

D   (i) only

257   A builder has produced a quote for some alterations. The price is made up as follows:

		$
Direct materials	100 kg @ $4 per kg	400
Direct labour	5 hours @ $10 per hour	50
	15 hours @ $5 per hour	75
Hire of machine	1 day @ $100 per day	100
Overheads	20 hours @ $8 per hour	160
		———
Total cost		785
Profit @ 20% of cost 0.2 × $785		157
		———
Price quoted		$942

Actual costs for the job were as follows:

Direct materials	120 kg @ $4 per kg
Direct labour	3 hours @ $10 per hour
	20 hours @ $5 per hour
Hire of machine	2 days @ $100 per day

What was the actual profit/(loss) made on the job?

A $52 loss

B $28 loss

C $28 profit

D $52 profit

258 A business operates a job costing system and prices its jobs by adding 10% to the total cost of the job. The prime cost of a job was $2,840 and it had used 45 direct labour hours. The fixed production overheads are absorbed on the basis of direct labour hours. The budgeted overhead absorption rate was based upon a budgeted fixed overhead of $5,000 and total budgeted direct labour hours of 500.

What should the job be sold for?

A $3,124

B $3,290

C $3,619

D $3,656

259 A company operates a job costing system. Job 874 requires 110 hours of labour at $8 per hour. Materials and other expenses amount to $1,700. There are 3 employees whose basic hours are 30 hours a week. All work is to be completed in one week at the specific request of the customer. Overtime is paid at time and a quarter.

What is the total direct labour cost of Job 874?

A $880

B $920

C $2,580

D $2,620

260 **Which of the following would be considered a service industry?**

(i)   An airline company

(ii)   A railway company

(iii) A firm of accountants

A   (i) and (ii) only

B   (ii) and (iii) only

C   (i) and (iii) only

D   All of them

261   **Which TWO of the following are characteristics of service costing?**

   A   High levels of indirect costs as a proportion of total cost

   B   Use of equivalent units

   C   Use of composite cost units

   D   Long timescale from commencement to completion of the cost unit

262   **Which of the following is NOT likely to be used in a hospital run by a charitable foundation?**

   A   Cost per patient

   B   Cost per bed-day

   C   Bed throughput

   D   Profit per patient

263   A hotel calculates a number of statistics including average cost per occupied bed per day.

   The following information is provided for a 30-day period.

	Rooms with twin beds	Single rooms
Number of rooms in hotel	260	70
Number of rooms available to let	240	40
Average number of rooms occupied daily	200	30
Number of guests in period	6,450	
Average length of stay	2 days	
Payroll costs for period	$100,000	
Cost of cleaning supplies in period	$5,000	
Total cost of laundering in period	$22,500	

   What is the average cost per occupied bed per day for the period?

   A $9.90

   B $9.88

   C $7.20

   D $8.17

264 The following figures relate to two electricity supply companies.

Meter reading, billing and collection costs

	Company A	Company B
Total cost ($000)	600	1,000
Units sold (millions)	2,880	9,600
Number of consumers (thousands)	800	1,600
Sales of electricity (millions)	$18	$50

What do the figures given indicate?

A   Company A is more efficient than Company B

B   Company A is less efficient than Company B

C   Company A and Company B are as efficient as each other

D   That neither company is efficient

265 A hotel calculates a number of statistics including average room occupancy.

Average room occupancy is calculated as the total number of rooms occupied as a percentage of rooms available to let.

The following information is provided for a 30-day period.

	Rooms with twin beds	Single rooms
Number of rooms in hotel	260	70
Number of rooms available to let	240	40
Average number of rooms occupied daily	200	30

What is the average room occupancy?

A   69.7%

B   82.1%

C   82.7%

D   84.8%

266 **Which of the following are features of service organisations?**

(i)   High levels of inventory

(ii)   High proportion of fixed costs

(iii)   Difficulty in identifying suitable cost units

A   (i) and (ii) only

B   (i) and (iii) only

C   (ii) and (iii) only

D   All of these

ALTERNATIVE COSTING PRINCIPLES

267 **Which ONE of the following is an advantage of Activity Based Costing?**

A   It provides more accurate product costs

B   It is simple to apply

C   It is a form of marginal costing and so is relevant to decision making

D   It is particularly useful when fixed overheads are very low

268 **Quality control costs can be categorised into internal and external failure costs, inspection costs and prevention costs. In which of these four classifications would the following costs be included?**

- The cost of a customer service team
- The cost of equipment maintenance
- The cost of operating test equipment

	Internal failure costs	External failure costs	Inspection costs	Prevention costs
Cost of a customer service team				
Cost of equipment maintenance				
Cost of operating test equipment				

269 **In the context of quality costs, what would customer compensation costs and test equipment running costs be classified as?**

	Customer compensation costs	*Test equipment running costs*
A	Internal failure costs	Prevention costs
B	Internal failure costs	Appraisal costs
C	External failure costs	Appraisal costs
D	External failure costs	Prevention costs

270 The selling price of product K is set at $450 for each unit and the company requires a return of 20% from the product.

What is the target cost for each unit for the coming year?

A $300

B $360

C $400

D $450

271 In calculating the life cycle costs of a product, which of the following items would be excluded?

(i)   Planning and concept design costs

(ii)   Preliminary and detailed design costs

(iii)   Testing costs

(iv)   Production costs

(v)   Distribution and customer service costs

A   (iii)

B   (iv)

C   (v)

D   None of them

272 As part of a process to achieve a target cost, GYE Inc are interviewing prospective customers to determine why they would buy the product and how they would use it.

What term best describes this process?

A   Value analysis

B   Operational research

C   Total quality management

D   Lifecycle costing

273 A customer returns a faulty product to a firm for repair under a warranty scheme. The firm operates a total quality management system.

Which of the following best describes the cost of the repair?

A   An internal failure cost

B   An external failure cost

C   An appraisal cost

D   A prevention cost

SYLLABUS AREA D – BUDGETING

NATURE AND PURPOSE OF BUDGETING

274 **What are the main purposes of budgeting?**

(i)   to give authority to spend

(ii)   to control expenditure

(iii)   to aid decision making.

A   (i) only

B   (i) and (ii) only

C   (ii) only

D   (i), (ii) and (iii)

275 **Who does the budget committee contain?**

(i)   Purchasing manager

(ii)   The chief executive

(iii)   Sales manager

(iv)   Production manager

A   (i) and (ii) only

B   (iii) and (iv) only

C   (i), (ii) and (iii) only

D   All of the above

276 **A budget manual will include which of the following?**

(i)   An organisation chart

(ii)   A budget timetable

(iii)   Copies of budget forms

(iv)   Key assumptions to be used in the budget

A   (ii), (iii) and (iv)

B   (ii) and (iv)

C   (iii) and (iv)

D   All of the above

277 Which of the following is NOT a purpose of budgeting?

 A Planning

 B Co-ordination

 C Consultation

 D Communication

BUDGET PREPARATION

278 A business is preparing its production budget for the year ahead for product A998. It is estimated that 100,000 units of A998 can be sold in the year and the opening inventory is currently 14,000 units. The inventory level is to be reduced by 40% by the end of the year.

How many units of A998 need to be produced? ☐

279 What is the formula to calculate the production budget?

 A Sales budget + opening inventory – closing inventory

 B Sales budget – opening inventory + closing inventory

 C Sales budget – opening inventory – closing inventory

 D Sales budget + opening inventory + closing inventory

280 A process has a normal loss of 10% and budgeted output is 4,500 litres for the period. Opening inventory of raw material is 600 litres and is expected to increase by 20% by the end of the period.

What is the material usage budget?

 A 4,500 litres

 B 5,000 litres

 C 5,133 litres

 D 5,120 litres

281 What is the formula to calculate the material usage budget?

 A Production budget multiplied by the standard material quantity per unit

 B Sales budget multiplied by the standard material quantity per unit

 C Production budget less opening inventory plus closing inventory

 D Production budget plus opening inventory less closing inventory

282 A company has a budget for two products A and B as follows:

	Product A	Product B
Sales (units)	2,000	4,500
Production (units)	1,750	5,000

Labour:		
Skilled at $10/hour	2 hours/unit	2 hours/unit
Unskilled at $7/hour	3 hours/unit	4 hours/unit

What is the budgeted cost for unskilled labour for the period?

A $105,000

B $135,000

C $176,750

D $252,500

283 **What would be the principal budget factor for a footwear retailer?**

A The cost item taking the largest share of total expenditure

B The product line contributing the largest amount to sales revenue

C The product line contributing the largest amount to business profits

D The constraint that is expected to limit the retailer's activities during the budget period

284 A company makes 2 products, X and Y, which are sold in the ratio 1:2. The selling prices are $50 and $100 respectively. The company wants to earn $100,000 over the next period.

What should the sales budget be?

	X (units)	Y (units)
A	1,334	667
B	800	400
C	667	1,334
D	400	800

285 A business is preparing its production budget, materials usage and materials purchases budget for the forthcoming period. The following information is known:

Budgeted sales	2,300 units
Current inventory of finished goods	400 units
Required closing inventory of finished goods	550 units

Each unit of the product uses 6 kg of material X and details of this are as follows:

Current inventory of X	2,000 kg
Required closing inventory of X	2,600 kg

What is the production volume required for the forthcoming period to meet the sales demand?

A   3,050 units

B   2,450 units

C   2,300 units

D   2,150 units

286   A company makes three products, X, Y and Z. The following information is available:

	X	Y	Z
Budgeted production (units)	200	400	300
Machine hours per unit	5	6	2

Variable overheads	$2.30 per machine hour
Fixed overheads	$0.75 per machine hour

What is the total overhead budget?

A $12,200

B $12,000

C $11,590

D $10,980

The following information should be used for the next THREE questions

A toy manufacturer produces two products, a clockwork clown and a wind-up train. Standard cost data for the products are as follows:

	Clockwork clown	Wind-up train
Direct materials ($5 per kg)	2 kg	1 kg
Direct labour ($8 per hour)	18 minutes	30 minutes
Budgeted sales	450	550
Budgeted inventories are as follows:		
Finished goods		
Opening inventory	20	50
Closing inventory	30	40
Raw materials		
Opening inventory	50 kg	
Closing inventory	60 kg	

---

287   **What is the total direct material usage budget?**

A   1,540 kg

B   1,470 kg

C   1,460 kg

D   1,440 kg

288   **What is the total direct material purchases budget?**

    A $7,350

    B $7,300

    C $7,250

    D $7,200

289   **What is the total direct labour budget?**

    A $3,264

    B $3,280

    C $3,290

    D $3,296

290   A job requires 2,400 actual labour hours for completion but it is anticipated that idle time will be 20% of the total time required.

    If the wage rate is $10 per hour, what is the budgeted labour cost for the job, including the cost of the idle time?

    A $19,200

    B $24,000

    C $28,800

    D $30,000

291   **What is a continuous budget?**

    (i)   Prepared in advance for the period in question

    (ii)   Updated regularly by adding further periods

    (iii)   Also known as a rolling budget

    (iv)   Always prepared for a full year in advance

    A   (i), (ii) and (iii)

    B   (i), (iii) and (iv)

    C   (i), (iii) and (iv) only

    D   (i), (ii) and (iv)

292 Vincent is preparing a cash budget for July. His credit sales are as follows.

	$
April (actual)	40,000
May (actual)	30,000
June (actual)	20,000
July (estimated)	25,000

His recent debt collection experience has been as follows.

Current month's sales	20%
Prior month's sales	60%
Sales two months prior	10%
Cash discounts taken	5%
Irrecoverable debts	5%

How much may Vincent expect to collect from credit customers during July?

A $18,000

B $20,000

C $21,000

D $24,000

293 DRF's projected revenue for 20X9 is $28,000 per month. All sales are on credit. Receivables' accounts are settled 50% in the month of sale, 45% in the following month, and 5% are written off as irrecoverable debts after two months.

What are the budgeted cash collections for March?

A $24,500

B $26,600

C $28,000

D $32,900

294 A company anticipates that 10,000 units of product Z will be sold during January. Each unit of Z requires 2 litres of raw material W. Actual stocks as of 1 January and budgeted inventories as of 31 January are as follows.

	1 January	31 January
Product Z (units)	14,000	12,000
Raw material W (litres)	20,000	15,000

1 litre of W costs $4.

If the company pays for all purchases in the month of acquisition, what is the cash outlay for January purchases of W?

A $84,000

B $80,000

C $44,000

D $12,000

295 A company has a two-month receivables' cycle. It receives in cash 45% of the total gross sales value in the month of invoicing. Irrecoverable debts are 20% of total gross sales value and there is a 10% discount for settling accounts within 30 days.

What proportion of the first month's sales will be received as cash in the second month?

A   25%

B   30%

C   35%

D   55%

296 Spears makes gross sales of $40,000 per month, of which 10% are for cash, the rest on credit.

Experience shows that the credit sales are received as follows:

Receivables paying
within one month	40%
within two months	50%
Settlement discounts (for payment within one month)	4%

What will be the total expected cash receipts in any month?

A $35,824

B $36,400

C $38,560

D $40,000

297 Selected figures from a firm's budget for next month are as follows.

Sales	$450,000
Gross profit on sales	30%
Decrease in trade payables over the month	$10,000
Increase in cost of inventory held over the month	$18,000

What is the budgeted payment to trade payables?

A $343,000

B $323,000

C $307,000

D $287,000

298 A company has a current cash balance of $7,000, trade receivables of $15,000 and trade payables of $40,000. The company can sell goods costing $50,000 for $70,000 next month. One half of all sales are collected in the month of sale and the remainder in the following month. All purchases are made on credit and paid during the following month. Inventory levels will remain constant during the month. General cash expenses will be $60,000 during the month.

What is the cash balance at the end of the month?

A $25,000 overdrawn

B $26,000 overdrawn

C $33,000 overdrawn

D $43,000 overdrawn

299 **Which of the following would NOT be included in a cash budget?**

(i)   Depreciation

(ii)   Provisions for doubtful debts

(iii)   Wages and salaries

A   All three

B   (i) and (ii) only

C   (i) and (iii) only

D   (ii) and (iii) only

300 The following details have been extracted from the payables' records of X Limited:

Invoices paid in the month of purchase   25%
Invoices paid in the first month after purchase   70%
Invoices paid in the second month after purchase   5%

Purchases for July to September are budgeted as follows:

July $250,000
August $300,000
September $280,000

For suppliers paid in the month of purchase, a settlement discount of 5% is received.

What amount is budgeted to be paid to suppliers in September?

A $278,500

B $280,000

C $289,000

D $292,500

301 Galway Ltd budgeted to make sales of $1,500, $1,800 and $2,800 in its first three months of operation.

25% of its sales are expected to be for cash and another 25% of total sales will also be collected in the same month by offering a 10% discount; 40% will be collected in the following month, and the remainder the month after that.

How much cash did Galway Ltd budget to receive in its third month of operation?

A $1,800

B $2,200

C $2,270

D $2,800

302 **Budgeted production overhead expenditure for April and May is as follows:**

April	$93,000
May	$87,000

One third of the production overhead expenditure is fixed cost, including depreciation of production machinery of $8,000 per month.

Payments for variable production overhead expenditure are made 50% in the month they are incurred and 50% in the month following that in which they are incurred.

Payments for fixed production overhead expenditure are made in the month following that in which they are incurred.

How much would be shown in the cash budget for May in respect of payments for fixed production overhead and variable production overhead?

	Fixed ($)	Variable ($)
A	23,000	60,000
B	31,000	60,000
C	23,000	62,000
D	31,000	62,000

FLEXIBLE BUDGETS

303 **What is a flexible budget?**

A   a budget for semi-variable overhead costs only

B   a budget which, by recognising different cost behaviour patterns, is designed to change as volume of activity changes

C   a budget for a twelve month period which includes planned revenues, expenses, assets and liabilities

D   a budget which is prepared for a rolling period which is reviewed monthly, and updated accordingly

304   What is a purpose of a flexible budget?

A   to cap discretionary expenditure

B   to produce a revised forecast by changing the original budget when actual costs are known

C   to control resource efficiency

D   to communicate target activity levels within an organisation by setting a budget in advance of the period to which it relates

305   What is a fixed budget?

A   a budget for a single level of activity

B   a budget used when the mix of products is fixed in advance of the budget period

C   a budget which ignores inflation

D   an overhead cost budget

306   Which of the following statements are correct?

(i)   A fixed budget is a budget that considers all of an organisation's costs and revenues for a single level of activity.

(ii)   A flexible budget is a budget that is produced during the budget period to recognise the effects of any changes in prices and methods of operation that have occurred.

(iii)   Organisations can use budgets to communicate objectives to their managers.

A   (i) and (ii) only

B   (i) and (iii) only

C   (ii) and (iii) only

D   All of them

307   Oswald Press produces and sells textbooks for schools and colleges. The following budgeted information is available for the year ending 31 December 20X6:

	Budget	Actual
Sales (units)	120,000	100,000
	$000	$000
Sales revenue	1,200	995
Variable printing costs	360	280
Variable production overheads	60	56
Fixed production cost	300	290
Fixed administration cost	360	364
Profit	120	5

What does the flexed budget show?

A   a profit of $10,000

B   a loss of $10,000

C   a profit of $100,000

D   a loss of $100,000

308   **Which of the following statements is true?**

A   A fixed budget is a budget that remains the same from one accounting period to the next

B   A fixed budget is produced for one product for different levels of activity

C   A flexible budget is designed to change as activity levels change

D   A fixed budget is useful when comparing budget figures with actual figures

309   The following budgeted information comes from the accounting records of Smith

	Original budget
Sales units	1,000
	$
Sales revenue	100,000
Direct material	40,000
Direct labour	20,000
Variable overhead	15,000
Fixed overhead	10,000
Profit	15,000

In a period where the actual sales were 1,200 units, what would be the budgeted flexed profit?

A $17,000

B $20,000

C $22,000

D $35,000

310   **When budgeting, what are variable costs conventionally deemed to do?**

A   Be constant per unit of output

B   Vary per unit of output as production volume changes

C   Be constant in total when production volume changes

D   Vary in total, from period to period when production is constant

311 F Ltd makes a single product for which the budgeted costs and activity for a typical month are as follows:

Budgeted production and sales	15,000 units
Budgeted unit costs	$
Direct materials	30
Direct labour	46
Variable overheads	24
Fixed overheads	80
	180

The standard selling price of the product is $220 per unit. During October only 13,600 units were produced.

What is the total budget cost allowance contained in the flexed budget for October?

[ ]

312 The following extract is taken from the overhead budget of Y Ltd:

Budgeted activity	50%	75%
Budgeted overhead	$100,000	$112,500

What would the budgeted overhead cost be for an activity level of 80%?

A $115,000

B $120,000

C $160,000

D $360,000

313 Globe Ltd. has the following original budget and actual performance for product Bean for the year ending 31 December.

	Budget	Actual
Volume sold (litres)	4,000	5,000
	$000	$000
Sales revenue	1,500	1,950
Less costs:		
Direct materials	36	45
Direct labour	176	182
Fixed Overheads	89	90
Operating profit	1,199	1,633

What is the total production cost of the flexed budget?

$ [ ]

CAPITAL BUDGETING

314 The details of an investment project are as follows:

Cost of asset bought at the start of the project	$80,000
Annual cash inflow	$25,000
Cost of capital	5% each year
Life of the project	8 years

What is the net present value of the project?

A   −$120,000

B $120,000

C $81,575

D   −$81,575

315 A company is planning to open a new store in a new geographic location. An initial site evaluation has taken place at a cost of $5,000 and a store location has been found. The new store can be rented for $9,500 per annum. It will require refurbishment at a cost of $320,000.

Which of the following costs are relevant for an NPV calculation?

(i) $5,000

(ii) $9,500

(iii) $320,000

A   (i) only

B   (i) and (ii)

C   (ii) and (iii)

D   (iii) only

316 B Company is deciding whether to launch a new product. The initial outlay and the forecast possible annual cash inflows are shown below:

Year 0	(60,000)
Year 1	23,350
Year 2	29,100
Year 3	27,800

The company's cost of capital is 8% per annum.

Assume the cash inflows are received at the end of the year and that the cash inflows for each year are independent.

What is the net present value to the nearest $ for the product?

$ ☐

---

317 An education authority is considering the implementation of a CCTV (closed circuit television) security system in one of its schools. Details of the proposed project are as follows:

Life of project	5 years
Initial cost	$75,000
Annual savings:	
Labour costs	$20,000
Other costs	$5,000
NPV at 15%	$8,800

What is the internal rate of return for this project?

A   16%

B   18%

C   20%

D   22%

318 The following measures have been calculated to appraise a proposed project

The internal rate of return is 12%

The return on capital employed is 16%

The payback period is 4 years

Which of the following statements is correct?

A   the payback is less than 5 years so the project should go ahead

B   the IRR is lower than the return on capital employed so the project should not go ahead

C   the IRR is greater than the cost of capital so the project should go ahead

D   The IRR is positive so the project should go ahead

319 CC Company is considering an investment of $300,000 which will earn a contribution of $40,000 each year for 10 years at today's prices. The company's cost of capital is 11% per annum.

What is the net present value of the project?

A   ($64,440)

B $23,556

C $64,440

D $235,560

320 Sandwich Queen is looking to expand its restaurant facilities to increase its seating capacity a further 40%. Results for the current year are:

	$000	$000
Food sales	200	
Drink sales	170	
		370
Food costs	145	
Drink costs	77	
Staff costs	40	
Other costs	20	
		282
Cash flow		88

Sales and variable costs will increase in line with the seating capacity increase. The other costs are 40% fixed. An extra employee will be required to serve the extra seating capacity. There are currently 4 employees on an equal wage.

What is the relevant annual net cash flow to the nearest $000 of the proposed expansion?

$ [   ]

321 JAH Company is about to invest $400,000 in machinery and other capital equipment for a new product venture. Cash flows for the first three years are estimated as follows

Year	$000
1	210
2	240
3	320

JAH Company requires a 17% return for projects of this type.

What is the NPV of this venture?

A   −$154,670

B $45,010

C $220,450

D $154,670

322 A company has determined that the net present value of an investment project is $17,706 when using a 10% discount rate and $(4,317) when using a discount rate of 15%.

What is the internal rate of return of the project to the nearest 1%?

[   ] %

323 A company is considering an investment of $400,000 in new machinery. The machinery is expected to yield incremental profits over the next five years as follows:

Year	Profit ($)
1	175,000
2	225,000
3	340,000
4	165,000
5	125,000

Thereafter, no incremental profits are expected and the machinery will be sold. It is company policy to depreciate machinery on a straight line basis over the life of the asset. The machinery is expected to have a value of $50,000 at the end of year 5.

What is the payback period of the investment in this machinery?

A   0.9 years

B   1.3 years

C   1.5 years

D   1.9 years

324 **What is an interest rate that includes the effect of compounding known as?**

A   Nominal interest

B   Simple interest

C   Compound interest

D   Effective interest

325 **Which of the following statements about the IRR method are true?**

(i)   IRR considers the time value of money

(ii)   if the IRR exceeds the companies cost of capital the NPV at the company's cost of capital should be positive

(iii)   it is possible for one investment to have 2 IRRs

A   (i) only

B   (i) and (ii) only

C   (ii) and (iii) only

D   (i), (ii) and (iii)

326 **What is the effective annual rate of interest of 2.1% compounded every three months?**

A   6.43%

B   8.40%

C   8.67%

D   10.87%

327 A bank offers different bank accounts with different interest rates:

Bank account 1 = 10% interest per year, interest calculated quarterly

Bank account 2 = 12% interest per year, interest calculated monthly

Bank account 3 = 1.2% interest per month

Bank account 4 = 3% interest per quarter

Which account gives the highest annual effective interest rate?

A   1

B   2

C   3

D   4

BUDGETARY CONTROL AND REPORTING

328 **In a responsibility accounting system which of the following costs is most likely to appear on the performance report for the manager of a purchasing department?**

   A   Cost of direct labour

   B   Rent of machinery

   C   Repairs to machinery

   D   Cost of materials

329 **In a responsibility accounting system for which of the following should the production line manager be held responsible?**

   A   Raw material prices and labour wage rates

   B   Raw material usage and labour wage rates

   C   Raw material prices and labour hours worked

   D   Raw material usage and labour hours worked

330 **What term describes: 'the forecasting of differences between actual and planned outcomes, and the implementation of action, before the event, to avoid such differences'?**

   A   Feedforward control

   B   Variance analysis

   C   Budgeting

   D   Feedback control

331 Martin Mags produces and sells industry magazines. The following budgeted information is available for the year ending 31 December 20X6:

	Budget	Flexed budget	Actual
Sales (units)	120,000	100,000	100,000
	$000	$000	$000
Sales revenue	1,200	1,000	995
Variable printing costs	360	300	280
Variable production overheads	60	50	56
Fixed production cost	300	300	290
Fixed administration cost	360	360	364
Profit/(Loss)	120	(10)	5

What are the total expenditure and volume variances?

	Expenditure variance	Volume variance
A	$15,000 favourable	$130,000 adverse
B	$95,000 adverse	$115,000 favourable
C	$115,000 adverse	$95,000 favourable
D	$130,000 adverse	$15,000 favourable

332 Which of the following statements describes the volume variance?

A   The difference between the flexible budget and the actual results

B   The difference between the fixed budget and the flexible budget

C   The difference between the fixed budget and the actual results

D   The difference between the original budget and the actual results

333 Which of the following statements are correct?

(i)   An adverse variance increases profit

(ii)   A favourable variance increases profit

(iii)   A favourable variance will arise when actual revenue is greater than budgeted revenue

(iv)   An adverse variance will arise when actual costs are greater than budgeted costs

Options:

A   (i) only

B   (ii) only

C   (i), (iii) and (iv)

D   (ii), (iii) and (iv)

334 Complete the table below by calculating the missing figures.

Use minus signs where appropriate and put A into the table to denote an adverse variance and F to denote a favourable variance.

	Budgeted $	Actual $	Variance value $	A/F
RECEIPTS				
Cash sales	4,200	3,800		
Credit sales		48,000	5,900	F
Total receipts				
PAYMENTS				
Cash purchases	500		700	A
Credit purchases		35,100	7,100	A
Labour costs	2,500	3,200		
Capital expenditure	8,000	6,000		
General expenses	4,000		200	F
Total payments				
Net cash flow				

BEHAVIOURAL ASPECTS OF BUDGETING

335 Which of the following statements about imposed budgets are correct?

(i)   Imposed budgets are likely to set realistic targets because senior management have the best idea of what is achievable in each part of the business.

(ii)   Imposed budgets can be less effective than budgets set on a participative basis, because it is difficult for an individual to be motivated to achieve targets set by someone else.

(iii) Imposed budgets are generally quicker to prepare and finalise than participative budgets.

A   (i) and (ii) only

B   (i) and (iii) only

C   (ii) and (iii) only

D   (iii) only

336 **Which of the following is an NOT an advantage of top-down budgeting?**

A   It is less time consuming

B   It reduces budgetary slack

C   It is more likely to motivate managers

D   Budgets will be closer to the company's objectives

337 **In the context of budget preparation what does the term 'goal congruence' mean?**

A   the alignment of budgets with objectives using feed-forward control

B   the setting of a budget which does not include budget bias

C   the alignment of corporate objectives with the personal objectives of a manager

D   the use of aspiration levels to set efficiency targets.

338 **Which of the following is a disadvantage of participation in standard setting?**

A   Morale and performance are supressed

B   Staff may try to incorporate budget padding

C   Decision making will not improve

D   Budget requirements are not clearly communicated to staff

339 **Which of the following best describes 'budgetary slack'?**

A   The difference between what has been set as a budgetary objective and what has been achieved for the period.

B   The demotivating impact of a budgetary target that has been set too high.

C   The deliberate over-estimation of expenditure and/or under-estimation of revenues in the budgetary planning process.

D   Accumulated favourable variances reported against a specific item of budgeted expenditure.

340 **One of the purposes of a budget is to set targets to motivate managers and optimise their performance. Which of the following is most likely to motivate managers?**

A   The participation of managers in the budget setting process

B   Imposed budgets

C   The inclusion of budgetary slack

D   Easy budget targets

SYLLABUS AREA E – STANDARD COSTING

STANDARD COSTING SYSTEMS

341   When considering setting standards for costing which of the following would NOT be appropriate?

    A   The normal level of activity should always be used for absorbing overheads

    B   Average prices for materials should be used, encompassing any discounts that are regularly available

    C   The labour rate used will be the rate at which labour is paid

    D   Average material usage should be established based on generally-accepted working practices

342   What are performance standards that have remained unchanged over a long period of time known as?

    A   ideal standards

    B   current standards

    C   basic standards

    D   attainable standards

343   What are performance standards that allow for efficient but not perfect operating conditions known as?

    A   ideal standards

    B   current standards

    C   basic standards

    D   attainable standards

344   Which of the following statements are true and which are false?

Statement	True	False
A variance is the difference between budgeted and actual cost.		
A favourable variance means actual costs are less than budgeted.		
An adverse variance means that actual income is less than budgeted.		

VARIANCE CALCULATIONS AND ANALYSIS

345 A company uses standard marginal costing. Last month the standard contribution on actual sales was $10,000 and the following variances arose:

Total variable costs variance	$2,000 adverse
Sales Price variance	$500 favourable
Sales volume contribution variance	$1,000 adverse

What was the actual contribution for last month?

$ [   ]

346 A company uses standard marginal costing. Last month, when all sales were at the standard selling price, the standard contribution from actual sales was $50,000 and the following variances arose:

Total variable cost variance	$3,500 Adverse
Total fixed costs variance	$1,000 favourable
Sales volume contribution variance	$2,000 favourable

What was the actual contribution for last month?

A $46,500

B $47,500

C $48,500

D $49,500

347 The following information relates to labour costs for the past month:

Budget	Labour rate	$10 per hour
	Production time	15,000 hours
	Time per unit	3 hours
	Production units	5,000 units
Actual	Wages paid	$176,000
	Production	5,500 units
	Total hours worked	14,000 hours

There was no idle time.

What were the labour rate and efficiency variances?

	Rate variance	Efficiency variance
A	$26,000 adverse	$25,000 favourable
B	$26,000 adverse	$10,000 favourable
C	$36,000 adverse	$2,500 favourable
D	$36,000 adverse	$25,000 favourable

348 The following details relate to product T, which has a selling price of $44.00:

	$/unit
Direct materials	15.00
Direct labour (3 hours)	12.00
Variable overhead	6.00
Fixed overhead	4.00
	37.00

During April 20X6, the actual production of T was 800 units, which was 100 units fewer than budgeted. The budget shows an annual production target of 10,800, with fixed costs accruing at a constant rate throughout the year. Actual overhead expenditure totalled $8,500 for April 20X6.

Overheads are absorbed on the basis of units produced.

What were the overhead variances for April 20X6?

	Expenditure $	Volume $
A	367 A	1,000 A
B	500 A	400 A
C	100 A	1,000 A
D	100 A	400 A

349 A company operates a standard marginal costing system. Last month its actual fixed overhead expenditure was 10% above budget resulting in a fixed overhead expenditure variance of $36,000.

What was the actual expenditure on fixed overheads last month?

A $324,000

B $360,000

C $396,000

D $400,000

350 FGH has the following budgeted and actual data:

Budgeted fixed overhead cost	$120,000
Budgeted production (units)	20,000
Actual fixed overhead cost	$115,000
Actual production (units)	21,000

What was the fixed overhead volume variance?

A $4,500 adverse

B $5,500 favourable

C $6,000 favourable

D $10,500 favourable

351 A company budgeted to make 30,000 units of a product P. Each unit was expected to take 4 hours to make and budgeted fixed overhead expenditure was $840,000. Actual production of product P in the period was 32,000 units, which took 123,000 hours to make. Actual fixed overhead expenditure was $885,600.

What was the fixed overhead capacity variance for the period?

A $21,000 favourable

B $21,000 adverse

C $35,000 adverse

D $56,000 favourable

352 QRL uses a standard absorption costing system. The following details have been extracted from its budget for April 20X7:

Fixed production overhead cost	$48,000
Production (units)	4,800

In April 20X7 the fixed production overhead cost was under-absorbed by $8,000 and the fixed production overhead expenditure variance was $2,000 adverse.

What was the actual number of units produced?

A   3,800

B   4,000

C   4,200

D   5,400

353 A company has a higher than expected staff turnover and as a result staff are less experienced than expected.

As an indirect result of this, are the labour rate variance and material usage variance likely to be adverse or favourable?

	Labour rate	Material usage
A	Favourable	Favourable
B	Adverse	Favourable
C	Favourable	Adverse
D	Adverse	Adverse

354 A company is obliged to buy sub-standard materials at lower than standard price because nothing else is available.

As an indirect result of this purchase, are the materials usage variance and labour efficiency variance likely to be adverse or favourable?

	Materials usage	Labour efficiency
A	Favourable	Favourable
B	Adverse	Favourable
C	Favourable	Adverse
D	Adverse	Adverse

355 Fawley's direct labour cost data relating to last month were as follows:

Standard labour cost of actual hours worked	$116,000
Standard hours worked	30,000
Standard rate per hour	$4
Labour rate variance	$5,800 favourable
Labour efficiency variance	$4,000 favourable

What is the actual rate of pay per hour (to 2 decimal places)?

$ [   ]

356 Michel has the following results.

10,080 hours actually worked and paid costing $8,770

If the rate variance is $706 adverse, the efficiency variance $256 favourable, and 5,000 units were produced, what is the standard production time per unit?

A   1.95 hours

B   1.96 hours

C   2.07 hours

D   2.08 hours

357 An extract from the standard cost card for product CJ is as follows:

Direct labour (0.5 hours × $12) $6

710 units of CJ were produced in the period and staff worked 378 hours at a total cost of $4,725. Of these hours 20 were lost due to a material shortage.

What is the labour efficiency variance?

A $516 favourable

B $36 favourable

C $36 adverse

D $516 adverse

358 A company makes a single product. The following details are from the cost card for the product:

Direct labour	10 hours at $5 per hour
Variable overhead	10 hours at $1.50 per hour

The actual results for the last period are:

500 units produced

Labour	4,800 hours
Variable overheads	$7,700

What are the variable overhead expenditure and efficiency variances?

	Expenditure	Efficiency
A	$300 A	$500 F
B	$300 F	$500 A
C	$500 A	$300 F
D	$500 F	$300 A

359 **A company uses standard absorption costing. The following data relate to last month:**

	Budget	Actual
Sales and production (units)	1,000	900
	Standard	Actual
	$	$
Selling price per unit	50	52
Total production cost per unit	39	40

What was the adverse sales volume profit variance last month?

$	Adv

360 A company operates a standard marginal costing system. Last month actual fixed overhead expenditure was 2% below budget and the fixed overhead expenditure variance was $1,250.

What was the actual fixed overhead expenditure for last month?

A $61,250

B $62,475

C $62,500

D $63,750

361 **Under absorption costing the sales volume variance is calculated by multiplying the difference in sales volumes by which of the following?**

A Standard contribution per unit

B Standard cost per unit

C Standard profit per unit

D Standard selling price per unit

362 A business uses marginal costing to calculate variances. If they were to use absorption costing the current method of calculating the sales volume variance would be?

  A   Higher or the same

  B   Lower or the same

  C   The same

  D   Different but not able to say higher or lower

The following information relates to the next TWO questions

The standard direct material cost for a product is $50 per unit (12.5 kg at $4 per kg). Last month the actual amount paid for 45,600 kg of material purchased and used was $173,280 and the direct material usage variance was $15,200 adverse.

363 What was the direct material price variance last month?

  A $8,800 adverse

  B $8,800 favourable

  C $9,120 adverse

  D $9,120 favourable

364 What was the actual production last month?

  A   3,344 units

  B   3,520 units

  C   3,952 units

  D   4,160 units

365 A new machine is purchased which is more expensive, but requires less labour to operate per unit.

   What is the impact on the fixed overhead variances?

	Expenditure variance	Volume variance
A	Adverse	Adverse
B	Adverse	Favourable
C	Favourable	Favourable
D	Favourable	Favourable

366 QR has budgeted to produce 4,000 units in January. Actual production was 3,700 units with fixed production overheads of $10,300. The standard fixed overhead cost per unit was 1.5 hours at $2.40 per hour. 5,800 actual production hours were worked.

What was the fixed overhead volume variance?

A $1,080 favourable

B $480 favourable

C $480 adverse

D $1,080 adverse

367 **Which of the following could be the cause of an adverse sales volume variance for garden furniture?**

(i)   The company offers discounts on sales prices in order to maintain business.

(ii)   Poor weather leads to a reduction in sales.

(iii) A strike in the factory causes a shortage of finished goods.

A   (i) and (ii) only

B   (i) and (iii) only

C   (ii) and (iii) only

D   All of them

368 The following information relates to April production of product CK:

	Actual	Budget
Units produced	580	600
Input of material (kg)	1,566	1,500
Cost of material purchased and input	$77,517	$76,500

What is the materials usage variance?

A $2,349 favourable

B $3,366 adverse

C $5,742 adverse

D $5,916 adverse

369 For product DR, the material price variance for the month of August was $1,000 favourable and the material usage variance was $300 adverse.

The standard material usage per unit is 3 kg, and the standard material price is $2 per kg. 500 units were produced in the period. Opening inventories of raw materials were 100 kg and closing inventories 400 kg.

What were the material purchases in the period?

kg

370 The following information relates to a month's production of product CN:

	Budget	Actual
Units produced	600	580
Input of material P (kg)	1,500	1,566
Cost of material P purchased and input	$25,500	$25,839

What is the price variance for material P?

A $783 favourable

B $339 adverse

C $1,189 favourable

D $1,972 adverse

371 A company uses a standard absorption costing system. Last month budgeted production was 8,000 units and the standard fixed production overhead cost was $15 per unit. Actual production last month was 8,500 units and the actual fixed production overhead cost was $17 per unit.

What was the total adverse fixed production overhead variance for last month?

A $7,500

B $16,000

C $17,000

D $24,500

372 A company is reviewing actual performance to budget to see where there are differences. The following standard information is relevant:

	$ per unit
Selling price	50
Direct materials	4
Direct labour	16
Fixed production overheads	5
Variable production overheads	10
Fixed selling costs	1
Variable selling cost	1
Total costs	37
Budgeted sales units	3,000
Actual sales units	3,500

What was the favourable sales volume variance using marginal costing?

A $9,500

B $7,500

C $7,000

D $6,500

373 A company uses variance analysis to control costs and revenues.

Information concerning sales is as follows:

Budgeted selling price	$15 per unit
Budgeted sales units	10,000
Budgeted profit per unit	$5
Actual sales revenue	$151,500
Actual units sold	9,800

What was the sales volume profit variance?

A $500 favourable

B $1,000 favourable

C $1,000 adverse

D $3,000 adverse

374 A company operates a standard absorption costing system. The standard fixed production overhead rate is $15 per hour.

The following data relate to last month:

Actual hours worked	5,500
Budgeted hours	5,000
Standard hours for actual production	4,800

What was the fixed production overhead capacity variance?

A $7,500 adverse

B $7,500 favourable

C $10,500 adverse

D $10,500 favourable

375 Direct labour cost data relating to last month is as follows:

Actual hours worked	28,000
Total direct labour cost	$117,600
Direct labour rate variance	$8,400 adverse
Direct labour efficiency variance	$3,900 favourable

To the nearest thousand hours, what were the standard labour hours for actual production last month?

A   31,000 hrs

B   29,000 hrs

C   27,000 hrs

D   25,000 hrs

376 Which of the following variances would you find within an absorption costing system and which in a marginal costing system?

	Absorption costing	Marginal costing
Sales volume contribution variance		
Fixed overhead capacity variance		
Fixed overhead volume variance		
Sales volume profit variance		
Fixed overhead efficiency variance		

RECONCILIATION OF BUDGETED AND ACTUAL PROFIT

377 The budgeted contribution for last month was $43,900 but the following variances arose:

	$
Sales price variance	3,100 adverse
Sales volume contribution variance	1,100 adverse
Direct material price variance	1,986 favourable
Direct material usage variance	2,200 adverse
Direct labour rate variance	1,090 adverse
Direct labour efficiency variance	512 adverse
Variable overhead expenditure variance	1,216 favourable
Variable overhead efficiency variance	465 adverse

What is the actual contribution for last month? $ ☐

378 Below is a statement of variances for a business:

Sales price variance	$1,500F
Sales volume variance	$2,100A
Materials price variance	$4,200A
Materials usage Variance	$1,500F
Labour rate variance	$900F
Labour efficiency Variance	$450A
Fixed overhead expenditure variance	$1,750F
Fixed overhead volume variance	$1,800A

If the budgeted profit for the period was $250,000, what was the actual profit?

A $247,100

B $248,300

C $251,700

D $252,900

379 Below is a statement of variances for a business:

Sales price variance	$200F
Sales volume variance	$350F
Materials price variance	$250F
Materials usage Variance	$120A
Labour rate variance	$450A
Labour efficiency Variance	$800A
Fixed overhead expenditure variance	$600F
Fixed overhead volume variance	$860A

If the actual profit for the period was $7,170 what was the budget profit?

A $6,340

B $5,240

C $9,100

D $8,000

380 Below is a statement of variances for a business, including the budgeted and actual profit.

What is the missing value for the labour rate variance?

Budget profit	$19,000
Sales price variance	$1,200A
Sales volume variance	$2,000F
Materials price variance	$3,500F
Materials usage Variance	$4,200A
Labour rate variance	$ _____
Labour efficiency Variance	$1,500A
Fixed overhead expenditure variance	$1,500F
Fixed overhead volume variance	$750A
Actual profit	$21,100

SYLLABUS AREA F – PERFORMANCE MEASUREMENT

PERFORMANCE MEASUREMENT OVERVIEW

381   Which of the following are elements of a mission statement?

(i)   Purpose

(ii)   Strategy

(iii)   Values

(iv)   Culture

A   All of them

B   (i) and (ii) only

C   (ii) only

D   (ii) and (iv) only

382   An organisation is divided into a number of divisions, each of which operates as a profit centre.

Which TWO of the following would be useful measures to monitor divisional performance?

A   Contribution

B   Controllable profit

C   Return on investment

D   Residual income

383   When measuring performance which of the following could impact the overall results for the business?

(i)   A new competitor

(ii)   A change in local government

(iii)   An increase in interest rates

(iv)   A change in national government

A   (i) and (iv)

B   None of the above

C   (ii) and (iv)

D   All of the above

384 Which of the following performance measurements could be a result of government legislation?

A   Carbon footprint

B   Retention of customers

C   Return on capital employed

D   Capacity ratio

PERFORMANCE MEASUREMENT – APPLICATION

385 In the last year a division's controllable return on investment was 25% and its controllable profit was $80,000. The cost of finance appropriate to the division was 18% per annum.

What was the division's controllable residual income in the last year?

A $5,600

B $22,400

C $74,400

D $76,400

386 A government body uses measures based upon the 'three Es' to the measure value for money generated by a publicly funded hospital. It considers the most important performance measure to be 'cost per successfully treated patient'.

Which of the three E's best describes the above measure?

A   Economy

B   Effectiveness

C   Efficiency

D   Externality

387 A government is looking at assessing hospitals by reference to a range of both financial and non-financial factors, one of which is survival rates for heart by-pass operation.

Which of the three E's best describes the above measure?

A   Economy

B   Effectiveness

C   Efficiency

D   Externality

388 Which of the following measures would not be appropriate for a cost centre?

A   Cost per unit

B   Contribution per unit

C   Comparison of actual labour cost to budget labour cost

D   Under or over absorption of overheads

389 A government is looking at assessing state schools by reference to a range of both financial and non-financial factors, one of which is average class sizes.

   Which of the three E's best describes the above measure?

   A   Economy

   B   Effectiveness

   C   Efficiency

   D   Externality

390 **For operational purposes, for a company operating a fleet of delivery vehicles, which of the following would be most useful?**

   A   Cost per mile run

   B   Cost per driver hour

   C   Cost per tonne mile

   D   Cost per kg carried

391 A division has a residual income of £240,000 and a net profit before imputed interest of £640,000.

   If it uses a rate of 10% for computing imputed interest on its invested capital, what is its return on investment (ROI) to the nearest whole number?

   A   4%

   B   10%

   C   16%

   D   27%

392 JKL Inc budgeted to make 1,000 units in May using 2,000 hours of direct labour. Actual output was 1,100 units which took 2,300 hours.

   What is the production/volume ratio?

   A   91%

   B   105%

   C   110%

   D   115%

393 RL Inc budgeted to make 200 units in June with a standard labour usage of 0.6 hours per unit. Actual output was 180 units which took 126 hours.

   What is the efficiency ratio?

   A   86%

   B   90%

   C   105%

   D   116%

394 CAP Inc budgeted to make 50 units in July with a standard labour usage of 1.2 hours per unit. Actual output was 49 units which took 61 hours.

What is the capacity ratio?

A   96%

B   98%

C   100%

D   102%

395 HH plc monitors the % of total sales that derives from products developed in the last year.

Which part of the balanced scorecard is this measure classified under?

A   Financial perspective

B   Customer perspective

C   Internal perspective

D   Learning perspective

396 **Which of the following KPIs would be used to assess the liquidity of a company?**

(i)   Return on capital employed

(ii)   Gross profit percentage

(iii)   Acid test ratio

(iv)   Gearing ratio

A   (i) and (ii) only

B   (iii) only

C   (iv) only

D   (iii) and (iv) only

397 K Class has calculated the following indictors

(i)   Return on capital employed

(ii)   Training costs as a percentage of total costs

Which of the balanced scorecard perspectives would these measures relate to?

	(i)	(ii)
A	Financial	Financial
B	Financial	Internal
C	Internal	Learning and growth
D	Financial	Learning and growth

398 Area 27 are a pizza delivery company and have asked you to suggest some performance indicators that could be used to measure the customer perspective and the internal perspective of the balanced scorecard.

Which of the following would be appropriate?

	Customer	Internal
A	Number of customer complaints	Time taken from order to delivery pizza
B	Cost per pizza	Cost of time spent on training
C	Number of late deliveries	Profit per pizza
D	Cost of delivery vehicles	Gross profit percentage

Use the following information for the next SEVEN questions

Extracts from a company's accounts show the following balances:

	£000		£000
Inventories	150	Revenue	2,700
Receivables	300	Cost of sales	1,300
Cash	25	Gross profit	1,400
Payables	230	Admin costs	500
Overdraft	90	Distribution costs	350
		Operating profit	550
		Finance cost	75

399 What is the company's current ratio (to the nearest two decimal places)?

A 1.48

B 1.41

C 1.96

D 1.02

400 What is the company's quick ratio (to the nearest two decimal places)?

A 1.41

B 1.02

C 1.48

D 1.30

401 **What is the receivables' payment period in days (to the nearest day)?**

    A   41 days

    B   84 days

    C   78 days

    D   45 days

402 **What is the payables' payment period in days (to the nearest day)?**

    A   31 days

    B   65 days

    C   60 days

    D   35 days

403 **What is the inventory holding period (to the nearest day)?**

    A   4 days

    B   10 days

    C   24 days

    D   42 days

404 **What is the return on sales for the company?**

    A   52%

    B   39%

    C   20%

    D   25%

405 **What is the interest cover of the company?**

    A   4.67 times

    B   5.67 times

    C   7.33 times

    D   6.50 times

Use the following information for the next FIVE Questions

Extracts from a company's accounts show the following:

	£000	£000		
Non-Current assets		30,000		
Current assets				
Inventory	22,000			
Trade receivables	12,506		Additional Notes	£000
Cash	5,006		Revenue	64,323
		39,512	Profit before interest and taxation	27,657
Total assets		**69,512**		
Equity				
Share capital		100		
Revaluation reserve		12,000		
Retained earnings		26,412		
Non-current liabilities				
Loans		16,000		
Current liabilities				
Trade payables		15,000		
Total equity and liabilities		**69,512**		

406 **What is the gearing ratio (total debt/equity) of the company?**

   A   44.3%

   B   41.5%

   C   60.6%

   D   57.1%

407 **What is the company's current ratio (to the nearest two decimal places)?**

   A   2.63

   B   1.27

   C   1.61

   D   1.17

408 **What is the company's quick ratio (to the nearest two decimal places)?**

   A   0.83

   B   1.27

   C   1.17

   D   2.57

409 **What is the ROCE of the company (return on capital employed)?**

    A   72%

    B   92%

    C   47%

    D   51%

410 **What are the receivable days of the company (to the nearest whole day)?**

    A   14 days

    B   18 days

    C   71 days

    D   90 days

Use the following information for the next SIX questions

Extracts from a company's accounts show the following:

Statement of profit or loss	£000	Statement of financial position	£000	£000
Revenue	2,250	Non-current assets		700
Cost of sales	1,000	Current assets		
Gross profit	1,250	Inventory	150	
Distribution costs	275	Trade receivables	240	
Administrations	150	Cash	100	
Operating profit	825			490
Finance cost	80	Long term loans		200
Profit before Tax	745	Trade payables		275
Tax	90			
Profit for the year	655			

411 **What is the gross profit margin?**

    A   55.6%

    B   36.7%

    C   33.1%

    D   29.1%

412 **What is the return on sales?**

    A   55.6%

    B   36.7%

    C   33.1%

    D   29.1%

413 **What is the current ratio?**

   A   1.2

   B   0.9

   C   1.4

   D   1.8

414 **What are the receivable days?**

   A   88 days

   B   80 days

   C   70 days

   D   39 days

415 **What are the payable days?**

   A   100 days

   B   80 days

   C   143 days

   D   45 days

416 **What is the inventory turnover in days?**

   A   24 days

   B   55 days

   C   44 days

   D   66 days

417 A division has a residual income of $50,000 and a net profit before imputed interest of $80,000.

   If it uses a rate of 10% for computing imputed interest on its invested capital, what is its return on investment (ROI) to the nearest whole number?

   A   4%

   B   10%

   C   16%

   D   27%

418 A division of a company has capital employed of $2m and its return on capital is 12%. It is considering a new project requiring capital of $500,000 and is expected to yield profits of $90,000 per annum. The company's interest rate is 10%.

If the new project is accepted, what will the residual income of the division be?

A $40,000

B $80,000

C $30,000

D $330,000

419 The following information relates to a small production unit during a period:

Budgeted hours	9,500 hours
Actual hours worked	9,200 hours
Standard hours of work produced	9,300 hours

What is the efficiency ratio for the period?

A   97%

B   98%

C   99%

D   101%

420 A company makes a product for which the standard labour time is 2 hours per unit. The budgeted production hours for a given week were 820. During the week the production staff were able to produce 380 units of product. Staff worked and were paid for 800 hours. During the week 20 production hours were lost due to a shortage of material.

What is the efficiency ratio?

A   95.00%

B   95.12%

C   97.44%

D   97.50%

421 A company has calculated that its activity ratio is 103.5% and that its efficiency ratio is 90%.

What is the capacity ratio?

A   86.96%

B   93.15%

C   115.00%

D   193.50%

422 **How is the activity (production volume) ratio calculated?**

A   Actual hours ÷ Budgeted hours

B   Budgeted hours ÷ Actual hours

C   Standard hours for actual output ÷ Actual hours

D   Standard hours for actual output ÷ Budgeted hours

423 The direct labour capacity ratio for a period was 104%.

What could have caused this?

A   Actual hours worked being greater than budgeted hours

B   Actual hours worked being less than budgeted hours

C   Standard time for actual output being greater than budgeted hours

D   Standard time for actual output being less than budgeted hours

424 Green division is one of many divisions in the Colour group. At its year-end, the non-current assets invested in Green were $30 million, and the net current assets were $5 million.

Included in this total was a new item of plant that was delivered three days before the year end. This item cost $4 million and had been paid for by Colour, which had increased the amount of long-term debt owed by Green by this amount. The profit earned in the year by Green was $6 million before the deduction of $1.4 million of interest payable to Colour.

What is the most appropriate measure of ROI for the Green division?

A   13.1%

B   14.8%

C   17.1%

D   19.4%

425 Division M has produced the following results in the last financial year:

		$000
Net profit		360
Capital employed:	Non-current assets	1,500
	Net current assets	100

For evaluation purposes all divisional assets are valued at original cost. The division is considering a project which will increase annual net profit by $25,000, but will require average inventory levels to increase by $30,000 and non-current assets to increase by $100,000. There is an 18% capital charge on investments.

Given these circumstances, will the evaluation criteria of Return on Investment (ROI) and Residual Income (RI) motivate Division M management to accept this project?

	ROI	RI
A	Yes	Yes
B	Yes	No
C	No	Yes
D	No	No

426 **Which TWO of the following performance indicators could be used to measure the quality of a service?**

A   Number of customer complaints

B   Customer retention

C   Overtime worked

D   Number of sick days

427 Which balanced scorecard perspective would the performance indicator 'Training costs as a % of total costs' come under?

    A   Financial

    B   Customer

    C   Learning and growth

    D   Internal

428 A company wants to measure performance under the 'Internal' perspective of the balanced scorecard. Which of the following would be an appropriate measure?

    A   ROI

    B   Warranty claims

    C   New products developed

    D   Labour capacity ratio

429 Which TWO of the following would be a suitable measure of resource utilisation for a private sector college?

	Tick
Average class size	
Tutor grading by students	
Pass rates	
Percentage room occupancy	

430 A business is concerned that not all the employees are making the best use of their time. Consider the following information:

	Budget operations	Actual operations	Budget employees	Actual employees
Department A	800	1,000	4	5
Department B	700	660	5	3
Department C	1,200	1,050	8	7
Department D	300	400	4	5

Which department is making the best use of the employees' time when compared to budget?

    A   A

    B   B

    C   C

    D   D

COST REDUCTIONS AND VALUE ENHANCEMENT

431 **Which two of the following could be used to control costs?**

	Tick
Setting targets for cost centre managers	
Reducing the cost budget	
Cost variance analysis	
Increasing sales volume	

432 **Value analysis looks to do which of the following?**

	Tick
Control costs	
Reduce costs	
Improve sales	
Increase the value of the product	

433 **Which of the following is defined as 'the body of knowledge concerned with the analysis of the work methods and the equipment used in performing a job, the design of an optimum work method and the standardisation of proposed work methods'?**

A Work study

B Work measurement

C Job study

D Method measurement

434 **Which of the following relates to Value analysis and which to value engineering?**

	value analysis	value engineering
Reviews current products to reduce costs		
Reviews products at the design stage to reduce costs		

435 **Which of the following techniques would be useful for controlling costs?**

(i) Actual versus flexed budget

(ii) Variance analysis

(iii) Trend of costs analysis

A (i) and (ii) only

B (i) and (iii) only

C (ii) and (iii) only

D (i), (ii) and (iii)

MONITORING PERFORMANCE AND REPORTING

436 Copenhagen is an insurance company. Recently there has been concern that too many quotations have been sent to clients either late or containing errors.

The department concerned has responded that it is understaffed, and a high proportion of current staff has recently joined the firm. The performance of this department is to be carefully monitored.

Which of the following non-financial performance indicators would NOT be an appropriate measure to monitor and improve the department's performance?

A   Percentage of quotations found to contain errors when checked

B   Percentage of quotations not issued within company policy of three working days

C   Percentage of department's quota of staff actually employed

D   Percentage of budgeted number of quotations actually issued

437 **A company wants to encourage an investment centre to make new investments. Performance measurement using which of the following KPIs would achieve this?**

A   ROI

B   ROCE

C   RI

D   IRR

438 **Why would a company want to encourage the use of non-financial performance indicators?**

A   To encourage short termism

B   To look at the fuller picture of the business

C   To enable results to be easily manipulated to the benefit of the manager

D   To prevent goal congruence

439 **Which of the following is not a type of benchmarking?**

A   Internal

B   Strategic

C   International

D   Functional

440 **In a responsibility accounting system which of the following costs is least likely to appear on the performance report for the manager of a production department?**

A   Cost of direct labour

B   Rent of machinery

C   Repairs to machinery

D   Cost of materials used

441 In a responsibility accounting system for which of the following should the purchasing manager be held responsible?

A   Raw material prices

B   Raw material usage

C   Labour hours worked

D   Labour wage rates

442 The operating statement used by an organisation to measure the performance of its divisions is structured as follows.

	$	$	$
External sales		X	
Internal transfers		X	
		___	
Variable cost of sales	(X)		
Other variable divisional costs	(X)		
		(X)	
Contribution		X	
Depreciation on controllable non-current assets	(X)		
Other controllable fixed costs	(X)		
	___	(X)	
		___	
Controllable operating profit			X
Depreciation on other divisional non-current assets	(X)		
Other traceable divisional costs	(X)		
	___	(X)	
		___	
Traceable divisional profit		X	
Apportioned head office cost		(X)	
		___	
Divisional net profit			X

Which of the following would provide the best basis for measuring the performance of a manager of an investment centre?

A   Contribution

B   Controllable operating profit

C   Traceable divisional profit

D   Divisional net profit

443 Classify the following as either a measure of effectiveness, efficiency or economy according to the 3Es framework for an NHS hospital

	Effectiveness	Efficiency	Economy
Have the waiting lists been reduced?			
What was the average cost per patient treated?			
Have mortality rates gone down?			
Did the hospital spend more or less on drugs this year?			
What was the average spend per bed over the period?			
Did the hospital spend more or less on nurses' wages?			

444 **YU is a charity based in country K which aims to offer value for money. It has been set up to manage an area of woodland on behalf of the local population.**

YU aims to have around 3,000 visitors to the woodland every year, but in the last year it has only had around half of this number. YU has spent more on advertising than in previous years, but has moved from using leaflets to radio advertisements. While YU was able to buy a large amount of radio advertising, YU's directors were unaware that the chosen station had relatively low numbers of listeners.

With reference to value for money, the low number of visitors indicates that YU has failed with regards to _____1_____ over the past year. Its poor use of its advertising budget also indicates a lack of _____2_____.

Which of the options below can be used to fill in the missing words in gaps 1 and 2?

Note that each term can be used more than once.

A   Effectiveness

B   Economy

C   Ethics

D   Efficiency

E   Expertise

445 **Which of the following statements are correct?**

A   Non-financial performance indicators can be used easily to compare one organisation to another

B   Financial performance indicators encourage a long-term view of performance

C   Financial performance indicators provide all the analysis of progress needed

D   Non-financial performance indicators are difficult to determine

446 How can short-termism be prevented?

A   Focus performance measurement on financial performance only

B   Focus performance measurement on non-financial performance only

C   Focus performance measurement on both financial and non-financial performance

D   Create budgets for more than one year at a time.

447 **The management process which involves comparison of competences with best practice within and outside the organisation is known as?**

A   Balanced scorecard

B   Benchmarking

C   Productivity

D   Resource analysis

448 VG is planning to introduce a new benchmarking procedure within its organisation, but is unsure which type of benchmarking would be most appropriate. It is aware that each type of benchmarking has certain drawbacks.

VG has identified that _____1_____ benchmarking is often difficult to undertake as it is difficult to convince the other party to share information about their operations.

_____2_____ benchmarking is unlikely to suggest any truly innovative solutions and is typically only useful where the organisation feels that conformity of service is crucial to its operations.

Finally, _____3_____ benchmarking often fails to provide data on the benchmarking company's core functions as it requires the organisation to benchmark itself against an organisation in a different industry.

Which of the options below can be used to fill in the missing words in gaps 1, 2 and 3?

A   Functional

B   Internal

C   Competitive

449 KV operates a van rental company through a chain of around 35 stores. It has received a number of complaints from customers about the service they have received. KV's investigation has revealed that different stores are offering radically different levels of service to customers.

KV is the current market leader in the van rental market, with a market share which is significantly ahead of its nearest rival. KV's managers are still keen to ensure their market share does not fall and have decided to undertake a benchmarking process to help the business standardise the level of service it offers to customers across its business.

Which type of benchmarking would be most appropriate for KV to adopt?

A   Functional

B   Strategic

C   Competitive

D   Internal

SECTION B-TYPE QUESTIONS

BUDGETING

450 Globe Ltd. has the following original budget and actual performance for product Bean for the year ending 31 December.

(a) **Complete the table below to show a flexed budget and the resulting variances against the budget for the year. Show the actual variance amount, for sales and each cost, in the column headed 'Variance' (to the nearest $000).**

Note:

- Adverse variances must be denoted with a minus sign or brackets
- Enter 0 where any figure is zero.

	Original budget	Flexed budget	Actual	Variance
Volume sold	4,000		5,000	
	$000	$000	$000	$000
Sales revenue	1,500		1,950	
Less costs:				
Direct materials	36		45	
Direct labour	176		182	
Variable overheads	92		90	
Profit from operations	1,196		1,633	

(6 marks)

(b) **Referring to your answer for part (a), which one of the following has had the least impact in increasing the profit from operations?**

A   Sales revenue

B   Direct materials

C   Direct labour

D   Variable overheads   **(2 marks)**

(c) **Which of the following might have caused the variance for sales revenue?**

A   An increase in units produced

B   Offering a bulk discount

C   Increased competition from other companies

D   An increase in selling price   **(2 marks)**

(Total: 10 marks)

451 Daps Co makes spades and forks. The following budgeted information is available:

	Month one	Month two
Fork production	220 units	240 units
Spade production	170 units	180 units

Each fork uses 1.5 kg of steel, and each spade uses 2 kg of steel.

No finished goods inventory is held, but Daps Co's raw material inventory policy is to hold enough material to cover half of the next month's production requirements.

A spreadsheet for the material purchases budget is being prepared for month one:

	A	B
1	Steel required for production	Gap 1
2	Opening inventory	Gap 2
3	Closing inventory	Gap 3
4	Material purchases	

Required:

(a) Calculate the figure that should be entered into (to the nearest whole kg):

    (i)   Gap 1   Kg   **(2 marks)**

    (ii)   Gap 2   Kg   **(2 marks)**

    (iii) Gap 3   Kg   **(1 mark)**

(b) State the formula that should be entered into cell B4

    (1 mark)

(c) Are the following statements true or false?

	True	False
The master budget includes the capital expenditure budget		
Continuous budgets are also known as rolling budgets		
Scenario planning is mainly used in the short term		
The mission of an organisation is the target to be met in the medium term.		

(2 marks)

(d) Which TWO of the following are the main aims of budgeting?

    A   Controlling costs

    B   Identifying objectives

    C   Evaluating manager's performance

    D   Introducing budgetary bias   **(2 marks)**

(Total: 10 marks)

452 Mr Grob started trading in 20X3, selling one product, wheelbarrows, on credit to small retail outlets. The following budgeted information for 20X4 has been gathered:

	January 20X4	February 20X4	March 20X4
Credit sales	$12,000	$15,000	$21,000

Receivables have recently been settling their debts 50% in the month following sale, and 50% two months after sale. A prompt payment discount of 3% is offered to those receivables paying within one month.

The gross profit margin is expected to be 25%. Due to an anticipated continued increase in sales, Mr Grob intends to increase inventory levels in March 20X4 by $2,000, and it is intended that the payables balance is increased by $3,000 to ease cash flow in the same month.

Required:

(a) Calculate the budgeted cash that will received in March 20X4 (to the nearest $)

$ _____ (3 marks)

(b) Calculate the budgeted payment to suppliers in March 20X4 (to the nearest $)

$ _____ (3 marks)

(c) Calculate the chain base index for sales in February 20X4 and March 20X4 (to nearest whole number) (2 marks)

	February 20X4	March 20X4
Index		

(d) The following incomplete statement has been made.

The product life cycle has **(gap 1)** stages. Mr Grob's business is in the **(gap 2)** phase of the product lifecycle.

Required:

Select the correct words to complete the sentence.

Gap 1

A   Four

B   Five (1 mark)

Gap 2

A   Introduction

B   Growth (1 mark)

(Total: 10 marks)

453 A company manufactures a single product and has the following flexible production cost budgets for a period.

Production quantity	12,000 units	15,000 units	18,000 units
Direct material AB	$3,600	$4,500	$5,400
Direct material CD	$17,760	$22,200	$26,196
Labour (direct and indirect)	$25,700	$29,900	$35,150
Overhead (excluding indirect labour)	$12,400	$13,180	$13,960

The budget includes the following assumptions:

(i)   Each unit of the product requires:

        Material AB   0.2 kg
        Material CD   0.4 kg
        Direct labour   0.2 hours

(ii)   The supplier of Material CD gives a 10% discount on the excess of purchases over 6,000 kg per period.

During the period, the company manufactured 17,000 units of the product and incurred the following production costs:

Direct materials:

        Material AB $5,025
        Material CD $25,118
        Labour (direct and indirect) $32,889
        Overhead (excluding indirect labour) $13,315

Required:

(a)   Calculate the budgeted cost per kg of Material CD on the excess of purchases over 6,000 kg per period (to 2 decimal places).   **(3 marks)**

        $

(b)   Calculate the flexed statement for the period showing for each of the four items of cost and calculate the variance indicating if it is favourable (f) or adverse (a) (to the nearest whole $)

	Flexed budget	Actual cost	Variance
Activity level	17,000	17,000	0
Costs	$	$	$
Material AB		5,025	
Material CD		25,118	
Labour		32,889	
Overhead		13,315	

(4 marks)

(c)   The purchase price of Material AB in the period was as per budget.

       Calculate the material usage variance (in kg) for Material AB (to the nearest whole kg).   **(3 marks)**

Kg Fav/Adv

(Total: 10 marks)

454 Tathbone plc is preparing its budgets for the coming year. It expects to be able to sell 5,000 units of its only product, the Graham, in January 20X7. Sales are then expected to rise to 5,500 units in February and 7,000 units in March, and then remain stable for the rest of the year.

Tathbone plc aims to carry a finished goods inventory at the end of each month equal to 10% of the following month's sales. Each Graham takes four labour hours to make.

Tathbone's 138 production workers are employed on contracts that require them to work a minimum of 160 hours per month and are each paid $1,280 per month. Production workers are highly skilled and require a minimum of one year's training. In the short term it is not possible to recruit any more production workers. Any labour hours required in excess of 160 hours per worker are made up by overtime that is paid at basic rate plus an overtime premium of 50%.

Required:

(a)   **Calculate the a production budget in units, showing opening and closing inventories of finished goods (to the nearest whole number).**

Production budget 20X7   **Units**

	January	February	March
Sales			
Closing inventory			
Opening inventory			
Production units			

(4 marks)

(b)   **Calculate the labour budget showing both hours and labour cost (to the nearest whole number).**

(Assume that all production workers work at least 160 hours per month.)

Labour budget 20X7

	January	February	March
Total hours			
Basic hours available			
Overtime hours needed			

	January $	February~ $	March $
Basic rate payment			
Overtime payment			
Total labour cost			

(6 marks)

(Total: 10 marks)

455 J Co is considering investing in a new machine costing $18,750, payable immediately. The scrap value will be zero, and the machine will be depreciated on a straight line basis. Output would be 1,000 units per year for each of the six years of the machine's life. Each unit earns a contribution of $5.

Required:

(a) **Assuming that the cash flows arise evenly throughout the year, what is the payback period in years and months?** **(2 marks)**

years	months

(b) The management of J Co have heard about the concept of the time value of money.

Required:

(i) **Complete the gaps in the following statement:**

The time value of money means that $1 now is worth **(Gap 1)** than $1 in the future. The reasons for this are risk, **(Gap 2)** and potential for earning a return e.g. interest. **(2 marks)**

(ii) **Using a discount rate of 8%, and assuming that the cash flows arise at the end of a year, what is the discounted payback period?** **(2 marks)**

years	months

(c) **Using a discount factor of 8%, what is the net present value of purchasing the new machine (to the nearest $)?** **(2 marks)**

$

(d) **Are the following statements about investment appraisal true or false?**

Statement one: If the cost of capital increased to 10%, the net present value of purchasing the new machine would decrease.

Statement two: The payback method of investment appraisal is a useful method to consider time risk.

	Statement 1	Statement 2
A	True	False
B	True	True
C	False	False
D	False	True

(2 marks)

(Total: 10 marks)

456 A company is considering investment in several projects. The following information relates to three of the projects:

Project 1: Investment of $119,000 at the start of the project.

Net cash inflow of $13,500 per annum in perpetuity.

Project 2: Investment of $241,000 at the start of the project.

Net present value (NPV) at 20% of ($23,000) i.e. negative, based on net cash inflows of:

1st year	$60,000
2nd year	$65,000
3rd year	$70,000
4th year	$100,000
5th year	$85,000

Project 3: Investment of $186,000 at the start of the project.

Constant annual net cash inflows for five years.

Internal rate of return (IRR) of 14%.

Assume that net cash inflows occur at the end of each year.

The company's cost of capital is 10%.

Required:

(a) **Calculate the net present value (NPV) of Project 1 at the company's cost of capital (to the nearest $).** **(2 marks)**

$

(b) **Calculate the estimated internal rate of return (IRR) of Project 2 (to 1 decimal place)** **(3 marks)**

	%

(c) **Calculate the annual net cash inflow of Project 3 (to the nearest $).** **(3 marks)**

$

(d) **If the company's cost of capital increased to 15%, which project would be invested in?** (tick your chosen answer)

Project 2	
Project 3	

(2 marks)

(Total: 10 marks)

457 A company is considering an investment in new machinery. The incremental annual profits (losses) relating to the investment are estimated to be:

	$000
Year 1	(11)
Year 2	3
Year 3	34
Year 4	47
Year 5	8

Investment at the start of the project would be $175,000. The investment sum, assuming nil disposal value after five years, would be written off using the straight-line method. The depreciation has been included in the profit estimates above, which should be assumed to arise at each year end.

Required:

(a) **What is the total cash flows to be included in the investment appraisal (to the nearest $)?** **(2 marks)**

$ [   ]

(b) **What is the net present value (NPV) of the investment at a discount rate of 10% per annum (to the nearest $)?** **(2 marks)**

$ [   ]

(c) **If 10% is the company's required return what would be the decision regarding the investment?** **(2 marks)**

	Invest	Do not invest
Decision		

(d) The future value (S) of a sum invested now can be calculated using the formula:

$S = X(1 + r)^n$

What would be the future value of $5,000 if it was invested today for four years at a compound rate of interest of 8% per annum (to the nearest $). **(2 marks)**

$ [   ]

(e) **What is the effective annual rate of interest of 2.1% compounded every three months?**

A   6.43%

B   8.40%

C   8.67%

D   10.87%

(2 marks)

(Total: 10 marks)

STANDARD COSTING

458 Cabrinda Co manufactures bulbs. The following figures are available:

- 500 kg of direct materials were actually purchased

- The standard cost per kg is $2.25, leading to a standard cost of actual purchases of $1,125

- The direct materials price variance is $125 favourable

- The direct materials usage variance is $45 adverse

Required:

(a) **From the information provided calculate**

   (i) **The actual price paid per kg for the direct material (to 2 decimal places)**

     | $ |

     (2.5 marks)

   (ii) **The standard quantity that should have been used for actual production (to the nearest whole kg).**

     | kg |

     (2.5 marks)

(b) **Which of the following is likely to lead to the variances stated above?**

   A   lower quality direct material has been purchased

   B   higher quality direct material has been purchased   **(1 mark)**

(c) The following graph shows the standard price and quantity and the actual and price and quantity relating to the direct material for the manufacture of the bulbs.

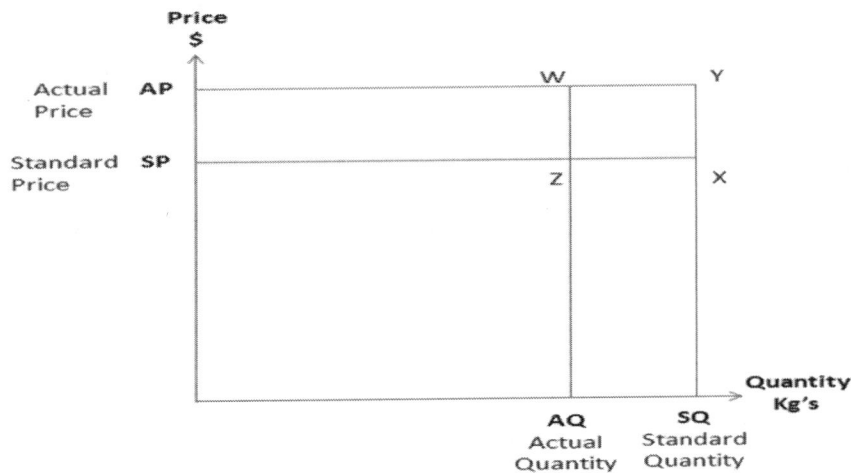

Required:

Which area correctly represents the direct material price variance?

   A   APWZSP

   B   APYXSP

   C   AQWYSQ

   D   AQZXSQ   **(2 marks)**

(d) The following spreadsheet has started to be completed for direct materials, with a ✔ showing where data has been entered.

	A	B	C
		Standard	Actual
1		Standard	Actual
2	Production in units	✔	✔
3	Kg's per unit	✔	
4	Cost per kg ($)	✔	✔
5	Total kg's purchased		C6/C4
6	Total material cost		✔

Required:

What will be the formula for the materials usage variance?

A   =(C5xC4)–(B2xB3xB4)

B   =(C5xB4)–(B2xB3xB4)

C   =(C5xC4)–(C2xB3xC4)

D   =(C5xB4)–(C2xB3xB4)

(2 marks)

(Total: 10 marks)

459 The following is a proforma operating statement for Wick Co, a company manufacturing candles.

	$
Budgeted profit	
Sales volume variance	
Standard profit on actual sales	_____
Sales price variance	
	_____

	Favourable ($)	Adverse ($)
Cost variances		
Materials price		
Materials usage		
Labour rate		
Labour efficiency		
Variable overhead rate		
Variable overhead efficiency		
Fixed overhead expenditure		
Fixed overhead capacity		
Fixed overhead efficiency	_____	
Total		_____
Actual profit		_____

(a)   **Which of the following THREE statements are correct?**

A   Wick Co uses standard profit per unit to calculate the sales volume variance.

B   The fixed overhead expenditure variance is the same figure as the over or under absorption of fixed overheads

C   Wick Co absorbs fixed overheads on an hourly basis.

D   The efficiency variances will all either be favourable or adverse   **(2 marks)**

(b)   The following information is available for Wick Co for month 1

Budgeted

Fixed overheads	$20,000 to be absorbed at $10/hr
Time to make one unit	4 hours

Actual

Fixed overheads	$23,000
Time taken to make 550 units	2,475 hours

Required:

Calculate the fixed overhead (to the nearest whole number):

(i)   **Expenditure variance and state if it is favourable or adverse**   **(2 marks)**

$ ☐

(ii)   **Capacity variance and state if it is favourable or adverse.**   **(2.5 marks)**

S ☐

(iii)   **Efficiency variance and state if it is favourable or adverse.**   **(2.5 marks)**

$ ☐

(c)   **Is the following statement true/false?**

'A favourable fixed overhead capacity variance is likely to arise if a new machine is bought to replace an unreliable one.'

A   True

B   False   **(1 mark)**

(Total: 10 marks)

460 Bogh Co manufactures wooden picture frames.

The company's information system produces an operating statement, and on the basis of the variances calculated, managers are assessed and bonuses paid.

The standard material cost for each picture frame is $8. This is made up:

Wood	0.5 kg @ $10 per kg	$5
Glass	0.25 kg @ $12 per kg	$3

In July, Bogh manufactured 300 picture frames, and purchased:

Wood	170 kg	$2,040
Glass	70 kg	$860

Required:

(a) **Using the information above, calculate (to the nearest whole number):**

    (i) **The total materials price variance and state if it is adverse or favourable.**

        $ _____

        (2.5 marks)

    (ii) **The total materials usage variance and state if it is adverse or favourable**

        $ _____

        (2.5 marks)

(b) The managers have now been told that although the levels of glass inventory did not change during July, wood inventory rose by 15 kg.

    Which manager will need to have this fact accounted for in their performance appraisal?

    A   Purchasing manager

    B   Production manager   **(1 mark)**

(c) **In the following graph, which area arises because both the material quantity and price are above standard levels?**

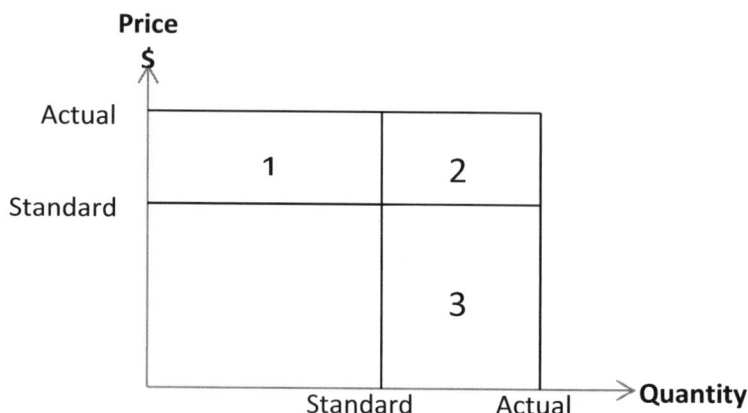

    A   Area 1 only

    B   Area 2 only

    C   Area 2 and 3

    D   Area 1 and 2   **(2 marks)**

(d) **Are the following statements true or false?**

Statement one: A flexed budget cannot be produced for non-manufacturing costs such as sales commission.

Statement two: All costs can be controlled in the long term.

	Statement one	Statement two
A	True	True
B	True	False
C	False	True
D	False	False

(2 marks)

(Total: 10 marks)

461 An operating statement has been partially completed for a company that makes pies and pasties:

	$
Budgeted contribution	5,075
Sales volume variance	175 (F)
Standard contribution on actual sales	5,250
Sales price variance	750 (A)
	4,500

	Favourable ($)	Adverse ($)
Cost variances		
Materials price		700
Materials usage	600	
Labour rate		724
Labour efficiency	650	
Variable overhead rate		
Variable overhead efficiency		
GAP 1		
Fixed overhead expenditure		
Total		

Required:

(a) For the following variances, state whether it is true or false that the variance stated above could be caused by better quality ingredients being purchased for the pies:

		True	False	
(i)	Sales volume			**(1 mark)**
(ii)	Materials price			**(1 mark)**
(iii)	Labour rate			**(1 mark)**
(iv)	Materials usage			**(1 mark)**
(v)	Sales price			**(1 mark)**

(b) What should the title be in Gap 1? **(1 mark)**

(c) Using the following information, calculate the variable overhead rate and efficiency variances, and state if they are favourable or adverse.

Actual production was 1,500 units which were completed in 3,620 hours at a variable overhead cost of $11,000.

The budget was that each pie would take 2.5 hours to make and the variable overhead absorption rate would be $3 per hour. **(4 marks)**

Variable overhead rate variance	$
Variable efficiency variance	$

(Total: 10 marks)

PERFORMANCE MEASUREMENT

462 Tel Co manufactures televisions and sells them to large retailers. Due to high staff turnover, no liquidity ratios have been calculated for the year ahead.

The bank is concerned about the forecast increase in Tel Co's overdraft to $40,500 at 30 November 20X4, and has suggested that the ratios be calculated. The following forecast information is available for the year ended 30 November 20X4:

	$
Revenue	343,275
Cost of sales	284,000
Purchases	275,000
Closing Inventory	35,000
Receivables	37,400
Payables	35,410

Required:

(a) For Tel Co for the year ended 30 November 20X2 calculate:

    (i) The inventory holding period (to the nearest day)   **(1.5 marks)**

days

    (ii) The receivables collection period (to the nearest day)   **(1.5 marks)**

days

    (iii) The payables period (to the nearest day)   **(1.5 marks)**

days

    (iv) The current ratio (to 3 decimal places)   **(1.5 marks)**

days

(b) Tel Co's quick ratio is 0.49.

If they sell half of their inventory to pay off part of the bank overdraft, what will happen to their quick ratio?

    A   Stay the same

    B   Increase

    C   Decrease   **(2 marks)**

(c) In an attempt to improve their liquidity position, Tel Co is considering offering an early settlement discount to its customers.

Which TWO of the following outcomes may occur as a result of offering the early settlement discount?

    A   Sales increase

    B   Bad debts increase

    C   Administration cost decrease

    D   Receivables decrease   **(2 marks)**

                    (Total: 10 marks)

463 Drive Co is a diverse business, one division of which runs a courier business using a fleet of small vans. The following information has been produced by the manager of the division for the year ended 30 June 20X4:

Revenue	$500,000
Gross profit	$120,000
Operating profit	$50,000
Loan (8% per year)	$60,000
Asset turnover	4

Required:

(a) Using the information provided, calculate (to 2 decimal places):

    (i)   **Interest cover**   **(1.5 marks)**

        [   ]

    (ii)   **Return on capital employed**   **(2.5 marks)**

        [%]

    (ii)   **Gearing**   **(2 marks)**

        [%]

(b) The manager of the courier division is retiring this year and his bonus is being paid based on the ROCE percentage of the division.

Which TWO of the following actions could the manager of the courier division have taken in order to improve his bonus?

    A   Delay repairs to the fleet of vans.

    B   Understate the closing inventory of fuel held in the depot.

    C   Include all the revenue for an uncompleted new contract.

    D   Overstate the bad debt provision   **(2 marks)**

(c) The management of Drive Co would like to introduce some more operational measures for performance evaluation.

Which of the following measures would be most useful?

    A   Cost per tonne mile

    B   Cost per driver hour

    C   Van idle time percentage

    D   Driver idle time percentage   **(2 marks)**

(Total: 10 marks)

464 Mal Co currently sells 25 styles of sports watches. The market has remained static with an overall revenue of $50 million.

Mal Co is always trying to bring out new designs and colours to try and increase market share or at least maintain it. In order to not fall behind their competitors, Mal Co tries to bring new products to the market quickly. Therefore Mal Co undertakes market research one year, and the results of that market research are incorporated in the new styles/colours that are launched the next year.

Historically, Mal Co have measured their performance by looking for an increase in the revenue and net profit figures and ensuring that there is cash in the bank. A new financial manager has been appointed who is keen to increase the range of performance measures used by Mal Co.

The following data is available:

	Year ended 31 October 20X3	Year ended 31 October 20X4
Revenue	$5.75 million	$6 million
Number of styles	22	25
Net profit	$345,000	$348,000
Market research costs	$200,000	$150,000

Required:

(a) **Calculate:**

   (i) **Net profit percentage for 20X4 (to 1 decimal place)** (1.5 marks)

%

   (ii) **Market share for 20X4 (to 1 decimal place)** (1.5 marks)

%

   (iii) **Increase in revenue (to 2 decimal places)** (1.5 marks)

%

   (iv) **Revenue per style of watch for 20X4 (to the nearest whole $)** (1.5 marks)

$

   (v) **Increase in sales per $ of market research (to 2 decimal places)** (2 marks)

(b) Mal Co are considering setting up another division selling expensive watches. The two divisions would be run as profit centres, with head office costs being allocated to each division. Managers' bonuses will be dependent on the divisions meeting their targets. Targets that are being considered are:

   (i)   Gross profit percentage

   (ii)   Contribution

   (iii) Net profit for the division

   (iv)   Return on capital employed

Which of the targets should be used to assess the performance of the divisional manager and provide motivation?

A   (i) only

B   (i) and (ii) only

C   (i), (ii) and (iii) only

D   All of them   **(2 marks)**

(Total: 10 marks)

465   Grub Co is a fast food restaurant. Historically they have always relied upon financial measures of performance, concentrating on ratios such as the number of burgers sold and the profit made per burger sold.

Grub Co is now considering implementing a balanced scorecard approach.

Required:

(a)   **Complete the following statements about the balanced scorecard approach, choosing from the options available:**

Before a balanced scorecard approach can be considered, an organisation needs to first have **(gap1)**. The balanced scorecard approach focuses on **(gap 2)**

Gap 1

A   key performance indicator's agreed with management

B   a mission statement

C   operational plans in place   **(1 mark)**

Gap 2

A   short term improvements for the business.

B   the long term success of the business.   **(1 mark)**

(b)   **For each of the following measures, state if they are measuring the financial, customer, internal, or learning perspective of Grub Co's balanced scorecard:**

	Financial	Customer	Internal	Learning perspective
Profit made per burger				
Time taken from the customer ordering food to food being passed to the customer				
Percentage of employees with higher level food hygiene certificates				
Percentage of burgers cooked but not sold as they are inedible				

(4 marks)

(c)   The following explanation of benchmarking is incomplete:

There are four types of benchmarking, being **(gap 1)**, competitive, functional and strategic. Comparing the results of Grub Co with McDonalds would be a form of **(gap 2)** benchmarking

State the words that fill the gaps.   **(2 marks)**

(d)   **Select the option that has the steps in a systematic benchmarking exercise in the correct order:**

A   analysis→ planning→ action→ review

B   review→ planning→ action→ analysis

C   planning→ analysis→ action→ review

D   analysis→ action→ review→ planning   **(2 marks)**

(Total: 10 marks)

466   The directors of Donny Co are reviewing the performance of two of its divisions. The following information is available for the year ending 31 March 2009.

	South division	North division
	$000	$000
Sales	50,000	3,200
Operating profit	700	840
Capital employed	3,500	4,000
Cost of capital	12%	12%

South division is a food retailer that sells low priced food from a number of stores that are rented on short-term contracts. North division sells luxury motor vehicles, which it manufactures in a fully automated production plant.

Required:

Calculate the following performance measures for the two divisions (to 1 decimal place):

		South division	North division	
(a)	**Return on capital employed**			**(2 marks)**
(b)	**Return on sales**			**(2 marks)**
(c)	**Asset turnover**			**(3 marks)**
(d)	**Residual income**			**(3 marks)**

(Total: 10 marks)

467 During a period, the actual hours worked by the employees of SCRMA totalled 31,630. Budgeted hours were 29,470 hours. The standard hours for the work totalled 30,502.

(a) **Calculate the production volume ratio (to 1 decimal place)** (1 mark)

	%

(b) **Calculate the efficiency ratio (to 1 decimal place)** (1 mark)

	%

(c) **Calculate the capacity ratio (to 1 decimal place)** (1 mark)

	%

SCRMA has 2 divisions with the following information:

Division A of SCRMA has been offered a project costing $100,000 and giving returns of $20,000. The company's cost of capital is 15%. Divisional performance is judged on ROI and the ROI related bonus is sufficiently high to influence the managers' behaviour. Without the project Division A has the following details:

	Division A
	$
Profit	90,000
Capital employed	300,000
ROI	30%

(d) **What decision will be made by management of the division if they act in the best interests of their division (and in the best interest of their bonus)?** (3 marks)

	Invest	Do not invest
Decision		

(e) **What should the managers do if they act in the best interests of the company as a whole?** (1 mark)

	Invest	Do not invest
Decision		

One of SCRMA's investment centres has net assets of $800,000, and made profits before interest of $160,000. The notional cost of capital is 12%. An opportunity has arisen to invest in a new project costing $100,000 that would make profits of $15,000 each year.

(f) **What would be the residual income with the investment (to nearest $)?** (2 marks)

$

(g) **Would the investment centre manager wish to undertake the investment? (1 marks)**

	Invest	Do not invest
Decision		

(Total: 10 marks)

468 NFS hospital is located in a country where healthcare is free, as the taxpayers fund the hospitals which are owned by the government. Two years ago management reviewed all aspects of hospital operations and instigated a number of measures aimed at improving performance and overall 'value for money' for the local community.

- To reduce the number of complaints

- To reduce the number of existing patients

- To reduce the cost per patient

The following data have been provided:

	Year 1	Year 2
Total patients	8,800	9,100
of which - new	1,300	700
of which - existing	7,600	8,400
Complaints	560	565
Total cost	$14.08m	$14.287m

(a) **What proportion of total patients are new in year 2 (to 2 decimal places)? (1 mark)**

	%

(b) **What is the percentage change in existing patients from year 1 to year 2 (to 2 decimal places)?**   **(1 mark)**

	%

(c) **Which TWO of the following statements regarding NFS's performance are true?**

  A   NFS has failed to succeed in meeting any of its goals

  B   NFS's cost per patient in Year 1 was $1,600

  C   NFS's number of complaints per patient in Year 2 was 0.062

  D   NFS's total cost has increased by 3.4%   **(2 marks)**

(d) **Select the correct term to complete the following sentences:**

  A   NFS's number of complaints has **increased/decreased** and its number of complaints per patient has **increased/decreased**.

  B   NFS's total cost has **increased/decreased** and its cost per patient has **increased/decreased**.

  C   NFS's number of new patients has **increased/decreased** and its number of existing patients has **increased/decreased**.   **(3 marks)**

Value for money can be assessed using the three Es. The three Es are:

- Efficiency

- Economy

- Effectiveness

NFS hospital has set the following performance goals:

- To maximise the bed occupancy rate

- To minimise patient waiting times

- To reduce the total staff cost while maintaining the level of service.

(e) **Match the goals to whether they relate to efficiency, effectiveness or economy.**

Efficiency
Economy
Effectiveness

To maximise the bed occupancy rate
To minimise patient waiting times
To reduce the total staff cost while maintaining the level of service

(3 marks)

(Total: 10 marks)

Section 3

ANSWERS TO SECTION A-TYPE QUESTIONS

SYLLABUS AREA A – THE NATURE, SOURCE AND PURPOSE OF MANAGEMENT INFORMATION

ACCOUNTING FOR MANAGEMENT

1   D

2   A

Reginald is only responsible for costs

3   A

Cost accounting can be used for inventory valuation to meet the requirements of both internal reporting and external financial reporting.

4   B

Cost accounting is not part of financial accounting.

5   A

Qualitative data is normally non-numerical. Information comes from both internal and external sources. Operational information is usually short-term (current) in nature. Quantitative data will be as accurate as possible.

6   C

The manager of a profit centre needs to know about the profits of the centre, i.e. revenues and costs. (Revenues only are appropriate for a revenue centre; costs only for a cost centre; and revenues, costs and assets employed for an investment centre.)

7   C

Lowering a selling price, presumably to increase sales volume, is a short-term decision/plan. The measures in A, B and D are not planning decisions at all: they are all monitoring/control activities.

8

	Management accounts	Financial accounts
Prepared yearly		✓
For internal use	✓	
Contains future information	✓	

9   B

Strategic planning is carried out by senior managers and is concerned with long-term planning. Both quantitative and qualitative information is used.

10   D

(i)   ROCE compares profit to capital employed and is not a suitable measure for a profit centre as the manager does not have responsibility for capital employed.

(ii)   Cost centres are found in all organisations.

(iii)   The manager of a revenue centre is only responsible for revenues, not costs.

11

	YES	NO
Control	✓	
Plan	✓	
Co-ordinate	✓	
Make decisions	✓	
Motivate	✓	

12   A

The mixing and pouring departments are cost centres. The paint is not poured into tins until after the colour adding department so a litre tin would not be a suitable cost unit.

SOURCES OF DATA

13   B

The information should be sufficiently accurate given time and cost constraints. Managers should be made aware of the degree of accuracy of the information.

14   B

Secondary data is used for one purpose, although it was originally collected for another purpose.

15

	Primary	Secondary
Data collected outside a polling station regarding voters choices	×	
An internet search for the cheapest fuel available in the area		×
Government statistics on the levels of unemployment		×
Data collected by observation on the number of cars flowing through a junction during peak travel hours	×	

16   **D**

17   **C and D**

18   **D**

Useful management information does not necessarily have to be presented in report format, supported by calculations or communicated in writing.

19   **D**

Data consists of numbers, letters, symbols, raw facts, events and transactions which have been recorded but not yet processed into a form which is suitable for making decisions. Information is data which has been processed in such a way that it has a meaning to the person who receives it, who may then use it to improve the quality of decision making.

20   **B**

Information is processed data. The distinction is that data is unprocessed whereas information is processed.

21   **A**

External information is obtained from sources outside the organisation. Statistics relating to the consumer price index come from the government. Information about price lists, production volumes and discounts to customers comes from sources within the organisation.

22   **A**

All of the others have been processed in some way and are information.

23   **C**

Primary data is data which is used solely for the purpose for which it was collected.

24   **D**

Information from the Institute of Directors, the tax authorities (e.g. HM Revenue and Customs in the UK) and a government department (national minimum wage) are all examples of external information – i.e. information from an external source.

25

	True	False
Big Data management involves using sophisticated systems to gather, store and analyse large volumes of data	✓	
Data can be in variety of structured and unstructured formats.	✓	
Big data does not include traditional data from internal sources such as sales history, preferences, order frequency and pricing information.		✓
Big Data does include information from external sources such as websites, trade publications and social networks.	✓	

26   A and B

27   A

28   B, C and D

Option A is incorrect in that Big Data does not refer to any specific financial amount.

29   B

30   B, C AND D

Note that the increasing use of electronic devices makes Big Data collection easier. Many organisations successfully gather information from social media sites such as Facebook and Twitter and use it to great effect within their decision-making processes.

31   C

PRESENTING INFORMATION

32   D

A simple bar chart would show five bars illustrating the different salaries in different regions.

33   C

The sales revenue is dependent on the money spent on advertising. The more advertising that is done the higher the sales revenue should be. Not vice versa

34   63°

241/1,384 × 360 = 62.69° = 63°

35   B

45°/360° × $800,000 = $100,000

36   D

A bar chart is a good way of illustrating total sales month by month. The length of the bar each month is a measure of total sales. The bar can be divided into three parts, to show the amount of sales achieved for each of the three products. This is called a component bar chart.

37   A

38   D

39

	True	False
Area 3 shows the best performance in Q3	✓	
Area 2 sales are consistent quarter on quarter		✓
Q4 has the largest volume of sales across all areas	✓	
Area 1 shows the best performance in Q2	✓	

40   The angle for Wheat would be 155° and the angle for Oats would be 43°

Wheat angle = (43 ÷ 100) × 360 = 155°

Oats angle = (12 ÷ 100) × 360 = 43°

COST CLASSIFICATION

41   D

Options B and C would begin from 0 and are clearly incorrect. Option A would be similar to the graph given except it would be flat at the top due to the maximum annual charge.

42   A

Variable cost per unit = [($274,000 − $250,000) ÷ (15,000 − 12,000)] = $8

Total fixed cost above 11,000 units = [$274,000 − (15,000 × $8)] = $154,000

Total fixed cost below 11,000 units = (10 ÷ 11) × $154,000 = $140,000

Total cost for 10,000 units = [(10,000 × $8) + $140,000] = $220,000

43   B

As the royalty relates to every unit produced, it is therefore classified as a direct expense.

44

Division	Cost centre	Profit centre	Investment centre
Car sales		✓	
Motorbike sales			✓
Manufacturing	✓		
Finishing			✓

45   B

Inventory is valued at full production cost which includes direct material, direct labour and production overheads.

46   A

Supervisor's wages are usually classified as a step cost because a supervisor may be responsible for supervising up to a specific number of workers. However, if output increases such that additional direct labour is required, then an extra supervisor will be required. Rates do step up in cost but that is in relation to time not output i.e. the rates may increase year on year.

47   C

C is the correct answer because a manager is not a cost object but may be linked to a cost centre in a responsibility accounting system.

48   B

Answers A, C and D are incorrect, leaving B as the only possible answer. Depreciation of fixtures is an overhead cost, and could be production, administration or selling and distribution overheads, depending on the nature of the fixtures.

49   D

The cost of the ingredients is a direct material cost.

50   A and B

The prime cost is the total of all direct costs which will include direct expenses as well as direct labour and materials.

51   C

The inventory valuation will be unchanged. Finished goods are valued at the total production cost and the rent of the warehouse would be classed as a distribution cost.

52

Cost	Fixed	Variable	Semi-variable
Director's salary	✓		
Wood		✓	
Rent of factory	✓		
Phone bill – includes a line rental			✓
Factory workers wage		✓	

53 A

The graph shows a reduction in unit variable costs beyond certain output levels. Only Answer A is consistent with this cost behaviour pattern.

54

Cost	Code
Salary of trainee IT consultant	B100
Planning costs to renew lease of the office	C200
Wages of the office manager	B200
Cleaning materials used by cleaner	A200

55

Cost	Materials	Labour	Expenses
Designer skirts	✓		
Heating costs			✓
Depreciation of fixtures and fittings			✓
Cashier staff salaries		✓	

56 B

Managers are not usually classified as direct labour.

57 C

Item B describes the costs of an activity or cost centre. Item A describes cost units. Item D describes budget centres. A cost centre is defined as 'a production or service location, function, activity or item of equipment for which costs are accumulated'.

58 $187,000

	$
Total cost of 18,500 hours	251,750
Total cost of 17,000 hours	246,500
Variable cost of 1,500 hours	5,250

Variable cost per machine hour = $5,250/1,500 machine hours = $3.50.

	$
Total cost of 17,000 hours	246,500
Less variable cost of 17,000 hours (× $3.50)	59,500
Balance = fixed costs	187,000

59   A

The cost is direct as it can be directly attributed to a job. It is an expense because it is invoiced to the company and not a payroll cost.

60   A

	Cost per unit ($) (125 units)	Cost per unit ($) (180 units)
T1	8.00	7.00
T2	14.00	14.00
T3	19.80	15.70
T4	25.80	25.80

Cost types T2 and T4 are variable and T1 and T3 are semi-variable.

61

Cost	Direct	Indirect
Machine operators wages	✓	
Supervisors wages		✓
Resin for golf balls	✓	
Salesmen's salaries		✓

62   A

	$
Total cost of 15,100 square metres	83,585
Total cost of 12,750 square metres	73,950
Variable cost of 2,350 square metres	9,635

Variable cost is $9,635/2,350 square metres = $4.10 per square metre.

Fixed costs can be found by substitution:

	$
Total cost of 12,750 square metres	73,950
Variable cost of 12,750 square metres (× $4.10)	52,275
Fixed costs	21,675

So for 16,200 square metres:

Overheads   = $21,675 + (16,200 × $4.10)

= $88,095

63   A

64   B

	$
Total cost of 10,000 units	400,000
Total cost of 5,000 units	250,000
Variable cost of 5,000 units	150,000

Therefore the variable cost per unit = $150,000/5,000 units = $30 per unit.

65   C

	Units		$
Total cost of	20,000	=	40,000
Total cost of	4,000	=	20,000
Therefore variable cost of	16,000	=	20,000

Variable cost per unit = $20,000/16,000 units = $1.25 per unit.

66   D

Graph D is consistent with the cost behaviour for total materials given.

Graph A implies that there is a certain range of activity (just above 15,000 units) when total materials cost is constant.

Graph B implies that total materials cost falls beyond 15,000 units of activity.

Graph C implies that the lower cost per unit for materials applies only to units purchased in excess of 15,000.

67

Cost	Production	Administration	Distribution
Purchases of plastic to make pens	✓		
Managing director's bonus		✓	
Depreciation of factory machinery	✓		
Salaries of factory workers	✓		
Insurance of sales team cars			✓

68 A

For the first 10 hours of calls only the fixed line rental is charged therefore the answer cannot be B or D, which show no costs until a number of hours have passed. Graph C shows a variable cost is charged from nil to a maximum number of hours which is incorrect. The answer is A.

69 C

Use the two levels of production above 1,100 units per month for the high-low analysis as at these levels fixed costs are the same.

Units	Total cost ($)
1,400	68,200
1,200	66,600
——	——
200	1,600
——	——

Variable cost per unit = ($1,600 ÷ 200) = $8

Total fixed cost (above 1,100 units) = [$68,200 − (1,400 × $8)] = $57,000

Total cost for 1,000 units = [($57,000 − $6,000) + (1,000 × $8)] = $59,000

70

Cost	Direct	Indirect
Bricks	✓	
Plant hire for long term contract	✓	
Builders' wages	✓	
Accountants' wages		✓

SYLLABUS AREA B – DATA ANALYSIS AND STATISTICAL TECHNIQUES

SAMPLING METHODS

71   C

72   C

This is the definition of systematic sampling.

73   B

Simple random sampling always eliminates selection bias but does not guarantee a representative sample.

74   D

Accountant first stratifies the invoices according to value and then selects randomly. Sampling method is stratified.

75   D

Option A is not random – it is a systematic sample.

Option B selects only those who are in a class – so it is NOT random.

Option C, again, is not random as it only selects from 10% of colleges (and therefore does not include home study, or the other 90%).

FORECASTING TECHNIQUES

76   A

As advertising will hopefully generate sales, advertising is the independent variable and sales revenue the dependent; i.e. advertising is x and sales revenue is y.

		$
High	Sales revenue from $6,500 of advertising	225,000
Low	Sales revenue from $2,500 of advertising	125,000
	Sales revenue from $4,000 of advertising	100,000

Sales revenue for each $1 of advertising = $100,000/$4,000 = $25.

	$
Sales revenue from $6,500 of advertising	225,000
Sales revenue from $6,500 of advertising (x $25)	162,500
Sales revenue with no advertising	62,500

This gives a function of sales revenue = $62,500 + $25x, where x is the spending on advertising.

77 C

In the formula C = 1,000 + 250P, 1,000 represents the weekly fixed costs and 250 the variable cost per unit.

78 2.04

C = F + Vx

14,520 = 7,788 + V(3,300)

6,732 = 3,300V

V = 2.04

79 A

Coefficient of determination = r^2 = 0.6 × 0.6 = 0.36 = 36%

80 A

$$a = \frac{\Sigma y}{n} - \frac{b\,\Sigma x}{n}$$

$$a = \frac{183,000}{5} - \frac{4,200 \times 21}{5} = [36,600 - 17,640] = 18,960.$$

If there are 2 salesmen in the month, expected costs will be: 18,960 + (4,200 × 2) = 27,360

81 A

This question is a simple test of your understanding of the meaning of the elements in a regression analysis formula. Statements (i) and (ii) are correct, but statement (iii) is wrong. The total value of x multiplied by the total value of y would be written as Σx Σy, not as Σxy.

82 0.69

You should use the formulae provided in the examination (formulae sheet)

$$b = \frac{(11 \times 13,467) - (440 \times 330)}{(11 \times 17,986) - (440)^2} = \frac{2,937}{4,246} = 0.6917 = 0.69$$

83 B

Σx = Σ Advertising expenditure = 100,000

Σy = Σ Sales revenue = 600,000

n = number of pairs of data = 5

84 A

85   **B**

$\Sigma y = 17,500 + 19,500 + 20,500 + 18,500 + 17,000 = 93,000$

$\Sigma x = 300 + 360 + 400 + 320 + 280 = 1,660$

$a = (93,000 \div 5) - (29.53 \times 1,660 \div 5) = 8,796.04$

86   **B**

+1 represents perfect positive correlation.

−1 represents perfect negative correlation.

The nearer to 0 the correlation coefficient the less correlation between the variables.

87   **A**

$$b = \frac{n\,\Sigma xy - \Sigma x\,\Sigma y}{n\,\Sigma x^2 - (\Sigma x)^2}$$

$$= [(5 \times 23,091) - (129 \times 890)] \div [(5 \times 3,433) - (129^2)] = 1.231$$

$$a = \frac{\Sigma y}{n} - b\frac{\Sigma x}{n}$$

$$= (890 \div 5) - [(1.231 \times 129) \div 5] = 146 \text{ (nearest whole number)}$$

88   In the equation y = a + bx, b represents the variable cost per unit.

Using the formula $b = [(6 \times 209,903) - (61.25 \times 20,430)]/[(6 \times 630.56) - 61.25^2] = \$254$

89   **B**

The correlation coefficient must be between +1 and −1.

90   **B**

91   **C**

92   **A**

Quarter	'Real' sales
1	$\dfrac{109}{100} \times 100 = 109.0$
2	$\dfrac{120}{110} \times 100 = 109.1$
3	$\dfrac{132}{121} \times 100 = 109.1$
4	$\dfrac{145}{133} \times 100 = 109.0$

The 'real' series is approximately constant and keeping up with inflation.

93   C

Current cost = $5 × 430 ÷ 150 = $14.33

94   The variable cost per unit = [($3,860 × 106/102) − ($3,098 × 106/104)]/(12 − 9) = $284

95   B

	Price index	Quantity weighting	Price index × Quantity
Flour	0.30/0.25 × 100 = 120	8,000	960,000
Eggs	1.25/1.00 × 100= 125	4,000	500,000
Milk	0.35/0.30 × 100 = 117	10,000	1,170,000
Potatoes	0.06/0.05 × 100 = 120	6,000	720,000
		28,000	3,350,000

Weighted price index = 3,350,000/28,000 = 119.6

96   A

	Quantity index	Revenue weighting	Quantity index × Revenue
Flour	10/8 × 100 = 125	0.25 × 8,000 = 2,000	250,000
Eggs	5/4 × 100= 125	1.00 × 4,000 = 4,000	500,000
Milk	10/10 × 100 = 100	0.30 × 10,000= 3,000	300,000
Potatoes	10/6 × 100 = 167	0.05 × 6,000 = 300	50,100
		9,300	1,100,100

Weighted quantity index = 1,100,100/9,300 = 118.3

97   C

See table below (226)

98   D

See table below

	Sales volume (units)	Trend	Variation
January	172,100		
February	149,600		
March	165,800	166,040	−240
April	182,600	171,040	11,560

May	160,100	176,040	−15,940
June	197,100	181,040	16,060
July	174,600	186,040	−11,440
August	190,800	191,040	−240
September	207,600	196,040	11,560
October		201,040	−15,940
November		206,040	16,060
December	199,600	211,040	−11,440

99 D

100 A

($2,000 × 120 ÷ 160) = $1,500

101 B

(5,000 + 23 × 4,000 − 1,500) = 95,500

102 B AND D

103 A

y = 3,000 + (150 × 3)

y = 3,450

Actual − trend = variation

3,500 − 3,450 = +50

104 C

y = 3,000 + (150 × 15)

y = 5,250

Trend + variation = actual

5,250 + 50 = 5,300

105 C

Development, Introduction, and Decline

106 C

	Price index	Quantity weighting	Price index × Quantity
F	11/12 × 100 = 92	25,000	2,300,000
G	22/26 × 100= 85	52,000	4,420,000
H	18/18 × 100 = 100	79,000	7,900,000
I	20/22 × 100 = 91	35,000	3,185,000
J	22/23 × 100 = 96	36,000	3,456,000
		227,000	21,261,000

Weighted price index = 21,261,000/227,000 = 93.7

107 B

	Quantity index	Revenue weighting	Quantity index × Revenue
F	21/25 × 100 = 84	12 × 25,000 = 300,000	25,200,000
G	56/52 × 100= 108	26 × 52,000 = 1,352,000	146,016,000
H	62/79 × 100 = 78	18 × 79,000= 1,422,000	110,916,000
I	29/35 × 100 = 83	22 × 35,000 = 770,000	63,910,000
J	31/36 × 100 = 86	23 × 36,000 = 828,000	71,208,000
		4,672,000	417,250,000

Weighted quantity index = 417,250,000/4,672,000 = 89.3

SUMMARISING AND ANALYSING DATA

108 Mean = **125 seconds**

Time taken (mid-point)	f	fx	fx^2
107.5	2	215.00	23,112.50
112.5	5	562.50	63,281.25
117.5	4	470.00	55,225.00
122.5	8	980.00	120,050.00
127.5	10	1,275.00	162,562.50
132.5	5	662.50	87,781.25
137.5	4	550.00	75,625.00
142.5	2	285.00	40,612.50
	40	5,000.00	628,250.00

Mean = $\Sigma fx \div \Sigma f$ = 5,000 ÷ 40 = 125 seconds

109 Standard deviation = **9.01**

$$S = \sqrt{\frac{\Sigma fx^2}{\Sigma f} - \left(\frac{\Sigma fx}{\Sigma f}\right)^2}$$

$$\text{Standard deviation} = \sqrt{\frac{628{,}250}{40} - \left(\frac{5{,}000}{40}\right)^2} = 9.01$$

110 x = **24kg**

Mean = 20 kg

Samples size = 10

so 15 + x + 22 + 14 + 21 + 15 + 20 + x + 18 + 27 = 200

so 152 + 2x = 200

2x = 48

x = 24

111 The complete sentences are:

- The **mode** is the value which appears with the highest frequency

- The **mean** is calculated by adding all of the values and dividing the total by the number of values

- The **median** is the middle of a set of values

112 The standard deviation is **1.16.**

Orders (x)	Frequency	fx	fx^2
1	3	3	3
2	5	10	20
3	10	30	90
4	14	56	224
5	8	40	200
Total	40	139	537

$$S = \sqrt{\frac{\Sigma fx^2}{\Sigma f} - \left(\frac{\Sigma fx}{\Sigma f}\right)^2}$$

$$S = \sqrt{\frac{537}{40} - \left(\frac{139}{40}\right)^2}$$

$$= \sqrt{13.43 - 12.08}$$

$$= \sqrt{1.35} = 1.16$$

113 C

To make calculation easier subtract 500

So $500 + \dfrac{4+6+1+5+7+6+4+8+3+5+2+4}{12}$

$= 500 + \dfrac{55}{12} = 504.6$

114 B

Arranging in numerical order we have

501, 502, 503, 504, 504, 504, 505, 505, 506, 506, 507, 508

Median = (504 + 505) ÷ 2 = 504.5

115 A

The modal weight is 504 since it appears more times than any other

116 The complete frequency distribution is shown below

Time	Frequency
105 > 110	2
110 > 115	**6**
115 > 120	4
120 > **125**	7
125 > 130	**10**
130 > 135	5
135 > **140**	4
140 > 145	2

117 The correct matching is:

A Data has to be arranged in order of size which is time consuming – **Median**

B It may give undue weight or be influenced by extreme values – **Mean**

C Data has to be arranged to ascertain which figure appears the most often – **Mode**

The arithmetic mean is calculated by taking the total value of all items divided by the total number of items.

The median is the value of the middle item in a distribution once all the items have been arranged in order of magnitude.

The mode is the value that occurs most frequently amongst all the items in the distribution.

118 C and E

119 D

Expected value = $\sum PX$

= (0.3 × $10) + (0.3 × $50) + (0.4 × $80)

= $50

120 The council would make a **$1,000 saving**

Cost of new machine = $20,000

Expected saving   = (0.2 × 40,000) + (0.5 × 20,000) + (0.3 × 10,000)

= $8,000 + $10,000 + $3,000

= $21,000

Based purely on expected value theory, the council should buy a new snow plough since they could expect to save $1,000.

121 Expected profit from new product is **$27,000**

(0.1 × $100,000) + (0.5 × $50,000) + (0.4 × −20,000)

= $27,000

122 B

$$Z = \frac{x - \mu}{\sigma}$$

$$Z = \frac{330 - 360}{15} = -2$$

From normal distribution table, look up 2, which gives 0.4772

So probability Z < $330   = 0.5 − 0.4772 = 0.0228 or 2.3%

123 D

Required area is between 370 and 400

$$Z = \frac{400 - 360}{15} = 2.666$$

From table, Z = 2.666 gives 0.4962

$$Z = \frac{370 - 360}{15} = 0.667$$

From table, Z = 0.667 gives 0.2486

0.4962 − 0.2486 = 0.2476 or approximately 25%.

124 The probability that the cake selected is chocolate flavoured is **25%**.

In each batch of 100, 25 of the cakes will be chocolate flavoured.

The probability of selecting a chocolate cake will be 25 in 100 = 0.25 or 25%.

125 A and D

The median is the value of the middle item. So if the numbers are put in order:

3, 6, 10, 14, 17, 19, 22

The median is 14.

The arithmetic mean = (3 + 6 + 10 + 14 + 17 + 19 + 22) ÷ 7 = 13

126 B

Project	EV	Workings
	$000	
L	500	(500 × 0.2) + (470 × 0.5) + (550 × 0.3)
M	526	(400 × 0.2) + (550 × 0.5) + (570 × 0.3)
N	432.5	(450 × 0.2) + (400 × 0.5) + (475 × 0.3)
O	398	etc.
P	497.5	

∴ Project M will maximise expected cash.

127

	Disadvantage of EVs?
Expected values only provides the most likely result	
It ignores attitudes to risk	✓
Only two possible outcomes can be considered	
Probabilities are subjective	✓
The answer provided may not exist	✓

128 2.74%

$$Z = \frac{x - \mu}{\sigma}$$

$$Z = \frac{823 - 800}{12} = 1.92$$

From table, Z = 1.92 gives 0.4726

There is a 47.26% probability that an item would weigh from 800g up to 823g but only a 2.74% chance that it would weigh more.

0.5 − 0.4726 = 0.0274 = 2.74%

129 B

The probability of a sale worth more than $120 is 0.0119 therefore the probability of a sale between $110 and $120 is 0.5 − 0.0119 = 0.4881

Using the normal distribution tables z = 2.26

$$Z = \frac{x - \mu}{\sigma}$$

$$2.26 = \frac{120 - 110}{\sigma}$$

$\sigma = (120-110) / 2.226 = \$4.42$

130   26.67%

$$Z = \frac{x - \mu}{\sigma}$$

If the weight is 7.985kg

$$Z = \frac{7.985 - 8}{0.02}$$

Z = -0.75 which gives 0.2734 from the tables

If the weight is 8.035

$$Z = \frac{8.035 - 8}{0.02}$$

Z = 1.75 which gives 0.4599 from the tables

We want to know the probability outside this range so 0.2734 + 0.4599 = 0.7333

Therefore faulty items outside this range has the probability of 1 − 0.7333 = 0.2667 = 26.67%

131   A

If 7% of the population is above 510 litres then we get a z score of 0.5 − 0.07 = 0.43. Using the tables Z = 1.48

$$1.48 = \frac{510 - 500}{\sigma}$$

$\sigma = (510 -500) / 1.48 = 6.76$

132   1.32%

$$Z = \frac{500 - 498}{0.9}$$

Z = 2.22

Using the tables 2.22 = 0.4868

We want to know the probability of the volume being greater than 500ml so 0.5 – 0.4868 = 0.0132 = 1.32%

133   0.62%

$$Z = \frac{47 - 37}{4}$$

Z = 2.5

From the table 2.5 = 0.4938

Therefore the probability of customer taking longer that 47 days to pay = 0.5 – 0.4938 = 0.0062 = 0.62%

SPREADSHEETS

134   B and C

A database (rather than a spreadsheet) contains records and files and is most suitable for storing large volumes of data

135   C

The formula for correlation is $r = \dfrac{n\Sigma xy - (\Sigma x)(\Sigma y)}{\sqrt{\{n\Sigma x^2 - (\Sigma x)^2\}\{n\Sigma y^2 - (\Sigma y)^2\}}}$

Here n is 7 and to construct the formula we need to identify the appropriate totals from row 11.

A and D are wrong because they use n = 6.

B is wrong because it lacks the square root required for the bottom of the formula.

136 B

All are said to be advantages of spreadsheet software with the exception of (i) security.

A computer-based approach exposes the firm to threats from viruses, hackers and general system failure.

137 D

Budgeted production for a period = budgeted sales for the period –opening inventory of finished goods for the period + closing inventory of finished goods for the period.

Sales	F3
(Opening Inventory)	(10% F3)
Closing Inventory	10% F4
Production	90% F3 + 10% F4

Or [(0.9*F3) + (0.1*F4)]

138 B

Using graphics is usually done using the chart wizard not the format cells option.

SYLLABUS AREA C – COST ACCOUNTING TECHNIQUES

ACCOUNTING FOR MATERIALS

139 $4,350

{[Buffer Inventory + (EOQ ÷ 2)] × Annual holding cost per component}

= [700 units + (1500 units ÷ 2)] × $3.00 = $4,350

140 C

Materials inventory account

	$000s		$000s
Opening inventory	15	Issued to production	165
Payables for purchases	176	Returned to suppliers	8
Returned to stores	9	Written off	4
		Closing balance (balancing item)	23
	200		200

141 D

Option A: A stores ledger account records details of receipts and issues

Option B: A stores requisition will also detail quantity required

Option C: Lead time is the time between placing an order and receiving goods

142 B

Perpetual inventory involves recording, as they occur, receipts, issues and the resulting balances of individual items of inventory, in either quantity, or quantity and value.

143 B

Indirect materials are overhead costs so debit production overhead. An issue of materials is a credit from the material control account

144

	Materials Requisition	Purchase Requisition	Goods received note	Goods returned note
Material returned to stores from production				✓
Form completed by the stores department detailing inventory requirements		✓		
Materials returned to supplier				✓

	Materials Requisition	Purchase Requisition	Goods received note	Goods returned note
Form completed by stores on receipt of goods			✓	
Form completed by production detailing inventory requirements.	✓			

145 C

A goods requisition note (materials requisition) will be raised by the production department requesting that the stores department obtain material from suppliers. A purchase order will then be raised by the purchasing department and sent to the supplier. Delivery notes and goods received notes are used when supplies are delivered.

146 $131,000

Materials inventory account

	$000s		$000s
Opening inventory	23	Issued to production	144
Purchases (bal fig)	131		
Returned to stores	5		
		Closing balance	15
	159		159

147 B

Standard costs are used to help control the costs of purchases. Regular stocktakes and physical security help to minimise losses from stores.

148 A

In times of rising prices FIFO will give a higher valuation of the closing inventory as the older lower prices will be issued to production.

Opening inventory + units purchased	440
Units sold	(290)
	———
Closing inventory (units)	150
	———

FIFO Closing inventory: 150 units @ $2.78 — $417

AVCO	Weighted average cost	$
	100 units @ $2.52	252
	140 units @ $2.56	358
	200 units @ $2.78	556
	———	———
	440	1,166
	———	———

Average cost per unit	1,166/440	$2.65

Closing inventory: 150 units @ $2.65	$397.50
FIFO higher by (417 – 397.50)	**$19.50**

149 B

- If prices have fallen during the year, AVCO will give a higher value of closing inventory than FIFO, which values goods for resale at the latest prices.

- Where the value of closing inventory is higher, profits are higher.

150 B

	Items	Unit value	
		$	$
Opening inventory	6	15	90
January: purchases	10	19.80	198
	———		———
	16	18	288
February: sales	(10)	18	(180)
	———		———
	6	18	108
March: purchases	20	24.50	490
	———		———
	26	23	598
March: sales	(5)	23	(115)
	———		———
	21	23	483
	———		———

		$
Sales (15 × $30)		450
Cost of sales		
Opening Inventory	90	
Purchases	688	
Closing Inventory	(483)	
		(295)
Gross profit		155

151 **$1,110**

Date		Units	Unit value $	Inventory value $
1 October	Opening inventory	60		720
8 October	Purchase 40 units at $15	40		600
14 October	Purchase 50 units at $18	50		900
		150	14.80	2,220
21 October	Sold 75 units: cost	(75)	14.80	(1,110)
31 October	Closing inventory	75	14.80	1,110

152 **D**

The closing inventory of 12 items (15 − 5 + 10 − 8) comprise

	$
10 items at $3.50 each	35.00
2 items at $3 each	6.00
Cost on a FIFO basis is	41.00

153 **A**

When prices are rising, FIFO will give a higher valuation for closing inventory, because the closing inventory will consist of the most recently-purchased items. Higher closing inventory means lower cost of sales and higher profit.

154 **A**

The formula for the EOQ has the holding cost as the denominator. If this increases, the EOQ will be lower. A lower EOQ means that more orders will have to be placed each year; therefore, the total annual ordering cost will increase.

155 C

		$
Purchase costs	(20,000 units × $40)	800,000
Order costs	(20,000/500 orders × $25/order)	1,000
Holding costs	(500/2 average units × $4/unit)	1,000
		_____
Total costs		802,000
		_____

156 7,800

Maximum usage × maximum lead time = 520 × 15 = 7,800 units

157 B

Average inventory   = ROQ/2 + minimum inventory

= 100/2 + 20 = 70 chairs

158 D

The economic batch quantity determines the batch size for products manufactured internally. The EBQ is the batch size which minimises the total of inventory holding costs and batch set-up costs.

159

Characteristic	FIFO	LIFO	AVCO
Potentially out of date valuation on issues.	✓		
The valuation of inventory rarely reflects the actual purchase price of the material.			✓
Potentially out of date closing inventory valuation.		✓	
This inventory valuation method is particularly suited to inventory that consist of liquid materials e.g. oil.			✓
This inventory valuation method is particularly suited to inventory that has a short shelf life e.g. dairy products.	✓		
This inventory valuation method is suited to a wheat farmer who has large silos of grain. Grain is added to and taken from the top of these silos.		✓	
In times of rising prices this method will give higher profits.	✓		
In times of rising prices this method will give lower profits.		✓	
In times of rising prices this method gives a middle level of profits compared to the other two.			✓
Issues are valued at the most recent purchase cost.		✓	
Inventory is valued at the average of the cost of purchases.			✓
Inventory is valued at the most recent purchase cost.	✓		

160   B

$$\text{Economic batch quantity} = \sqrt{\dfrac{2C_oD}{C_h\left(1-\dfrac{D}{R}\right)}}$$

$$= \sqrt{\dfrac{2(1,500)(40,000)}{25\left(1-\dfrac{40,000}{100,000}\right)}} = \sqrt{\dfrac{120\text{million}}{15}} = \sqrt{8,000,000}$$

= 2,828 units.

161   A and C

The EOQ model distinguishes between holding costs (A and C) and ordering costs B and D)

162   C

Annual holding cost = {[Buffer inventory + (EOQ ÷2)] × Annual holding cost per component}

$$= \{[500 + (2000 \div 2)] \times 2\} \qquad = 3,000$$

163 $4.49

Let Co = ordering cost

$185 = \sqrt{\{[2 \times Co \times (4 \times 2,000)] \div [0.05 \times 42]\}}$

$185 = \sqrt{(16,000 \times Co \div 2.1)}$

$Co = 185^2 \times 2.1 \div 16,000 = \$4.49$

Note that the period for demand must be the same as that given for holding cost. As holding cost is given as an annual figure quarterly demand must be converted to annual demand by multiplying by 4.

164

Statement	True	False
In periods of rising prices, FIFO gives a higher valuation of closing inventory than LIFO or AVCO.	✓	
In periods of falling prices, LIFO gives a higher valuation of issues of inventory than FIFO or AVCO.		✓
AVCO would normally be expected to produce a valuation of closing inventory somewhere between valuations FIFO and LIFO.	✓	
FIFO costs issues of inventory at the most recent purchase price.		✓
AVCO costs issues of inventory at the oldest purchase price.		✓
LIFO costs issues of inventory at the oldest purchase price.		✓
FIFO values closing inventory at the most recent purchase price.	✓	
LIFO values closing inventory at the most recent purchase price.		✓
AVCO values closing inventory at the latest purchase price.		✓

165 C

Using the formula given: EOQ = √[(2 × 120 × 48,000) ÷ (0.10 × 80)] = 1,200 units

166 A

	$
Purchasing cost (48,000 × $80)	3,840,000
Ordering cost (48,000 ÷ 1,200) × $120	4,800
Holding costs [(1,200 ÷ 2) × $80 × 0.10]	4,800
Total cost	3,849,600

167 C

	$
Purchasing cost (48,000 × $80 × 0.99)	3,801,600
Ordering cost (48,000 ÷ 2,000) × $120	2,880
Holding costs [(2,000 ÷ 2) × $80 × 0.99 × 0.10]	7,920
Total cost	3,812,400

Annual total saving = $(3,849,600 − 3,812,400) $37,200

168 C

Order quantity = 750 units

		$
Order cost	600 × 12 × 8.75/750 =	84
Holding cost	0.1 × 2.24 × 750/2 =	84
Purchase cost	600 × 12 × 2.24 =	16,128
Total cost		16,296

Order quantity = 2,000 units

		$
Order cost	600 × 12 × 8.75/2,000 =	31.50
Holding cost	0.1 × 2.24 × 0.95 × 2,000/2 =	212.80
Purchase cost	600 × 12 × 2.24 × 0.95 =	15,321.60
		15,565.90

Change in cost = $16,296 − $15,566 = saving of $730.

169 C

Annual production rate = 500 × 50 = 25,000

Using the economic batch quantity formula given,

2,000 = √{(2 × setup cost × 5,000)/(1.5 × (1–5,000/25,000))}

$2,000^2$ = 2 × setup cost × 5,000/1.5 × 0.8

Setup cost = $2,000^2$ × 1.5 × 0.8 /2 × 5,000

Setup cost = $480

170 A

The sales process may begin with an enquiry from a potential customer. The customer then places the order. When the order is delivered, the customer is sent an invoice. The customer is then required to pay the invoice within the credit period allowed.

171 C

A purchase originates with a requisition for goods, by either the stores department or a user department. The buying department negotiates purchase terms and issues a purchase order to send to the supplier. The supplier processes the order and delivers the goods. A delivery note is provided with the goods when delivered. The stores department then produces its own document to record the goods received (the goods received note), which includes additional details such as the code for the item of inventory. The supplier sends the invoice when the goods are delivered. Invoices received from suppliers are called purchase invoices.

When the invoice has been checked and confirmed as correct, a cheque requisition might be prepared, for a senior manager to sign, asking the relevant section of the accounts department to prepare a cheque and send it to the supplier.

172 A

Option B describes a purchase requisition note. Option C describes a delivery note. Option D describes a material requisition note.

173 A and C

174 B

A material requisition note is a document used internally for requisitioning a quantity of inventory from the stores.

175 A and B

An invoice is matched to a goods received note and a purchase order before payment is made.

176 A

The introduction of buffer inventory would increase average stockholding. So (iii) is correct. Total holding cost would increase but holding costs per unit should stay the same or may even decrease so (i) is incorrect. The Economic Order Quantity is dependent on the cost of ordering per order, annual demand and unit holding costs, none of which should change so EOQ should not be affected. Total ordering cost should not be affected.

177 A

The EOQ calculation does not include safety inventory.

178 C

A materials returned note is used to record materials sent back to stores from production. A materials requisition note is a request from production to stores for material. A goods received note is produced by the stores department to record the receipt of goods into stores and a delivery note is provided by the supplier when goods are delivered.

179 D

The price should be checked against a copy of the purchase order, or possibly against an official price list from the supplier. The purchase order should show the price the buyer has negotiated, including any discount. The quantity ordered might not be the same as the quantity delivered, so the quantity on the invoice should be checked against the goods received note. The goods received note is preferable to the delivery note, because the delivery note might be signed quickly, before the stores department has had time to check for faulty items or to carry out a detailed count of the items delivered.

ACCOUNTING FOR LABOUR

180 A

Statement (i) is correct, because extra spending would be incurred to pay the additional temporary staff. Statement (ii) is incorrect, because total spending on labour is unaffected when spare capacity is utilised and idle time reduced. Statement (iii) is also incorrect, because total labour costs will not be increased by switching labour from working on one product to working on another product. However, there is an opportunity cost in switching labour. This is the total contribution forgone by no longer producing and selling the original product. This opportunity cost would be a relevant cost in evaluating a decision to switch the labour from one product to the other. Even so, as worded, statement (iii) is incorrect.

181 B

Unless the overtime can be traced to a specific product or job, it will be treated as an indirect production cost and absorbed into units using the normal absorption basis.

182 B

The employee took 44 hours to perform 94 operations. The standard time allowed per operation is 37.5 minutes, giving a standard time of (94 × [37.5/60]) = 58.75 hours to perform 94 operations. The time saved is therefore (58.75 − 44) = 14.75 hours. The bonus payable will be:

(time taken/time allowed) × time saved × hourly rate

= (44/58.75) × 14.75 × $6.50 = $71.80 (rounded).

The gross wage for Week 24 will therefore be (44 hours × $6.50) + $71.80 = $357.80.

183 A

Direct labour costs are credited to wages and salaries and debited to work-in-progress.

184

Cost	Direct	Indirect
Basic pay for production workers	✓	
Supervisors wages		✓
Bonus for salesman		✓
Production workers overtime premium due to general pressures.		✓
Holiday pay for production workers		✓
Sick pay for supervisors		✓
Time spent by production workers cleaning the machinery		✓

185 $300,000

(4,800 units × 5 hours × $10 per hour) ÷ 0.80 = $300,000

186 C

If direct labour is working at below the agreed productivity level, this will lead to lower output than planned. This could have been caused by factors which resulted in idle time, such as (ii) and (iii) but would not lead to idle time.

187 B

40 × $15 = $600. Note that the basic element of overtime is classified as a direct cost. The normal treatment of overtime premium is for it to be treated as an indirect cost.

188 B

Average employment during the year was (5,250 + 5,680)/2 = 5,465

The labour turnover rate = 360/5,465 × 100 = 6.6%

189 D

Expected hours to make actual output/actual hours = 192/180 × 100% = 106.7%

190 D

Actual hours/budget hours = 180/185 × 100% = 97.3%

191 C

Expected hours to make actual output/budget hours = 192/185 × 100 = 103.8%

192

Payment method	Basic rate	Overtime premium	Overtime payment
This is the amount paid above the basic rate for hours worked in excess of the normal hours.		✓	
This is the total amount paid per hour for hours worked in excess of the normal hours.			✓
This is the amount paid per hour for normal hours worked.	✓		

193 B

	$
600 units at $0.40	240.00
50 units at $0.50	25.00
10 units at $0.75	7.50
For 660 units	272.50

194 B

Piecework is an incentive-based pay scheme, because employees are paid more for producing more, and so have an incentive to be more productive. A day rate scheme, in which employees receive a basic rate of pay, does not offer any incentive to be more productive.

195 A

(500 × 0.50) + (100 × 0.55) + (20 × 0.60) = $317

196

Payment method	Time-rate	Piecework	Piece-rate plus bonus
Labour is paid based solely on the production achieved.		✓	
Labour is paid extra if an agreed level of output is exceeded.			✓
Labour is paid according to hours worked.	✓		

197   C and D

A timesheet and a job card are used to allocate labour costs to cost units. An attendance record card is used for payroll purposes and an employee record card details all of the information relating to an employee.

198   D

Grade B labour costs are an indirect labour cost. Grade A labour costs are direct costs for the basic pay, but overtime premium is treated as an indirect cost if the overtime hours are worked as general overtime. If overtime is worked for a specific purpose, such as a customer order, the cost of the overtime premium paid to direct labour is treated as a direct cost. The direct labour cost for the week is therefore:

	$
30 hours worked in overtime	
Cost of basic pay, Grade A labour (30 × $10)	300
Cost of overtime premium for hours on specific order (10 × 50% of $10)	50
	——
	350
	——

199   D

Good units = 512 – 17 – 495

200 units at $0.15 + 295 units at $0.20 = $89

200   C

Labour turnover ratio = 8/55 × 100% = 14.55%

ACCOUNTING FOR OVERHEADS

201 $58,540

Reapportion service cost centre K first as it does work for service cost centre J but not vice versa.

	G	H	J	K
Overhead cost ($)	40,000	50,000	30,000	18,000
Reapportion K	9,000	7,200	1,800	(18,000)
			——	
			31,800	
Reapportion J	9,540		(31,800)	
	——			
	$58,540			

202   C

An absorption rate is used to determine the full cost of a product or service. Answer A describes overhead allocation and apportionment. Absorption does not control overheads, so answer D is not correct.

203 D

X = 46,000 + 0.1Y

Y = 30,000 + 0.2X

X = 46,000 + 0.1(30,000 + 0.2X) = 46,000 + 3,000 + 0.02X

0.98X = 49,000 and X = 50,000

Y = 30,000 + 0.2(50,000) = 40,000

P = 95,000 + 0.4(50,000) + 0.3(40,000) = 127,000

Alternatively use the repeated distribution method as follows:

	P	Q	X	Y
Overhead cost ($)	95,000	82,000	46,000	30,000
Reapportion X	18,400	18,400	(46,000)	9,200
Reapportion Y	11,760	23,520	3,920	(39,200)
Reapportion X	1,568	1,568	(3,920)	784
Reapportion Y	235	470	78	(784)
Reapportion X	31	31	(78)	16
Reapportion Y	5	9	2	(16)
Rounding	1	1		
	$127,000			

204 B

	$
Actual expenditure	56,389
Absorbed cost (12,400 × 1.02 × $4.25)	53,754
Total under-absorption	2,635

205 A

Under- or over-absorption is determined by comparing the actual overhead expenditure with the overhead absorbed.

206 D

Fixed production overheads are over-absorbed when actual expenditure is less than budget and/or actual production volume is higher than budget.

207 D

Over-absorbed overheads increase profit, and so are recorded as a credit entry in either an over-absorbed overhead account or directly as a credit in the statement of profit and loss. The matching debit entry could be either in the WIP account or the production overhead control account, depending on the costing system used.

208 C

Indirect labour is a costing concept. The double entry is:

Wages control		**Overhead control**	
	Indirect labour × (overheads)	Indirect labour × (wages)	

209 $18.00

Machining hours	=	(4,000 × 0.5 hour) + (4,000 × 1.0 hour)
	=	6,000 hours
Assembly hours	=	(4,000 × 0.2 hour) + (4,000 × 0.25 hour)
	=	1,800 hours
Machining absorption rate	=	$\dfrac{\$120,000}{6,000\,\text{hours}}$
	=	$20 per hour
Assembly absorption rate	=	$\dfrac{\$72,000}{1,800\,\text{hours}}$
	=	$40 per hour
Fixed overhead per unit of Pye	=	(0.5 hour × $20) + (0.2 hour × $40)
	=	$18

210 D

Cost apportionment is concerned with sharing costs according to benefit received.

211 B

	$
Actual overheads	694,075
Under recovery	(35,000)
Overhead absorbed	659,075

$$\text{OAR} = \frac{\$659,075}{32,150}$$

$$= \$20.50$$

212 B

	$
Actual overheads	245,600
Over-absorption of overheads	6,400
Overheads absorbed	252,000

Absorption rate = $252,000/45,000 hours = $5.60 per direct labour hour.

213 $14.00

	$
Actual overhead	138,000
Over-absorbed overhead	23,000
Therefore amount of overhead absorbed	161,000

Hours worked = 11,500.

Therefore absorption rate per hour = $161,000/11,500 hours = $14 per hour.

214 C

Let the overhead apportioned from service department C be $C.

Let the overhead apportioned from service department D be $D.

$$C = 3,200 + 0.20D \quad .....(1)$$
$$D = 4,600 + 0.10 C \quad ....(2)$$

Substitute (1) in (2)

$$D = 4,600 + 0.10 (3,200 + 0.20D)$$
$$D = 4,600 + 320 + 0.02D$$
$$0.98D = 4,920$$
$$D = 5,020.$$

Substitute in (1)

$$C = 3,200 + 0.20 (5,020)$$
$$C = 4,204.$$

Total overhead for department X = 5,000 + 0.50C + 0.20D

$$= 5,000 + 0.50 (4,204) + 0.20 (5,020)$$
$$= 5,000 + 2,102 + 1,004$$
$$= 8,106.$$

Note: You could have reached the same answer by using the repeated distribution method.

215 B

Fixed overhead absorption rate = $36,000/18,000 = $2 per direct labour hour.

Variable overhead absorption rate = $9,000/18,000 = $0.50 per direct labour hour.

	$	$
Overheads absorbed:		
Fixed (20,000 × $2)		40,000
Variable (20,000 × $0.50)		10,000
Total overhead absorbed		50,000
Overheads incurred:		
Fixed	39,000	
Variable	12,000	
Total overhead incurred		51,000
Under-absorbed overhead		1,000

216 B

$$(\$3,000 \times \frac{700}{8,000}) + (\$11,000 \times \frac{80}{400}) + (\$7,000 \times \frac{20}{70}) = \$(262.50 + 2,200 + 2,000) = \$4,462.50$$

217 C

$$60 \times \frac{12}{120} + 100 \times \frac{8}{100} = \$14$$

ABSORPTION AND MARGINAL COSTING

218 C

Total variable cost	= $(4 + 5 + 3 + 3) = $15
Contribution per unit	= $20 − $15 = $5
Total contribution earned	= $5 × 800 = $4,000

219 D

If a sales value of $100 per unit is assumed then the original and revised situations will be:

	Original	Revised
	$	$
Selling price	100	110
Variable cost/unit	60	60
Contribution/unit	40	50

Fixed costs do not affect contribution and if sales volume is unchanged then the overall change in contribution can be measured using the contribution per unit:

$$\frac{(50 - 40)}{40} \times 100 = 25\%$$

220 12,500 UNITS

Absorption costing profit = $2,000 > Marginal Costing profit = $(3,000)

Therefore Production > Sales by $5,000

$5,000 = OAR × number of units change in inventory

$5,000 = $2 × number of units change in inventory

Therefore number of units change in inventory = $\dfrac{\$5,000}{\$2}$ = 2,500

If Sales = 10,000 units, therefore Production = Sales + 10,000 units = 12,500 units.

221 B

Contribution per unit = $(10 − 6) = $4.

	$
Total contribution (250,000 × $4)	1,000,000
Fixed overheads (200,000 × $2)	400,000
	_____
Profit	600,000
	_____

222 B

Fixed production overhead per unit = $48,000/12,000 units = $4.

Sales volume is less than production volume by 280 units.

In absorption costing, this means that some fixed overheads will be carried forward in the closing inventory value. Fixed overheads in this addition to inventory = 280 units × $4 = $1,120.

In marginal costing, all fixed overheads incurred in a period are charged as an expense against profit. Marginal costing profit would therefore be lower than the absorption costing profit by $1,120.

223 $56,850

As inventory decreases over the period, the cost of sales will be higher with absorption costing, since they will include fixed overhead in the opening inventory now sold. The extra cost of sales (and thus reduction in profit) = (8,500 − 6,750) × $3 = $5,250.

This means that since profit will be lower with absorption costing by $5,250, the absorption costing profit will be $(62,100 − 5,250) = $56,850.

224 C

There was an increase in inventory in the period; therefore the absorption costing profit is higher than the marginal costing profit (because a larger amount of fixed overhead is carried forward in the closing inventory value).

	$
Marginal costing profit	72,300
Less: fixed costs in opening inventory (300 units × $5)	(1,500)
Add: fixed costs in closing inventory (750 units × $5)	3,750
Absorption costing profit	74,550

225

	Marginal costing	Absorption costing
The cost of a product includes an allowance for fixed production costs.		✓
The cost of a product represents the additional cost of producing an extra unit.	✓	

226 B

Production volume exceeded sales volume, so the profit with absorption costing is higher than the profit with marginal costing.

Fixed overheads in inventory = $30,000/750 = $40 per unit, therefore total fixed overhead in closing inventory (absorption costing) = 250 units × $40 = $10,000. Profit with marginal costing is therefore lower by $10,000.

227 D

		$000
Variable production cost of boats	45/750 × 700	42
Fixed production costs (absorbed)	30/750 × 700	28
Production costs of 700 boats		70
Closing inventory of 100 boats		(10)
Production cost of 600 sold		60
Under-absorbed overhead	30–28	2
Variable selling costs	5/500 × 600	6
Fixed selling costs		25
		93
Profit		15
Sales revenue	90/500 × 600	108

228 B

In an absorption costing system, the fixed cost per unit would be $3,000/15,000 units = $0.20 per unit.

Budgeted profit with marginal costing = Contribution – Fixed costs

= $26,000 – $3,000 = $23,000.

By switching to absorption costing, in a period when inventory levels increase by 2,000 units, absorption costing profit would be higher by 2,000 units × fixed cost per unit, i.e. by 2,000 × $0.20 = $400.

Absorption costing profit = $23,000 + $400 = $23,400.

229 A

Total contribution will increase as sales volume increases, but the contribution per unit will be constant as long as the sales price and variable cost per unit are unchanged. Overhead is not absorbed to product unit so there is no under/over absorption of overhead. Marginal costing does provide useful information for decision making because it highlights contribution, which is a relevant cash flow for decision-making purposes.

230 C

Increase in inventory of 34,000 – 31,000 = 3,000 units.

Difference in profits of $955,500 – $850 500 = $105,000

OAR = $105,000/3,000 = $35 per unit

Level of activity = $1,837,500/£35 = 52,500 units

231 A

Profit figures only differ if inventory changes in the period.

232 B

Suppose we start with the following situation.

	$ per unit
Selling price	100
Variable cost	(60)
Contribution	40

Sales 1,000 units; total contribution $40,000

A, B and C would have the following effects.

	A	B
	$ per unit	*$ per unit*
Selling price	100	110
Variable cost	(54)	(60)
Contribution	46	50
Total contribution	$46,000	$50,000

C : Total contribution   = $40,000 × 1.1

                     = $44,000

Fixed costs are irrelevant since we are concerned with *contribution*.

233 **$78.10**

Inventory is valued at full production cost i.e. both fixed and variable production costs.

$(33.00 + 45.10) = $78.10

COST ACCOUNTING METHODS

234 C

	Job 812
	$
Direct materials	60
Direct labour	40
Direct expenses	20
Prime cost	120
Production overheads ($40 ÷ 8) × $16	80
Non-production overheads (0.6 × $120)	72
Total cost – Job 812	272

235 D

Statement A is correct. Job costs are identified with a particular job, whereas process costs (of units produced and work in process) are averages, based on equivalent units of production.

Statement B is also correct. The direct cost of a job to date, excluding any direct expenses, can be ascertained from materials requisition notes and job tickets or time sheets.

Statement C is correct, because without data about units completed and units still in process, losses and equivalent units of production cannot be calculated.

Statement D is incorrect, because the cost of normal loss will usually be incorporated into job costs as well as into process costs. In process costing this is commonly done by giving normal loss no cost, leaving costs to be shared between output, closing inventory and abnormal loss/gain. In job costing it can be done by adjusting direct materials costs to allow for normal wastage, and direct labour costs for normal reworking of items or normal spoilage.

236 D

	Job 1	Job 2	Total
	$	$	$
Opening WIP	8,500	0	8,500
Material in period	17,150	29,025	46,175
Labour for period	12,500	23,000	35,500
Overheads (see working)	43,750	80,500	124,250
	81,900	132,525	214,425

Working

Total labour cost for period = $(12,500 + 23,000 + 4,500) = $40,000

Overhead absorption rate = $140,000/$40,000 = 3.5 times the direct labour cost.

237 C

	Job 3
	$
Opening WIP	46,000
Labour cost for period	4,500
Overheads (3.5 × $4,500)	15,750
Total production costs	66,250
Profit (50%)	33,125
Selling price of 2,400 boards	99,375

Selling price of one board = $99,375/2,400 = $41.41

238 $21,150

This can be calculated as a balancing figure in the process account.

Process account

	kg		$		kg		$
Input (balance)	3,000		21,150	Output	2,800	(× 7.50)	21,000
Abnormal gain	100	(× 7.50)	750	Normal loss	300	(× 3)	900
			21,900				21,900

Alternatively:

	$
Cost of output (2,800 × 7.50)	21,000
Scrap value of normal loss (300 × 3)	900
	21,900
Less: Value of abnormal gain (100 × 7.50)	(750)
Cost of input	21,150

239 B

	Units
Input	13,200
Less: Normal loss (13,200 × 10/110)	1,200
Expected output	12,000

	$
Process costs	184,800
Less: scrap value of normal loss (1,200 × $4)	4,800
Cost of good output	180,000

Cost for each expected unit of output = $180,000/12,000 = $15.

Finished units of output, and also abnormal loss and abnormal gain units will be valued at this amount.

240 $11.60

Cost per unit = net process costs/expected output

= (9,000 + 13,340 − 300)/2,000 − 100

= $22,040/1,900 = $11.60.

241 A

	$
Opening WIP	1,710
Completion of opening WIP (300 × 0.40 × $10)	1,200
Units started and completed in the month	
(2,000 – 300) × $10	17,000
	———
Total value (2,000 units)	19,910
	———

242 C

	Materials equivalent units
Opening inventory completed (400 × 0%)	0
Units started and finished in the period (800 – 400)	400
Closing inventory (600 × 75%)	450
	———
Total equivalent units produced in the period	850
	———

243 $77,616

Sales value of production:

Product W: (12,000 × 10) = $120,000

Product X: (10,000 × 12) = $120,000

Therefore joint production costs are apportioned W:X in the ratio 1:1

Amount apportioned to product X is (776,160 ÷ 2) = $388,080

20% of X's production is in closing inventory @ (0.2 × 388,080) = $77,616

244 D

	Units
J: (6,000 – 100 + 300) =	6,200
K: (4,000 – 400 + 200) =	3,800
	———
	10,000
	———

Joint costs apportioned to J: (6,200 ÷ 10,000) × $110,000 = $68,200

245 C

Total sales revenue = ($18 × 10,000) + ($25 × 20,000) + ($20 × 20,000) = $1,080,000

Joint costs to be allocated	= $277,000 – ($2 × 3,500)
	= $270,000

Allocation rate = ($270,000/1,080,000) = 0.25 of sales revenue.

Joint costs allocated to product 3	= 0.25 × ($20 × 20,000)
	= $100,000
	= ($100,000/20,000 units) $5 per unit

246 C

		$
Prime cost		6,840.00
Fixed overhead	$300,000/60,000 × 156	780.00
		7,620.00
Profit	20% × 7,620.00	1,524.00
Job price		9,144.00

247 D

Abnormal loss units are valued as one equivalent unit of cost, the same as units of good production. This cost is credited to the process account and debited to the abnormal loss account. The scrap value of abnormal loss is then credited to the abnormal loss account (with the matching debit to bank).

248 A

		kg
Input		12,750
Output	Normal loss	510
	Finished goods	12,700
		13,210
Abnormal gain		460

249 A

	kg
Material input	2,500
Normal loss (10%)	(250)
Abnormal loss	(75)
Good production achieved	2,175

250 C

Direct labour hours = $400 ÷ $8 = 50 hours

	$
Prime cost (300 + 400)	700
Production overheads (50 × $26)	1,300
	———
Total production cost	2,000
Non-production overheads (1.20 × 700)	840
	———
Total cost	2,840
	———

251 B

Finished output = (20,000 + 110,000 – 40,000) = 90,000 units.

Closing WIP = 40,000 units 50% complete = 20,000 equivalent units.

Cost per equivalent unit (in $000) = $132,000/(90,000 + 20,000)

= $1,200 per equivalent unit/finished car.

252 B

The total value of WIP will increase. The number of equivalent units will increase which will cause the cost per unit to decrease.

253 C

Normal loss is 10% of input = 20 kg.

Actual loss = 50 kg

Abnormal loss = 50 – 20 = 30 kg

Equivalent units of output:

	Total	Materials	Conversion
Finished output	150	150	150
Abnormal loss	30	30	15
Total EUs	180	180	165

Cost per equivalent unit:

Material cost = 200 × $ 4 = $800

Labour and overheads cost = 100 × $ 15 + $1,000 = $2,500

Materials   = $800/180 = $4.44

Conversion = $2,500/165 = $15.15

Total cost of completed unit = $(4.44 + 15.15) = $19.59

254 10,200 EU

Flow of units

2,000 + 12,000 = 11,000 (bal) + 3,000

Units started and finished = 11,000 – 2,000	=	9,000
Closing WIP = 3,000 × 20%	=	600
Opening WIP = 2,000 × 30%	=	600
		————
		10,200
		————

255 C

Cost per unit = ($1,200 + $3,500 – $30)/(200 – 30) = $27.47 per kg

$27.47 × 190 = $5,219

256 A

Process costing is used for companies producing large quantities of similar products (homogeneous output) and these are valued at average cost.

257 A

	$
Direct materials 120 kg @ $4 per kg	480
Direct labour: 3 hours @ $10 per hour	30
20 hours @ $5 per hour	100
Hire of machine: 2 days @ $100 per day	200
Overhead 23 hours @ $8 per hour	184
	————
	994
Price charged	942
	————
Loss	(52)
	————

258 C

		$
Prime cost		2,840.00
Fixed overhead	$5,000/500 × 45	450.00
		————
		3,290.00
Profit	10% × 3,290.00	329.00
		————
Job price		3,619.00
		————

259 B

Basic hours = 110 ×$8 = $880

Overtime hours = 110 – (3 × 30) = 20 hours

Overtime premium = 20 × 8 × 0.25 = $40

Total direct labour cost = $880 + $40 = $920

260 D

A service industry is an industry not involved in agriculture, mining, construction or manufacturing. Transport industries are service industries.

261 A and C

Services are usually (but not always) associated with labour and labour costs, low material costs and relatively high indirect costs. Service costing also makes use of composite cost units, such as the cost per guest/day, cost per patient/day, cost per passenger/mile and so on.

262 D

A charitable foundation will be a not-for-profit organisation.

263 B

Average cost per occupied bed per day

$$= \frac{\text{Total cost}}{\text{Number of beds occupied}}$$

$$= \frac{\$100,000 + \$5,000 + \$22,500}{6,450 \times 2} = \$9.88$$

or 127,500/(200 × 2 + 30) × 30 = \$9.88

264 B

Cost per:	Company A $	Company B $
Millions of units sold	208	104
Thousand consumers	750	625
$m of sales	33,333	20,000

The cost per unit sold, per consumer and per $m of sales are all higher for Company A than for Company B indicating that Company A is less efficient than Company B.

265 B

$$\text{Room occupancy \%} = \frac{\text{Total number of rooms occupied daily}}{\text{Rooms available to be let}} \times 100\%$$

$$= \frac{200 + 30}{240 + 40} \times 100\% = 82.1\%$$

266 C

A service is intangible and inventory cannot be held. Services generally have a high level of fixed costs and there are often difficulties in identifying a suitable cost unit.

ALTERNATIVE COSTING PRINCIPLES

267 A

ABC is fairly complicated, is a form of absorption (not marginal) costing and is particularly useful when fixed overheads are high and not primarily volume driven.

268

	Internal failure costs	External failure costs	Inspection costs	Prevention costs
Cost of the a customer service team		✓		
Cost of equipment maintenance				✓
Cost of operating test equipment			✓	

A customer service team deals with customer queries and complaints from outside the organisation, typically after goods have been delivered to the customer. The costs of this team arise from quality failures and are preventable. They are external failure costs. Maintenance is intended to prevent machine breakdowns and so to prevent quality failures, and they are therefore prevention costs. Test equipment is used for inspection.

269 C

External failure costs are those incurred due to poor quality of goods delivered to customers; therefore this includes compensation costs.

Appraisal costs are those incurred in the measuring of quality of output; therefore this includes test equipment running costs.

270 B

	$
Sales revenue: 600 units × $450	450
Return required: 20% × $450	90
	———
Target cost per unit:	360

271 D

A product's life cycle costs are very inclusive; none of these would be excluded.

272 A

Value analysis involves identify why and how customers value a product to enable cost savings to be made without compromising the value to the customer.

273 B

SYLLABUS AREA C – BUDGETING

NATURE AND PURPOSE OF BUDGETING

274 B

The main purposes of budgeting are to plan and control. Budgets also usually give authority to spend up to the budget limit. Budgets are not primarily used for decision making.

275 D

The budget committee is made up from senior managers of each function in the organisation.

276 D

A budget manual will include all of the options.

277 C

BUDGET PREPARATION

278 94,400

Units required	100,000
Less: opening inventory	(14,000)
Add: closing inventory required (14,000 × 0.6)	8,400
	94,400

279 B

The production budget is the sales budget **minus** opening inventory of finished goods **plus** closing inventory of finished goods.

280 B

4,500/0.9 = 5,000 litres.

Note that opening and closing inventories are relevant to the material purchases budget, not the material usage budget.

281 A

The material usage budget is the material requirement for the units produced.

282 C

		$
Product A	1,750 units × 3 hours/unit × $7 /hour	36,750
Product B	5,000 units × 4 hours/unit × $7 /hour	140,000
		176,750

283 D

A principal budget factor is defined as the factor acting as the constraint on the overall level of activity in a period. It is often sales demand, but could be a key production resource or cash.

284 D

If 1X and 2Y are sold, this earns $250. Call this a batch.

The company wants to earn $100,000.

$100,000/250 = 400 batches.

This is 400 X and 800 Y

285 B

	Units
Budgeted sales	2,300
Current inventory	(400)
Closing inventory required	550
Production	2,450

286 A

Machine hours required:

X	1,000 hours
Y	2,400 hours
Z	600 hours
Total	4,000

Overhead budget:

Variable: 4,000 × $2.30 = $9,200

Fixed: 4,000 × $0.75 = $3,000

Total = $(9,200 + 3,000) = $12,200

287 C

	Clockwork clown	Wind-up train	Total
Budgeted sales	450	550	
+ Closing inventory	30	40	
– Opening inventory	(20)	(50)	
	———	———	
Production budget	460	540	
Material usage	× 2 kg	× 1 kg	
Material usage budget	920 kg	540 kg	1,460 kg

288 A

Total material usage	1,460 kg
+ Closing inventory	60
– Opening inventory	(50)
Total material purchases	1,470 kg
Material purchases budget = 1,470 × $5	$7,350

289 A

	Clockwork clown	Wind-up train
Budgeted sales	450	550
+ Closing inventory	30	40
– Opening inventory	(20)	(50)
	———	———
Production budget	460	540
Labour	× 18/60	× 30/60
	138 hours	270 hours
Total	408 hours × $8 = $3,264	

290 D

Paid hours including idle time = 2,400 × 100/80 = 3,000

Budgeted labour cost = 3,000 hours × $10 = $30,000

291 A

A continuous budget does not have to be prepared for a whole year; the budget period could be a month or a quarter.

292 B

	$
July's sales $25,000 × 20%	5,000
June's sales $20,000 × 60%	12,000
May's sales $30,000 × 10%	3,000
	20,000

293 B

	$
February sales 45% × $28,000	12,600
March sales 50% × $28,000	14,000
	26,600

294 C

	Units
Sales of Z	10,000
Opening inventory	(14,000)
Reduction in inventory	12,000
Production	8,000

	Litres
Usage at 2 litres per Z	16,000
Opening inventory	(20,000)
Closing inventory	15,000
Purchases	11,000

Therefore cash cost is 11,000 × $4 = $44,000.

295 B

Consider sales of $100

Cash receipt in month of sale = 45% × 100 = $45

This is after a discount of 10%, so must represent 45/0.9 = $50 of sales value

Irrecoverable debts = 20% of any month's sales = $20

The receipts in month 2 must be the rest of the sales = 100 − 50 − 20 = $30

$$\$30/\$100 \times 100 = 30\%$$

296 A

	$
Cash sales 10% of $40,000	4,000
Receivables	
$36,000 × 40% × 96%	13,824
$36,000× 50%	18,000
	35,824

297 A

Payment = $(450,000 × 70% + 18,000 + 10,000) = $343,000

298 D

	$
Opening balance	7,000
Receipts from payables	
Re previous month's sales (= opening receivables)	15,000
Re this month's sales (= half this month's sales)	35,000
Payments to payables (= opening payables)	(40,000)
Expenses	(60,000)
Bank overdraft	(43,000)

299 B

Depreciation and the provision for doubtful debts are not cash flow items and so would not be included in a cash budget.

300 C

The amount budgeted to be paid to suppliers in September is $289,000.

		$
25% of September purchases	25% × $280,000, less 5% discount (i.e. x 95%)	66,500
70% of August purchases	70% × $300,000	210,000
5% of July purchases	5% × $250,000	12,500
Total payments		289,000

301 B

The cash received in the third month of trading was $2,200

	$
Cash sales in month 3: (25% of $2,800)	700
Cash from credit sales in month 3: (25% of $2,800, less 10%)	630
Cash from credit sales in month 2: (40% of $1,800)	720
Cash from credit sales in month 1: (10% of $1,500)	150
	2,200

302 A

The amount to be shown in the cash budget for May in respect of payments for fixed production overhead is $23,000.

Cash to be paid in May for April fixed overhead

$\quad$ = $(93,000/3) − $8,000 depreciation

$\quad$ = $23,000

The amount to be shown in the cash budget for May in respect of payments for variable production overhead is $60,000.

Cash to be paid in May for April variable overhead = $(93,000 × 2/3)/2 $\quad$ = $31,000

Cash to be paid in May for May variable overhead = $(87,000 × 2/3)/2 $\quad$ = $29,000

$\qquad\qquad\qquad\qquad\qquad\qquad\qquad\qquad\qquad\qquad\qquad\qquad\quad$ $60,000

FLEXIBLE BUDGETS

303 B

Option C is a fixed budget and option D is a rolling budget. Option A is incorrect as a flexible budget includes all costs.

304 C

A flexible budget helps to control resource efficiency by providing a realistic budget cost allowance for the actual level of activity achieved. Control action can therefore be more effective because the effects of any volume change have been removed from the comparison.

305 A

A fixed budget is a budget prepared for a planned single level of activity. It does not ignore inflation (option C is incorrect) and it includes direct costs as well as overhead costs (option D is incorrect). A fixed budget can be prepared for a single product as well as a mix of products (option B is incorrect).

306 B

Statement (i) is correct. A fixed budget is prepared for a single level of activity.

Statement (ii) is incorrect. A flexible budget is prepared during the budget period but it recognises only the effects of changes in the volume of activity.

Statement (iii) is correct. A major purpose of the budgetary planning exercise is to communicate an organisation's objectives to its managers.

307 B

Flexed budget:

	Budget	Flexed Budget	Actual
Sales (units)	120,000	100,000	100,000
	$000	$000	$000
Sales revenue	1,200	1,000	995
Variable printing costs	360	300	280
Variable production overheads	60	50	56
Fixed production cost	300	300	290
Fixed administration cost	360	360	364
Profit/(Loss)	120	(10)	5

308 C

309 B

	Original Budget	Flexed Budget
Sales units	1,000	1,200
	$	$
Sales revenue	100,000	120,000
Direct material	40,000	48,000
Direct labour	20,000	24,000
Variable overhead	15,000	18,000
Fixed overhead	10,000	10,000
Profit	15,000	20,000

310 A

Variable costs are conventionally deemed to be constant per unit of output.

311 $2,560,000

Total variable cost per unit = Direct material + Direct labour + Variable overheads

Total variable cost per unit = 30 + 46 + 24 = $100

Flexed for 13,600 units = $1,360,000

Total fixed costs for the period = $80 × 15,000 units = 1,200,000

Total cost for 13,600 units = $1,360,000 + $1,200,000 = $2,560,000

312 A

VC per unit = (112,500 − 100,000)/(75 − 50) = $500

Fixed cost in total = 100,000 − (500 × 50) = $75,000

Total overhead for 80% activity = $75,000 + (500 × 80) = $115,000

313 $354,000

(36,000 + 176,000)/4,000 × 5,000 = 265,000

265,000 + 89,000 = $354,000

CAPITAL BUDGETING

314 C

	$	AF	$
Outflow	(80,000)	1.000	(80,000)
Cash inflow $25,000 each year for 8 years	25,000	6.463	161,575
Present value of project			$81,575

315 C

The $9,500 and $320,000 are future incremental cash flow figures so are relevant. The $5,000 is sunk (past) cost so it is not a relevant cost.

316 $8,634

Year	Cash inflow/(outflow)	Discount factor @ 8%	Present value $
0	(60,000)	1.000	(60,000)
1	23,350	0.926	21,622
2	29,100	0.857	24,939
3	27,800	0.794	22,073
Net present value			8,634

317 C

Try 20%

Year	Cash $	20%	PV $
0	(75,000)		(75,000)
1 – 5	25,000	2.991	74,775
			(225)

$$\text{IRR} = 15 + \frac{8,800}{(8,800 - -225)} \times 5$$

$$\text{IRR} = 15 + \frac{8,800}{9,025} \times 5$$

IRR   = 19.88% therefore 20% to the nearest 1%

318 C

Statement A is not correct as there is no company policy to confirm the payback is appropriate. Statement B is not correct as the IRR and ROCE are not comparable. Statement D is not correct as the IRR is always a positive whether the project is acceptable or not.

Statement C is correct as the IRR must be greater than the cost of capital (the discount rate) used to appraise the project as the project has a return therefore a positive NPV at the company's cost of capital so the project should go ahead.

319 A

Year	Cash $	11%	PV $
0	(300,000)		(300,000)
1 – 10	40,000	5.889	235,560
			(64,440)

320 $44,000

	Current			Expansion	
	$000	$000		$000	$000
Food sales	200		× 40%	80	
Drink sales	170		× 40%	68	
		370			148
Food costs	145		× 40%	58	
Drink costs	77		× 40%	31	
Staff costs	40		40/4 × 1	10	
Other costs	20		× 60% × 40%	5	
		282			104
Cash flow		88			44

321 D

Year	Cash ($000)	17% discount factor	Present value ($000)
0	(400)	1.000	(400.00)
1	210	0.855	179.55
2	240	0.731	175.44
3	320	0.624	199.68
			154.67

322 14%

$$10 + \frac{\$17,706}{(\$17,706 - -\$4,317)} \times (15-10) = 14\%$$

323 C

Depreciation is not a cash flow so needs to be added back to profit to calculate cash flows.

Depreciation on straight line basis = ($400,000 – $50,000)/5 = $70,000 per year

Year	Profit ($)	Cash flow ($)	Cumulative cash flow ($)
0		(400,000)	(400,000)
1	175,000	245,000	(155,000)
2	225,000	295,000	140,000

Payback period = 1 + 155/295 years = 1.5 years to nearest 0.1 years

324 D

325 D

326 C

Using the formula $[(1.021)^4 – 1] \times 100 = 8.67\%$

327 C

$(1 + 0.1/4)^4 - 1 \times 100 = 10.38\%$

$(1 + 0.12/12)^{12} - 1 \times 100 = 12.68\%$

$(1 + 0.012)^{12} - 1 \times 100 = 15.39\%$

$(1 + 0.03)^4 - 1 \times 100 = 12.55\%$

BUDGETARY CONTROL AND REPORTING

328 D

329 D

The production-line manager does not control prices or rates

330 A

Feedforward control compares the budgeted outcome with the current best forecast of what actual results will be. For example, suppose that the budgeted sales for the year are 1,000 units. After six months, actual sales for the year to date might be 450 units, and the current estimate of what actual sales will be for the year might be 900 units. Using feedforward control, management will identify a difference of 100 units in sales (1,000 – 900 units) and try to take measures for increasing sales up to the 1,000 target by the end of the year, by selling 550 units in the second half of the year.

331   A

The expenditure variance is measured by the difference between the flexed budget and the actual cost.

The expenditure variance is $15,000 favourable.

The volume variance is measured by the difference between the original budget and the flexed budget.

The volume variance is $130,000 adverse.

332   B

The volume variance is the difference between the fixed and flexible budget.

333   D

334

	Budgeted $	Actual $	Variance value $	A/F
RECEIPTS				
Cash sales	4,200	3,800	400	A
Credit sales	42,100	48,000	5,900	F
Total receipts	46,300	51,800	5,500	F
PAYMENTS				
Cash purchases	500	1,200	700	A
Credit purchases	28,000	35,100	7,100	A
Labour costs	2,500	3,200	700	A
Capital expenditure	8,000	6,000	2,000	F
General expenses	4,000	3,800	200	F
Total payments	43,000	49,300	6,300	A
Net cash flow	3,300	2,500	800	A

BEHAVIOURAL ASPECTS OF BUDGETING

335   C

Statement (i) is incorrect. Managers at an operational level are more likely to know what is realistically achievable than a senior manager imposing budget targets from above. Statement (ii) is arguably correct: participation in budgeting could improve motivation. Statement (iii) is correct: imposed budgets should be much quicker to prepare, because less discussion time and negotiation time is required than with participative budget-setting.

336   C

Top-down budgeting are imposed budgets so are less likely to motivate managers. Bottom –up budgeting involve more participation from managers, therefore they are more likely to motivate managers.

337   C

Where there is goal congruence, managers who are working to achieve their own personal goals will automatically also be working to achieve the organisation's goals. Although the use of aspiration levels to set targets (option D) is likely to help in the achievement of goal congruence, it is not of itself a definition of the term.

338   B

A is incorrect as participation in the budget procedure should improve morale and thus improve performance. C is incorrect as more knowledge at base level will improve decision making. D is incorrect as the staff themselves can be involved in the budget process so will have input and knowledge of the budget.

339   C

Budgetary slack is also called budget bias. Budget holders may sometimes try to obtain a budget that is easier to achieve. They may do this either by bidding for expenditure in excess of what they actually need or, in the case of sales budgets, by deliberately setting easy revenue targets.

340   A

Managers are more likely to be motivated to achieve the target if they have participated in setting the target. Participation can reduce the information gap that can arise when targets are imposed by senior management. Imposed targets are likely to make managers feel demotivated and alienated and result in poor performance. Participation however can cause problems; in particular, managers may attempt to negotiate budgets that they feel are easy to achieve which gives rise to 'budget padding' or budgetary slack, this can result in budgets that are unsuitable for control purposes. If targets are too easy then managers will not need to be motivated to achieve their goals.

SYLLABUS AREA D – STANDARD COSTING

STANDARD COSTING SYSTEMS

341 C

The standard labour rate should be the expected rate/hour, but allowing for standard levels of idle time. For example, if the work force is paid $9 per hour but idle time of 10% is expected, the standard labour rate will be $10 per hour, not $9.

342 C

This is a definition of 'basic standards'. Basic standards are not widely used in practice.

343 D

This is a definition of 'attainable standards'. Attainable standards are widely used in practice.

344

Statement	True	False
A variance is the difference between budgeted and actual cost.		✓
A favourable variance means actual costs are less than budgeted.	✓	
An adverse variance means that actual income is less than budgeted.	✓	

VARIANCE CALCULATIONS AND ANALYSIS

345 $8,500

Standard contribution on actual sales	$10,000
Add: favourable sales price variance	$500
Less: Adverse total variable costs variance	$(2,000)
Actual Contribution	**$8,500**

The standard contribution on actual sales has been obtained by adjusting the budgeted contribution by the sales volume contribution variance. Therefore, this variance should have been ignored in answering the question.

346 A

Sales contribution on actual sales	$50,000
Less adverse total variable costs variance	$3,500
Actual contribution	$46,500

No adjustment is required for the favourable sales volume contribution variance: it would have already been added to the budgeted contribution to arrive at the standard contribution from actual sales given in the question. The total fixed costs variance, along with budgeted fixed costs, appears in a reconciliation statement below the actual contribution.

347 D

Ah × Ar =	$176,000		
		Rate variance	$36,000 A
Ah × Sr = 14,000 hrs × $10	$140,000		
		Efficiency variance	$25,000 F
Sh × Sr = 3 hrs × 5,500 units × $10	$165,000		

348 D

Expenditure variance:

Monthly budgeted production (10,800/12) = 900 units

Monthly budgeted expenditure (Flexed budget)	$
Fixed costs (900 × $4)	3,600
Variable costs (800 × $6)	4,800
Total expected expenditure	8,400
Actual expenditure	8,500
	———
Expenditure variance	100 (A)
	———

Volume variance:

This only applies to fixed overhead costs:

Volume variance in units (900 – 800)	100 units (A)
Standard fixed overhead cost per unit	$4
Fixed overhead volume variance	$400 (A)

349 C

	$	
Expenditure variance	36,000	(A)
(= 10% of budgeted expenditure)		
Therefore budgeted expenditure 36,000/10 × 100	360,000	
	———	
Actual expenditure 36,000/10 × 110	396,000	
	———	

350 C

Fixed production overhead cost per unit = $120,000/20,000 units = $6 per unit.

Standard units ×	OAR	
21,000	$6	$126,000
Budget units ×	OAR	
20,000	$6	$120,000
		————
	Volume variance	$6,000 F

351 A

Budgeted hours of work = 30,000 units × 4 hours = 120,000 hours.

Fixed overhead absorption rate/hour = $840,000/120,000 hours = $7/hour.

Actual hours ×	OAR	
123,000	$7	$861,000
Budget hours ×	OAR	
120,000	$7	$840,000
		————
	Capacity variance	$21,000 F

352 C

Budgeted fixed overhead cost per unit = $48,000/4,800 units = $10.

	$	
Budgeted fixed overhead	48,000	
Expenditure variance	2,000	(A)
	————	
Actual fixed overhead	50,000	
	————	

	$
Actual fixed overhead	50,000
Under-absorbed fixed overhead	8,000
	————
Absorbed overhead	42,000
	————

Units produced = Absorbed overhead/Absorption rate per unit

= $42,000/$10 = 4,200 units.

353 C

Less experienced staff are likely to be paid at a lower rate and therefore the labour rate variance will be favourable.

Usage of materials is likely to be unfavourable as the staff are less experienced, thus there will be more wastage and a higher level of rejects.

354 D

Usage of materials is likely to be adverse as the materials are sub-standard, thus there will be more wastage and a higher level of rejects.

Time spent by the labour force on rejected items that will not become output leads to higher than standard time spent per unit of output.

355 $3.80

Ah × Ar = 29,000 × **$3.80**	$110,200	
	Rate variance	$5,800 F
Ah × Sr = 29,000 × $4	$116,000	
	Efficiency variance	$4,000 F
Sh × Sr = 30,000 × $4	$120,000	

356 D

Ah × Ar = 10,080 × $0.87	$8,770	
	Rate variance	$706 A
Ah × Sr = 10,080 × $0.80	$8,064	
	Efficiency variance	$256 F
Sh × Sr = **2.08** × 5,000 × $0.80	$8,320	

357 C

Standard hours ×	OAR	
710 × 0.5	$12	$4,260
Actual hours ×	OAR	
378 − 20	$12	$4,296
		_____
	Efficiency variance	$36 A

358 C

Ah × Ar = 4,800 × $1.60	$7,700	
	Expenditure variance	$500 A
Ah × Sr = 4,800 × $1.50	$7,200	
	Efficiency variance	$300 F
Sh × Sr = 500 × 10 × $1.50	$7,500	

359 $1,100

(Budgeted quantity − Actual quantity) × standard profit per unit

$(1,000 − 900) × ($50 − $39) = $1,100$

360 A

Fixed overhead expenditure variance = Actual cost − Budgeted cost	= $1,250
Actual overhead	= Budgeted cost − 2%
2%	= $1,250
Actual overhead = 1,250/2 × 98	= $61,250

361 C

362 A

The sales volume variance under marginal costing is based on standard contribution per unit and under absorption costing is based on standard profit per unit. Standard contribution is either greater than or the same as standard profit depending on the value of fixed costs. Therefore the variance will either be higher or the same.

363 D

See working below (326)

364 A

Aq × Ap =	$173,280
	Price variance **$9,120 F**
Aq × Sp = 45,600 ×$ 4	$182,400
	Usage variance $15,200 A
Sq × Sp = **3,344 units** × 12.5 kg × $4	$167,200

365 B

The purchase of the new machine is likely to result in improved efficiency but higher depreciation costs.

366 D

Standard hours ×	OAR	
3,700 × 1.5	$2.40	$13,320
Budget hours ×	OAR	
4,000 × 1.5	$2.40	$14,400
	Volume variance	$1,080 A

367 C

(i)   will affect the sales price variance.

368 D

Aq × Sp = 1,566 × (76,500/1,500)	$79,866
	Usage variance $5,916 A
Sq × Sp = (580 × 1,500/600) × (76,500/1,500)	$73,950

369   1,950 KG

Aq × Sp = **1,650** × $2 $3,300

                              Usage variance $300 A

Sq × Sp = 500 × 3 kg × $2 $3,000

500 units did use	**1,650**
Less opening inventory	(100)
Plus closing inventory	400
	___
Material purchases in kg	1,950
	___

370   A

Aq × Ap = $25,839

                                 Price variance $783 F

Aq × Sp = 1,566 × ($25,500/1,500) $26,622

371   C

Expenditure variance = Budget cost − actual cost   = (8,000 × 15) − (8,500 × 17)

                                                    = $24,500 A

Volume variance (8,500 − 8,000) × $15   = $7,500 F

Total variance   = $17,000 A

372   A

The standard contribution per unit is $(50 − 4 − 16 − 10 − 1) = $19.

Sales volume variance

= (Budgeted sales volume − actual sales volume) × Standard contribution per unit

= (3,000 − 3,500) × $19

= $9,500

373   C

Sales volume variance

= (Budgeted sales volume − actual sales volume) × Standard profit per unit

= (10,000 − 9,800) × $5

= $1,000 A

374 B

Actual hours ×	OAR	
5,500	$15	$82,500
Budget hours ×	OAR	
5,000	$15	$75,000

Capacity variance $7,500 F

375 B

Ah × Ar =   117,600
Rate variance $8,400 A

Ah × Sr = 28,000 × **$3.90** $109,200
Efficiency variance $3,900 F

Sh × Sr = **29,000** × $3.90 $113,100

376

	Absorption costing	Marginal costing
Sales volume contribution variance		✓
Fixed overhead capacity variance	✓	
Fixed overhead volume variance	✓	
Sales volume profit variance	✓	
Fixed overhead efficiency variance	✓	

RECONCILIATION OF BUDGETED AND ACTUAL PROFIT

377 $38,635

	$
Budgeted contribution	43,900
Sales price variance	(3,100)
Sales volume contribution variance	(1,100)
Direct material price variance	1,986
Direct material usage variance	(2,200)
Direct labour rate variance	(1,090)
Direct labour efficiency variance	(512)
Variable overhead expenditure variance	1,216
Variable overhead efficiency variance	(465)
Actual contribution	38,635

378 A

Budgeted profit	$250,000
Sales price variance	$1,500
Sales volume variance	($2,100)
Materials price variance	($4,200)
Materials usage Variance	$1,500
Labour rate variance	$900
Labour efficiency Variance	($450)
Fixed overhead expenditure variance	$1,750
Fixed overhead volume variance	($1,800)
Actual profit	$247,100

379 D

Actual profit	$7,170
Sales price variance	($200)
Sales volume variance	($350)
Materials price variance	($250)
Materials usage Variance	$120
Labour rate variance	$450
Labour efficiency Variance	$800
Fixed overhead expenditure variance	($600)
Fixed overhead volume variance	$860
Budgeted profit	$8,000

380 $2,750F

Budget profit	$19,000
Sales price variance	($1,200)
Sales volume variance	$2,000
Materials price variance	$3,500
Materials usage Variance	($4,200)
Labour efficiency Variance	($1,500)
Fixed overhead expenditure variance	$1,500
Fixed overhead volume variance	($750)
	$18,350
Actual profit	$21,100
Labour rate variance	$2,750F

SYLLABUS AREA E – PERFORMANCE MEASUREMENT

PERFORMANCE MEASUREMENT OVERVIEW

381   A

382   A and B

The manager of a profit centre can exercise control over revenues and controllable costs, but has no influence concerning the capital invested in the centre.
Contribution (A) would be a useful performance measure because a profit centre manager can exercise control over sales revenue and variable costs. Controllable profit (B) would also be useful as long as any overhead costs charged in deriving the profit figure are controllable by the profit centre manager. Apportioned central costs would not be deducted when calculating controllable profit. Return on investment (C), and residual income (D) would not be useful because they require a measure of the capital invested in the division.

383   D

384   A

PERFORMANCE MEASUREMENT – APPLICATION

385   B

Controllable assets = 80,000 ÷ 0.25 = $320,000

RI = $80,000 − ($320,000 × 0.18) = $80,000 − $57,600 = $22,400

386   C

Cost per patient is a measure of output related to input

387   B

Reducing mortality rates is likely to be a stated objective of the hospital and as such is a measure of output, or effectiveness

388   B

Contribution is calculated as sales revenue less variable costs. The manager of a cost centre will not be responsible for the revenue therefore this is not an appropriate measure.

389   C

Class sizes are the result of the number of pupils educated (output), the number of teachers employed (input) and how well the timetable is organised in using those teachers.

390 C

Revenue is most likely to be based on the quantity delivered and the distance travelled. Cost per tonne miles gives a measure of both quantity and distance

391 C

RI = Net profit before interest – (10% × invested capital)

Therefore £240,000 = £640,000 – (10% × invested capital)

So 10% × invested capital = £400,000

Therefore invested capital = £4m

$$\text{ROI} = \frac{\text{Net profit before interest}}{\text{Invested capital}} = \frac{£640,000}{£4,000,000} \times 100 = 16\%$$

392 C

Actual output in standard hours = 1,100 × 2 = 2,200 hours

Budgeted production hours = 2,000 hours

Production/volume ratio = 2,200/2,000 = 1.1 or 110%

393 A

Actual output in standard hours = 180 × 0.6 = 108 hours

Actual production hours = 126 hours

Efficiency ratio = 108/126 = 0.857 or 86%

394 D

Actual production hours = 61 hours

Budgeted production hours = 50 × 1.2 = 60 hours

Capacity ratio = 61/60 = 1.017 or 102%

395 D

396 B

(i) and (ii) are financial indicators and (iv) is a risk indicator

397 D

398 A

399 A

(150 + 300 + 25)/(230 + 90) = 1.48

400 B

(300 + 25)/(230 + 90) = 1.02

401 A

(300/2,700) × 365 = 40.55 days

402 B

(230/1,300) × 365 = 64.58 days

403 D

(150/1,300) × 365 = 42.12 days

404 C

(550/2,700) × 100 = 20.3%

405 C

550/75 = 7.33 times

406 B

16,000/38,512 = 41.5%

407 A

(22,000 + 12,506 + 5,006)/15,000 = 2.63

408 C

(12,506 + 5,006)/15,000 = 1.17

409 D

27,657/(38,512 + 16,000) × 100 = 50.7%

410 C

12,506/64,323 × 365 = 70.97 days

411 A

(1,250/2,250) × 100 = 55.6%

412 B

(825/2,250) × 100 = 36.7%

413 D

490/275 = 1.8

414 D

(240/2,250) × 365 = 39 days

415 A

(275/1,000) × 365 = 100 days

416 B

(150/1,000) × 365 = 55 days

417 D

RI = Net profit before interest − (10% × invested capital)

Therefore $50,000 = $80,000 − (10% × invested capital)

So 10% × invested capital = $30,000

Therefore invested capital = $300,000

ROI = 80,000/300,000 × 100 = 26.67 = 27% to the nearest whole number

418 B

Original profit	=	$2,000,000 × 12%	=	$240,000
New profit	=	$240,000 + $90,000	=	$330,000
New capital employed	=	$2,000,000 + $500,000	=	$2,500,000
Residual income	=	$330,000 − (10% × $2,500,000)	=	$80,000

419 D

Efficiency compares the standard hours produced with the hours actively worked

(9,300 hours ÷ 9,200 hours) × 100% = 101%.

420 C

421 C

Capacity ratio × Efficiency ratio = Activity ratio

Capacity ratio = 103.5/90 × 100% = 115%

422 D

This is the definition of the activity (PV) ratio.

423 A

The capacity ratio measures the number of hours actually worked compared to budget. A ratio that is greater than 100% means that more actual hours were worked than budget.

424 D

The most appropriate measure of ROI will include only assets available to earn profit during the year and will not include interest payable.

Thus ROI will be $6 million/($35 million – $4 million) = 19.4%

425 C

ROI before project	=	360/1,600	=	22.5%
ROI after project	=	385/(1,600 + 130)	=	22.3%

Therefore management would reject this project, if ROI is used as an evaluation criterion.

Residual value before project	=	360 – (1,600 × 0.18)	=	$72,000
Residual value after project	=	385 – (1,730 × 0.18)	=	$73,600

Therefore management would accept this project if residual income is used as an evaluation criterion.

426 A and B

427 C

428 D

ROI = financial

Warranty claims = customer

New products = learning and growth

429

Average class size	✓
Tutor grading by students	
Pass rates	
Percentage room occupancy	✓

430 B

Calculate the average number of operations per employee:

	Budget	*Actual*
Department A	200	200
Department B	140	220
Department C	150	150
Department D	75	80

COST REDUCTIONS AND VALUE ENHANCEMENT

431

Setting targets for cost centre managers	✓
Reducing the cost budget	Cost reduction
Cost variance analysis	✓
Increasing sales volume	Would lead to an increase in cost

432

Control costs	✓
Reduce costs	✓
Improve sales	VA looks at costs not sales
Increase the value of the product	The value of the product should not change if value analysis is applied correctly

433 A

434

	Value analysis	Value engineering
Reviews current products to reduce costs	✓	
Reviews products at the design stage to reduce costs		✓

435 D

All the techniques listed in the question could be used to monitor and control costs.

MONITORING PERFORMANCE AND REPORTING

436 D

Measuring the budgeted number of quotations actually issued would be monitoring the output and activity of the department but it would not be helpful in improving the department's performance in terms of the accuracy or speed of quotations in the scenario described.

437 C

438 B

439 C

440 B

Machine rental is more likely to be arranged at a higher level

441 A

The purchasing manager has some control of raw material prices

442 B

443

	Effectiveness	Efficiency	Economy
Have the waiting lists been reduced?	×		
What was the average cost per patient treated?		×	
Have mortality rates gone down?	×		
Did the hospital spend more or less on drugs this year?			×
What was the average spend per bed over the period?		×	
Did the hospital spend more or less on nurses' wages?			×

Effectiveness = links outputs with objectives, are the outputs achieving the objectives of the organisation.

Efficiency = links inputs to outputs, maximum output being achieved with the resources available

Economy = input measure, relationship between money spent and inputs

444 GAP 1 – EFFECTIVENESS, GAP 2 - EFFICIENCY

Effectiveness looks at results/outputs. The reduction in visitor numbers indicates poor effectiveness in YU. Inputs were constant (the same amount was spent on advertising as in previous years), suggesting YU was economical, but the medium used was less efficient than in previous years.

445 D

446 C

447 B

448 1 = COMPETITIVE, 2 = INTERNAL, 3 = FUNCTIONAL

449 D

Section 4

ANSWERS TO SECTION B-TYPE QUESTIONS

BUDGETING

450 (a)

	Original budget	Flexed budget	Actual	Variance
Volume sold	4,000	5,000	5,000	
	$000	$000	$000	$000
Sales revenue	1,500	1,875	1,950	75
Less costs:				
Direct materials	36	45	45	0
Direct labour	176	220	182	38
Variable overheads	92	115	90	25
Profit from operations	1,196	1,495	1,633	138

(b)　　B

(c)　　D

The flexed budget has already taken account of the increase in units sold, offering a bulk discount should increase sales volume but at a reduced price, increased competition from other companies could lead to a reduction in sales volume and prices

451 (a)　(i)　　Steel required for production = 220 × 1.5 kg + 170 × 2 kg = 670 kg

　　　　(ii)　　Opening inventory = (220 × 1.5 kg + 170 × 2 kg) × 0.5 = 335 kg

　　　　(iii)　　Closing inventory = (240 × 1.5 kg + 180 × 2 kg) × 0.5 = 360 kg

(b)　=B1 − B2 + B3

(c)　(i)　　False

　　　(ii)　　True

　　　(iii)　　False

　　　(iv)　　False

(d)　A and C

452 (a) Cash received in March = $15,000 × 0.5 × 0.97 + $12,000 × 0.5 = $13,275

(b) Payment to suppliers in March = $21,000 × 0.75 + $2,000 – $3,000 = $14,750

(c) Chain base index in February $15,000/$12,000 × 100 = 125

Chain base index in March $21,000/$15,000 × 100 = 140

(d) Gap 1 B

Gap 2 B

453 (a) To produce 12,000 units it would use 12,000 × 0.4 = 4,800 kg

Material CD, cost per kg up to 6,000 units = $17,760 / 4,800 kg= $3.70

Over 6,000 units discount 10%

Budgeted cost per kg of material CD = **$3.33**

Alternative method using 18,000 units

18,000 × 0.4 kg = 7,200 kg used

6,000 × 3.70 = $22,200

7,200kg cost $26,196

Difference = $3,996/1,200 kg = $3.33

(b)

	Flexed budget	Actual cost	Variance
Activity level or volume	17,000	17,000	0
Costs	$	$	$
Material AB	5,100	5,025	75 F
Material CD	24,864	25,118	254 A
Labour (W1)	33,570	32,889	681 F
Overhead (W2)	13,700	13,315	385 F

(W1) Labour (direct and indirect)

	High	Low	Difference
Activity	18,000 units	12,000 units	6,000 units
Cost	$35,150	$25,700	$9,450

Variable element of cost $9,450/6,000 units = $1.58 per unit.

Fixed cost:

Total variable cost at 18,000 units = 18,000 × $1.58 = $28,440

Fixed cost = $35,150 - $28,440 = $6,710

(W2) Overhead

	High	Low	Difference
Activity	18,000 units	12,000 units	6,000 units
Cost	$13,960	$12,400	$1,560

Variable element of cost $1,560/6,000 = $0.26 per unit

Fixed cost:

Total variable cost at 18,000 units = 18,000 × $0.26 = $4,680

Fixed cost = $13,960 - $4,680 = $9,280

(c)   Material usage variance for material AB

Standard usage of material AB

17,000 units × 0.2 kg = 3,400 kg
Actual usage = $5,025 / ($3,600/2,400kg) = 3,350 kg
Usage variance in kg **= 50 kg favourable**

454   (a)

Production budget 20X7		**Units**	
	January	February	March
Sales	5,000	5,500	7,000
Closing inventory (W1)	550	700	700
Opening inventory (W2)	(500)	(550)	(700)
Production units	5,050	5,650	7,000

Labour budget 20X7

	January	February	March
Total hours (W3)	20,200	22,600	28,000
Basic hours available (W4)	22,080	22,080	22,080
Overtime hours needed	0	520	5,920
	$	$	$
Basic rate payment (W5)	176,640	176,640	176,640
Overtime payment (W6)	0	6,240	71,040
Total labour cost	176,640	182,880	247,680

Workings

(W1) January closing inventory = February sales × 10% = 5,500 units × 10% = 550 units

(W2) January opening inventory = January sales × 10% = 5,000 units × 10% = 500 units

(W3) Production units × hours per unit

(W4) 138 workers × 160 hours per month = 22,080 hours

(W5) 138 workers × $1,280 = $176,640

(W6) Basic rate = $1,280 ÷ 160 hours = $8.00 per hour

Overtime rate = $8.00 × 150% = $12.00

Overtime payment February = 520 hours × $12.00 = $6,240

455 (a) Payback period = $18,750/$5,000 = 3.75 years = 3 years 9 months.

(b) (i)   Gap 1 more

Gap 2 inflation

(ii)

Year	Cash flow × DF	Cumulative cash flow
0	−18,750	−18,750
1	5,000 × 0.926 = 4,630	−14,120
2	5,000 × 0.857 = 4,285	−9,835
3	5,000 × 0.794 = 3,970	−5,865
4	5,000 × 0.735 = 3,675	−2,190
5	5,000 × 0.681 = 3,405	+1,215

As the cash flows arise at the end of the year payback will be 5 years

Alternative working

The project will payback when $18,750 = $5,000 × AF $_{1-n}$ @ 8%

AF$_{1-n}$=3.75

The annuity factor for 4 years is 3.312, and 5 years is 3.993. Therefore the payback must occur at 5 years as the cash flows arise at the end of the year.

(c)   Net present value = -$18,750 + ($5,000 × 4.623) = $4,365

(d)   B

456 (a) The present value of a cash flow in perpetuity (forever) is given by cash flow cost of capital (as a proportion).

In this case $13,500/0.1 = $135,000.

The net present value is therefore $135,000 – $119,000 = $16,000.

(b) At a cost of capital of 20% the NPV is negative.

Try calculating the NPV at 10%:

Year	Cash flow	Discount factor	Present value
	$000		$000
0	241	1.000	(241)
1	60	0.909	54.54
2	65	0.826	53.69
3	70	0.751	52.57
4	100	0.683	68.30
5	85	0.621	52.79
	Net present value		40.89

$$\text{IRR} = 10 + \left(\frac{40.89}{40.89 + 23} \right) \times (20 - 10) = 10 + 6.4 \times 10 = 16.4\%$$

(c)

	Cash flow	Discount factor at 14%	Present value
	$		$
Year 0	186,000	1	(186,000)
Year 1–5	?	3.432	186,000
			Nil

As the IRR is 14%, the net present value must be nil if the cash flows are discounted at this cost of capital.

The annual net cash inflow = $186,000/3.432 = $54,196

(d) Project 2

If the cost of capital increased to 15%, the investment in Project 2 will still be justified as the cost of capital would still be below the project's IRR of 16%. Any cost of capital below the IRR will result in a positive NPV. The investment in Project 3 will no longer be justified as the cost of capital would be higher than the Project's IRR. Discounting at 15% would result in a negative NPV for project 3.

457 (a) Annual depreciation = $175,000 ÷ 5 = $35,000

-11,000 + 3,000 +34,000 +47,000 + 8,000 + (5 × 35,000) = **$256,000**

(b) $187,000

Year	Cash inflow $000	Discount factor at 10%	Present value $000
1	24 [(11) + 35]	0.909	21.8
2	38 [3 + 35]	0.826	31.4
3	69 [34 + 35]	0.751	51.8
4	82 [47 + 35]	0.683	56.0
5	43 [8 + 35]	0.621	26.7
			———
			187.7
			———

(b) Net present value (NPV) = $187,700 − $175,000 = **$12,700**

(c) The investment is worthwhile because the NPV is positive when the incremental cash flows are discounted at the company's required rate of return.

(d) $5,000 × (1 + 0.08)^4 = **$6,802**

(e) **C**

$[(1.021)^4 − 1] × 100 = 8.67\%$

STANDARD COSTING

458 (a)

Aq × **Ap** = 500 × 2 (i)	= 1,000	
	Price = 125F	
Aq × Sp = 500 × 2.25	=1,125	
	Usage = 45A	
Sq × Sp = **480** (ii) × 2.25	=1,080	

(b) A

(c) A

(d) D

459 (a)   A, C and D

(b)   (i)   The expenditure variance is $23,000 – $20,000 = $3000 and is adverse

(ii)   The capacity variance is (2,475 hours × $10) – $20,000 = $4,750 and is favourable

(iii)   The efficiency variance is (550 units × 4 hours × $10) – (2,475 hours × $10) = $2,750 and is adverse

(c)   A

460 (a)

Wood	Aq × Ap = 170 × 12		= 2,040	
Glass	Aq × Ap = 70 × 12.29		= 860	= 2,900
				(i) Price = $360A
Wood	Aq × Sp = 170 × 10		= 1,700	
Glass	Aq × Sq = 70 × 12		= 840	= 2,540
				(ii) Usage = $140A
Wood	Sq × Sp = 300 × 0.5 × 10		= 1,500	
Glass	Sq × Sp = 300 × 0.25 × 12		= 900	= 2,400

(b)   B

(c)   B

(d)   C

461 (a)   (i)   True (better quality final product, sold more units)

(ii)   True (better quality ingredients cost more)

(iii)   False (nothing to do with the quality of ingredients)

(iv)   True (less wastage in the preparation process)

(v)   False (it is adverse, but better quality ingredients would imply a higher quality product and higher price)

(b)   Actual contribution

(c)

Ah × **Ar** = 3,620 × 3.04   = 11,000

Rate = 140A

Ah × Sr = 3,620 × 3   = 10,860

Usage = 390F

Sh × Sr = 1,500 × 2.5 × 3   = 11,250

PERFORMANCE MEASUREMENT

462 (a) (i) Inventory holding period = $35,000/$284,000 × 365 = 45 days

(ii) Receivables collection period = $37,400/$343,275 × 365 = 40 days

(iii) Payables period = $35,410/$275,000 × 365 = 47 days

(iv) Current ratio = ($35,000 + $37,400)/($40,500 + $35,410) = 0.954

(b) B

New quick ratio = $37,400/($35,410 + $40,500 − $17,500) = 0.64

(c) A and D

463 (a) Calculations:

(i) Interest cover = $50,000/0.08 × $60,000 = 10.42

(ii) Asset turnover = revenue/capital employed

4 = $500,000/CE therefore CE = $125,000

ROCE = $50,000/$125,000 × 100 = 40.00%

Or

ROCE = asset turnover × operating profit margin = 4 × $50,000/$500,000 = 40.00%

(iii) Gearing = debt/equity = $60,000/$125,000 = 48.00%

Or

Gearing = debt/debt + equity = $60,000/($60,000 + $125,000) = 32.43%

(b) A and C

(c) A

464 (a) Calculations

(i) Net profit percentage = $348,000/$6,000,000 = 5.8%

(ii) Market share $6,000,000/$50,000,000 = 12.0%

(iii) Increase in revenue = $0.25m/$5.75m = 4.35%

(iv) Revenue per style of watch = $6,000,000/25 = $240,000

(v) Increase in sales per $ of market research = $250,000/$200,000 = 1.25

(b) B – net profit for the division would include the allocated head office expenses which are not controllable, and would therefore affect motivation. ROCE is calculated using net profit so this would be misleading as well.

465 (a) Gap 1 B

Gap 2 B

(b)

	Financial	Customer	Internal	Learning perspective
Profit made per burger	✓			
Time taken from the customer ordering food to food being passed to the customer			✓	
Percentage of employees with higher level food hygiene certificates				✓
Percentage of burgers cooked but not sold as they are inedible			✓	

(c) Gap 1 Internal

Gap 2 Competitive

(d) C

466

		South division	North division
(a)	Return on capital employed		
	(Operating profit ÷ Capital employed × 100)		
	($700k ÷ $3,500k × 100)	20.0%	
	($840k ÷ $4,000k × 100)		21.0%
(b)	Return on sales		
	(Operating profit ÷ Sales × 100)		
	($700k ÷$50,000k × 100)	1.4%	
	($840k ÷$3,200k × 100)		26.3%
(c)	Asset turnover		
	(Sales ÷ Capital employed)		
	($50,000k ÷ $3,500k)	14.3	
	($3,200k ÷ $4,000k)		0.8
(d)	Residual income		
	(Operating profit – (capital employed × imputed interest charge))		
	($700k – ($3,500k × 12%) =	$280k	
	($840k – ($4,000k × 12%) =		$360k

467 (a) Production volume ratio = $\dfrac{30,502}{29,470} \times 100 =$ **103.5%**

(b) Efficiency ratio = $\dfrac{30,502}{31,630} \times 100 =$ **96.4%**

(c) Capacity ratio = $\dfrac{31,630}{29,470} \times 100 =$ **107.3%**

(d) ROI with investment

Profit = $90,000 + $20,000 = $110,000

CE = $300,000 + $100,000 = $400,000

New ROI = $110,000 ÷ $400,000 × 100 = 27.5%

The manager will not want to accept project as the ROI of the division reduces when the profit and capital employed are adjusted for the new investment

(e) Calculate the ROI of the project $20,000 ÷ $100,000 × 100 = 20%

The manager should accept a project giving a return of 20% as the cost of capital is only 15%.

(f)

	Without the investment	With the investment
Profit	$160,000	$175,000
Notional Interest	($800,000 × 12%) $96,000	($900,000 × 12%) $108,000
Residual Income	$64,000	$67,000

(g) The investment centre manager will want to undertake the investment because it will increase residual income.

468 (a) 700/9100×100=7.69%

(b) (8400 – 7600)/7600 × 100 = 10.53%

(c) B AND C

NFS has failed to reduce the number of complaints or to reduce the number of existing patients but it has succeeded in reducing the cost per patient. This reduced from $1,600 in Year 1 to $1,570 in Year 2.

NFS's total cost has increased by 1.47% and NFS's number of total patients has increased by 3.4%

(d) The completed sentences are:

A NFS's number of complaints has increased and its number of complaints per patient has decreased.

B NFS's total cost has increased and its cost per patient has decreased.

C NFS's number of new patients has decreased and its number of existing patients has increased.

(e) The correct matching is:

- To maximise the bed occupancy rate – **efficiency**

- To minimise patient waiting times – **effectiveness**

- To reduce the total staff cost while maintaining the level of service – **economy.**

Section 5

PRACTICE EXAM QUESTIONS

SECTION A

1   The following details are available for a company:

	Budgeted	Actual
Expenditure	$176,400	$250,400
Machine hours	4,000	5,000
Labour hours	3,600	5,400

The company absorbs overheads using labour hours.

What was the under or over absorption of the overheads?

A   Under-absorbed by $29,900

B   Under-absorbed by $14,200

C   Over-absorbed by $14,200

D   Over-absorbed by $64,990

2   **What type of sampling is defined as 'a sample taken in such a way that every member of the population has an equal chance of being selected'?**

A   Random

B   Stratified

C   Quota

D   Cluster

3   The following data is available for a company in period 2.

Actual overheads	$225,900
Actual machine hours	7,530
Budgeted overheads	$216,000

The budgeted overhead absorption rate was $32 per hour.

What were the number of machine hours (to the nearest hour) that were budgeted to be worked?

hours

4   **In overhead absorption which of the following is the final step relating overheads to units?**

A   Allocation

B   Apportionment

C   Absorption

D   Re-apportionment

5   ABC produces three main products.

Which would be the most appropriate chart or diagram for showing total revenue and product analysis month by month?

A   Z chart

B   Line graph

C   Pie chart

D   Component bar chart

6   **In times of decreasing prices, the valuation of inventory using the First In First Out method, as opposed to the Weighted Average Cost method, will result in which ONE of the following combinations?**

	Cost of sales	Profit	Closing inventory
A	Lower	Higher	Higher
B	Lower	Higher	Lower
C	Higher	Lower	Lower
D	Higher	Higher	Lower

7   A manufacturing company uses 28,000 components at an even rate during the year. Each order placed with the supplier of the components is for 1,600 components, which is the Economic Order Quantity. The company holds a buffer inventory of 800 components. The annual cost of holding one component in inventory is $3.50.

What is the annual cost of holding inventory of the component?

A $2,800

B $4,200

C $5,600

D $5,700

The following data relates to Questions 8 and 9.

Normal working week	36 hours
Basic rate of pay (direct)	$6.20 per hour
Overtime pay	$7.50 per hour

Last week, the total hours worked by all these workers was 936. The overtime hours worked was 108. All employees worked at least their basic 36 hours.

8   How many workers worked last week?

   A   was 23

   B   was 26

   C   was 29

   D   cannot be determined from the above data

9   What was the total direct labour charge?

   A $810.00

   B $5,133.60

   C $5,803.20

   D $6,210.00

10   Your firm values inventory using the weighted average cost method. At 1 October 20X9, there were 50 units in inventory valued at $15 each. On 8 October, 30 units were purchased for $20 each, and a further 40 units were purchased for $17 each on 14 October. On 21 October, 60 units were sold for $1,800.

   What was the value of closing inventory at 31 October 20X9 to the nearest $?

   $

11   Which of the following is service costing characterised by?

   A   high levels of indirect costs as a proportion of total

   B   identical output units

   C   the ability to store the units

   D   long shelf life of output

12 A Company has three departments – Assembly, Finishing and Maintenance. Budgeted data for each department is shown below:

	Assembly	Finishing	Maintenance
Allocated overheads	$90,000	$100,000	$10,000
Direct labour hours	5,000	6,000	Nil
Machine hours	10,000	3,000	2,000
Percentage of time spent maintaining machinery	60	40	Nil
Number of staff	60	120	10

What would be the most appropriate production overhead absorption rate to use in the Assembly department?

A $9.60 per machine hour

B $9.90 per machine hour

C $17.33 per labour hour

D $18.33 per labour hour

13 Products A and B are manufactured in a joint process. The following data is available for a period:

Joint process costs		$30,000
Output:	Product A	2,000 kg
	Product B	4,000 kg
Selling price:	Product A	$12 per kg
	Product B	$18 per kg

What is Product B's share of the joint process costs if the sales value method of cost apportionment is used?

A 7,500

B 18,000

C 20,000

D 22,500

The following data relates to Questions 14 and 15.

Budgeted production details for November are as follows:

	Product X	Product Y	Product Z
Units produced	2,000	1,600	2,200
Units sold	1,800	1,500	2,000
Variable cost/unit	100	80	120
Fixed overhead absorbed/unit	30	30	50
No. of labour hours	6	4.5	5

There was no opening inventory at the beginning of November.

14 **What were the budgeted fixed overheads for November?**

A $810,000

B $739,000

C $218,000

D $199,000

15 **Which of the following statements is true?**

A Absorption costing profit will be $19,000 lower than marginal costing profit

B Absorption costing profit will be $71,000 lower than marginal costing profit

C Absorption costing profit will be $19,000 higher than marginal costing profit

D Absorption costing profit will be $71,000 higher than marginal costing profit

16 The total costs incurred at various output levels in a factory have been measured as follows:

Output in units	Total cost
25	$5,500
30	$5,450
33	$5,550
44	$6,000
48	$6,500
55	$7,000

What are the variable cost per unit and the total fixed costs?

A Variable cost $50 per unit, Fixed costs $4,250

B Variable cost $53 per unit, Fixed costs $4,000

C Variable cost $56 per unit, Fixed costs $4,500

D Variable cost $59 per unit, Fixed costs £4,750

17 Which of the following statements are true and which are false when applied to fixed costs?

	True	False
Overhead costs are always fixed costs		
As production levels increase, fixed cost per unit decreases		
Fixed costs are always irrelevant in a decision making situation		
As the level of activity changes, fixed costs will also change		

18 A job is budgeted to require 3,300 productive hours but will incur 25% idle time.

If the total labour cost budgeted for the job is $36,300, what is the labour cost per hour (to the nearest cent)?

$

19 Which of the following statements about variable costs is correct?

Variable costs are conventionally deemed to:

A   be constant per unit of output

B   vary per unit of output as production volume changes

C   vary in total when production volume is constant

D   vary, in total, from period to period when production is constant

20 In quality related costs, which of the following are conformance costs and which are non-conformance costs?

	Conformance costs	Non-conformance costs
Internal failure costs		
Prevention costs		
Appraisal costs		
External failure costs		

21 A business is preparing its budget for the coming year by using time series analysis.

Using the following information and a 3-month moving average what is the seasonal variation for the month of October?

Month	Sales value (000s)
June	770
July	750
August	928
September	854
October	834
November	1012
December	938

A   −66

B   −38

C   +66

D   +38

22 D Ltd operates a total absorption costing system. Budgeted fixed overheads for 2007 were $175,000 and budgeted production was 5,000 units.

During 2007, the actual fixed overheads amounted to $186,000 and actual production was 6,000 units.

What is the over or under absorption of overheads?

A   under-absorbed by $24,000

B   under-absorbed by $11,000

C   over-absorbed by $11,000

D   over-absorbed by $24,000

23 Below is the standard cost card for one unit of product K.

	$/unit
Selling price	35
Direct materials	20
Direct labour	4
Variable overhead	1
Fixed overhead	6

Production was 50,000 units and sales 60,000 units. Opening inventory was 25,000 units. The profit calculated using marginal costing was $180,000.

What is the profit using absorption costing?

A $30,000

B $120,000

C $210,000

D $240,000

24 **Which of the following statements is true about direct costs?**

A   they can be directly identified with a product or service

B   they are directly under the control of a manager

C   they are incurred directly the factory is opened

D   they are directly charged to a department

25 **What is a cost pool in ABC?**

A   an activity that consumes resources and for which overhead costs are identified and allocated

B   an activity that causes a cost to change

C   an item of equipment that costs are charged to

D   an area of the business that is used to store output

26 A company is deciding between three projects A, B and C. The expected profit from each one is as follows:

Project A		Project B		Project C	
Profit	*Probability*	*Profit*	*Probability*	*Profit*	*Probability*
$5,000	0.5	$10,000	0.3	$6,000	0.4
$2,500	0.5	$1,000	0.7	$4,000	0.6

Rank projects in descending order by inserting 1 beside the highest ranked project, 2 beside the second and 3 beside the third.

	Rank
Project A	
Project B	
Project C	

27 Using an interest rate of 15% per year the net present value (NPV) of a project has been correctly calculated as $850.

If the interest rate is increased by 5% the NPV of the project falls by $900.

What is the internal rate of return (IRR) of the project?

A   14.7%

B   17.4%

C   19.7%

D   20.3%

28 Using data from 40 counties in England and Wales, it has been calculated that the correlation between the level of trampoline ownership and the number of neck injuries is 0.75.

Which TWO of the statements shown follow this?

A   High levels of trampoline ownership in a given county cause high levels of neck injuries.

B   There is a strong relationship between the level of trampoline ownership and the number of neck injuries.

C   56% of the variation in the level of neck injuries from one county to the next can be explained by the corresponding variation in the level of trampoline ownership.

D   75% of the variation in the level of neck injuries from one county to the next can be explained by the corresponding variation in the level of trampoline ownership.

29 The following statements refer to spreadsheets:

(1)   Spreadsheets can be used for budgeting.

(2)   Spreadsheets are very useful for word-processing.

(3)   Spreadsheets make the manipulation of data easier and quicker.

Which of these statements are correct?

A   (1) and (2)

B   (1) and (3)

C   (2) and (3)

D   (1), (2) and (3)

30 A company uses standard marginal costing. Last month, when all sales were at the standard selling price, the standard contribution from actual sales was $50,000 and the following variances arose:

Total variable costs variance	$3,500 adverse
Total fixed costs variance	$1,000 favourable
Sales volume contribution variance	$2,000 favourable

What was the actual contribution for last month?

A $46,500

B $47,500

C $48,500

D $49,500

31   A production worker is paid a salary of $650 per month, plus an extra 5 cents for each unit produced during the month.

What is the best description of the type of labour cost?

A   A variable cost

B   A fixed cost

C   A step cost

D   A semi-variable cost

32   A company achieves bulk buying discounts on quantities of raw material above a certain level. These discounts are only available for the units above the specified level and not on all the units purchased.

Which of the following graphs of total purchase cost against units best illustrates the above situation?

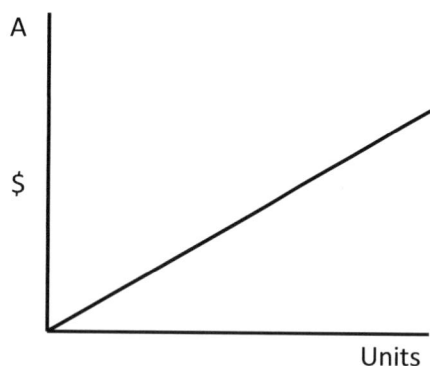

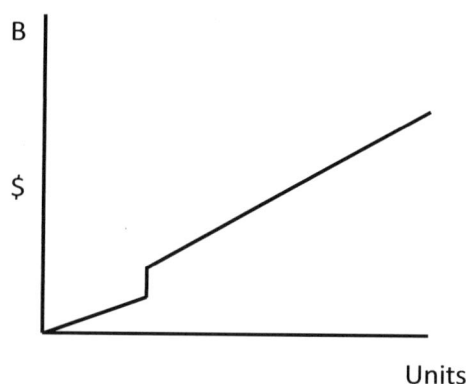

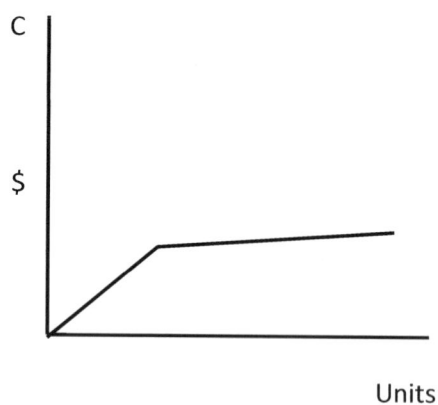

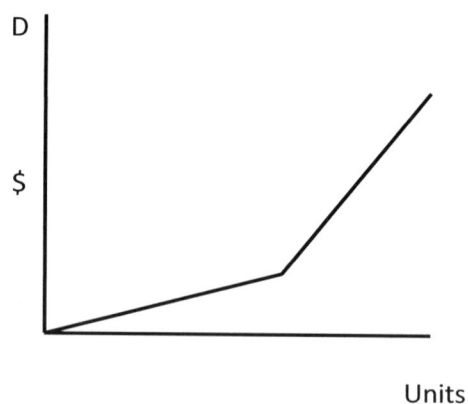

The following information relates to questions 33 and 34.

During the month of December, a manufacturing process incurs material costs of $8,000 and conversion costs of $4,500. 2,000 kgs of material was input. There is a normal loss of 10% and all losses have a scrap value of $1.75 per kg. During the period, 1700 kgs were output to finished goods. Opening and Closing inventories in the process were nil.

33   What was the cost per kg output?

   A $6.25

   B $6.75

   C $6.94

   D $7.35

34   What was the value of the abnormal loss written off in the statement of profit or loss?

   A $675

   B $175

   C $2,025

   D $500

35   Jojo is an assembly worker earning $12 per hour for a basic 35 hour week. Any overtime is paid at a premium of 50%.

In the last four-week period, Jojo was paid for 150 hours. During this time 15 hours were classed as idle due to a machine breaking down. Also included in the number of hours are four hours' overtime spent working for an urgent job at the request of the customer.

How much should be charged to the production overhead account for the four-week period?

   A $216

   B $240

   C $288

   D $360

SECTION B

ALL THREE QUESTIONS ARE COMPULSORY AND MUST BE ATTEMPTED

1   Mrs Glam wants to expand her clothes shop. Mrs Glam has commissioned a market research company at a cost of $3,000 to research her options for her. The company have offered two options:

Option 1

Remain in her the current premises and undertake an advertising campaign at a cost of $2,000 to increase the profile of the shop in the area. It is estimated that revenue will increase by 10% from its current level of $50,000 per year. The contribution earned on revenue is 30%.

Option 2

Move the shop to a more central location and undertake an advertising campaign to both increase the profile and the move to new premises. This more extensive campaign would cost $4,000 but revenue would be expected to increase by 18% from its current level. The level of contribution earned on revenue is not expected to change.

There would be further costs involved in moving location which have been estimated:

- Moving costs are estimated to be $1,500. This includes the cost of refitting the shop, and would be payable immediately

- New shop fittings will be required costing $2,500. These will be depreciated on a straight line basis.

- Rates of $4,000 will be payable yearly in advance. This cost is 15% higher than Mrs Glam currently pays, due to the location.

Other information

- Mrs Glam uses a cost of capital of 10%

- The expansion is to have a life of 4 years.

Required:

(a)   State if the following items relating to Mrs Glam's decision how to expand are relevant or irrelevant cash flows in a net present value calculation:

   (i)   The $3,000 market research fee   (1 mark)

   (ii)   Depreciation of $625 per year for the new shop fittings.   (1 mark)

   (iii)   The costs of $1,500 incurred in moving to the new premises.   (1 mark)

(b)   Calculate the present value of the INCREMENTAL contribution cash flow that will arise if option 2 is compared to option 1.   (2.5 marks)

(c)   Calculate the present value of the cash flows relating to the INCREMENTAL rates that will arise if option 2 is compared to option 1.   (2.5 marks)

(d) If Mrs Glam moved her clothes shop, she would finance the move with a small legacy of $10,000 that she has been left. She is wondering whether instead of moving the shop now, she should invest the money she has been left and use the lump sum in four years time to move to even bigger premises.

Required:

Calculate the value of the legacy in four years time, if it is invested at a compound interest rate of 10%. **(2 marks)**

(Total: 10 marks)

2 M Co is a small manufacturing company. The following information is available:

Budgeted
Labour rate per hour	$4
Fixed overhead absorption rate per hour	$2.50

Actual
Hours worked	3,000 hours
Fixed overheads	$9,000

Variances
Labour rate	300 favourable
Fixed overhead expenditure	200 favourable
Fixed overhead efficiency	500 adverse

Required:

(a) **Using the information available, calculate:**

  (i) **the budgeted fixed overhead expenditure and state if the fixed overhead capacity variance would be favourable or adverse.** **(2 marks)**

  (ii) **the labour efficiency variance** **(2 marks)**

  (iii) **the actual labour rate per hour** **(2 marks)**

(b) **Which of the following could have caused the fixed overhead efficiency variance to arise?**

  A **Sub contract staff being brought in to partially cover a strike by M Co's workforce**

  B **Incorrect estimation of standard absorption rate per hour.**

  C **A key piece of machinery breaking down and requiring repair before manufacturing could continue**

  D **The materials supplier failing to deliver raw materials into stock as required.** **(2 marks)**

(c) M co is aware that next month they will have to buy their materials from a different supplier. Although this supplier charges less per unit, M Co is aware that the material will be of a lesser quality. The management of M Co wants to understand the possible effect this purchase will have on their results.

Required:

As an indirect result of this purchase, what is likely to be the effect on the materials usage and labour efficiency variances?

	Materials usage	Labour efficiency
A	Adverse	Favourable
B	Adverse	Adverse
C	Favourable	Favourable
D	Favourable	Adverse

(2 marks)

(Total: 10 marks)

3   Play Co owns two indoor children's soft play centres one in Bromsgrove, one in Worcester. The following information about each centre is available:

	Bromsgrove	Worcester
Centre opened	3 years ago	6 years ago
Original cost including cost of site, building and equipment	$300,000	$150,000
Current value	$425,000	$425,000
Controllable profit	$55,000	$40,000
Depreciation policy set by head office	Reducing balance basis	Reducing balance basis

Managers are responsible for maintaining the centres to a high standard, and head office will do spot checks to ensure that no equipment is damaged.

Play Co uses an annual rate of 10% as the required return on investment and to determine residual income. Bonuses are paid if managers exceed their targets.

Required:

(a)   Using the information provided, calculate for Bromsgrove:

(i)   Return on investment using original cost   **(1 mark)**

(ii)   Residual income using original cost   **(2 marks)**

(b)   If the current values are used for the investment, what will happen to the return on investment and residual income figures for Bromsgrove?

	Residual income	Return on investment
A	Higher	Higher
B	Lower	Higher
C	Higher	Lower
D	Lower	Lower

(2 marks)

(c) The manager of the Worcester office is concerned that his controllable profit levels are so much lower than the Bromsgrove centre, despite the centres being the same size and having the same footfall. Which reason could account for the lower controllable profit:

A   Increased repair costs due to age of equipment.

B   Lower depreciation charge due to age of equipment

(1 mark)

(d) Are the following statements true or false?

Statement one: Residual income is of more use than return on investment when comparing divisions of different sizes.

Statement two: Residual income is more likely to encourage investment in new assets than return on investment is.

	Statement one	Statement two
A	True	True
B	True	False
C	False	True
D	False	False

(2 marks)

(e) Which sequence shows the level of managerial control decreasing?

A	Investment centre →	Profit centre →	Cost centre
B	Profit centre →	Investment centre →	Cost centre
C	Cost centre →	Profit centre →	Investment centre
D	Cost centre →	Investment centre →	Profit centre

(2 marks)

(Total: 10 marks)

Section 6

ANSWERS TO PRACTICE EXAM QUESTIONS

SECTION A

1 **C**

OAR = $176,400/3,600 = $49

	$
Amount absorbed = $49 × 5,400 =	264,600
Actual overhead	(250,400)
Over absorbed	14,200

2 **A**

3 **6,750 hours**

$$\text{Budgeted hours} = \frac{\$216,000}{\$32} = 6,750 \text{ hours}$$

4 **C**

5 **D**

A bar chart is a good way of illustrating total revenue month by month. The length of the bar each month is a measure of total revenue. The bar can be divided into three parts, to show the amount of sales achieved for each of the three products. This is called a component bar chart.

6 **C**

When prices are decreasing, FIFO will give a lower valuation for closing inventory, because the closing inventory will consist of the most recently-purchased items. Lower closing inventory means higher cost of sales and lower profit.

7   C

{[Buffer inventory + (EOQ ÷ 2)] × Annual holding cost per component}

= [800 units + (1,600 units ÷ 2)] × $3.50 = $5,600

8   A

Normal time = 936 − 108 = 828 hours

Number of employees = 23

9   C

Direct labour charge is **all** hours (including overtime) at normal rate:

936 × $6.20 = $5,803.20

10 $1,015

Date		Units	Unit value $	Inventory value $
1 October	Opening inventory	50	15.00	750
8 October	Purchase 30 units at $20	30	20.00	600
14 October	Purchase 40 units at $17	40	17.00	680
		120	16.92	2,030
21 October	Sold 75 units: cost	(60)	16.92	(1,015)
31 October	Closing inventory	60	16.92	1,015

11   A

12   A

	Assembly	Finishing	Maintenance
Allocated o/hs	90,000	100,000	10,000
Maintenance	6,000	4,000	(10,000)
	96,000	104,000	–

OAR for Assembly department = $96,000/10,000 machine hours = $9.60

13   D

	Output (kg)	Sales value ($)	Apportionment of joint costs ($)	
Product A	2,000	24,000	(24/96)	7,500
Product B	4,000	72,000	(72/96)	22,500
		96,000		30,000

14   C

($30 × 2,000) + ($30 × 1,600) + ($50 × 2,200) = $218,000

15   C

All inventories are increasing, so absorption costing profits will be higher by:

($30 × 200) + ($30 × 100) + ($50 × 200) = $19,000

16   A

	Units	Total costs
High	55	$7,000
Low	25	$5,500
Difference	30	$1,500

Therefore, Variable costs = $\dfrac{\$1,500}{30\,units}$ =$50 per unit

By substitution, we find FC = $4,250.

17

	True	False
Overhead costs are always fixed costs		✓
As production levels increase, fixed cost per unit decreases	✓	
Fixed costs are always irrelevant in a decision making situation		✓
As the level of activity changes, fixed costs will also change		✓

18 $8.25

Total hours worked, and paid = 3,300/0.75 = 4,400 hours

Hourly rate = $36,300/4,400 = $8.25

19   A

20   B

	Conformance costs	Non-conformance costs
Internal failure costs		✓
Prevention costs	✓	
Appraisal costs	✓	
External failure costs		✓

21   A

$$834 - [(854 + 834 + 1,012)/3] = -66$$

22   D

	$
Overheads incurred	186,000
Actual absorption $\dfrac{\$175,000}{5,000} \times 6,000$	210,000
	————
Over-absorbed	24,000

23   B

	$
Marginal costing profit	180,000
$(15,000 - 25,000) \times \$6$	(60,000)
Equals absorption costing profit	120,000

24   A

25   A

26   Ranking is

	Rank
Project A	**2**
Project B	**3**
Project C	**1**

Project A	$= (0.5 \times \$5,000) + (0.5 \times \$2,500)$
	$= \$3,750$
Project B	$= (0.3 \times \$10,000) + (0.7 \times \$1,000)$
	$= \$3,700$
Project C	$= (0.4 \times \$6,000) + (0.6 \times \$4,000)$
	$= \$4,800$

27   C

$$15 + [850/(850 - - 50)] \times (20 - 15) = 19.7\%$$

28   B and C

29   B

30   A

Sales contribution on actual sales	$50,000
Less: Adverse total variable costs variance	($3,500)
Actual contribution	$46,500

No adjustment is required for the favourable sales volume contribution variance, as it will have already been added to the budgeted contribution to arrive at the standard contribution from actual sales ($50,000) given in the question.

31   D

32   C

Raw materials are a variable cost so the graph will begin at the origin and increase at a gradient equal to the cost per unit. The cost per unit falls at a certain point so the gradient will become less and the graph will be flatter. Option D shows a situation where the cost per unit becomes greater above a certain volume.

33   B

Average cost = ($12,500 − $350)/(2,000 − 200) = $6.75

34   D

Statement of profit or loss value = 100 × ($6.75 − $1.75) = $500

35   A

Idle time + General overtime = (15 hours × $12) + ((10 hours − 4 hours) × $6) = $216

SECTION B

1   MRS GLAM

    (a)   (i)   Irrelevant (sunk cost)

         (ii)   Irrelevant (non-cash cost)

         (iii)   Relevant (future cash cost)

    (b)   Present value of the incremental contribution:

        $50,000 × 0.08 × 0.3 × 3.170 = $3,804

    (c)   Present value of the incremental rates

        Note: rates are paid in advance so payment will occur in years 0, 1, 2 and 3. The annuity factor is for years 0 to 3 = 1 + 2.487 = 3.487:

        ($4,000/115 × 15) × 3.487 = $1,819

    (d)   Value of legacy in four years time:

        $10,000 × 1.1^4 = $14,641

2   M CO

    (a)   Calculations:

        (i)   Fixed overhead expenditure = $9,000 + $200 = $9,200

              Capacity variance would be adverse

              Actual = 3,000 × $2.50 = $7,500

              Budget = 3,680 × $2.50 = $9,200

              Capacity = $7,500 – $9,200 = $1,700 Adverse

        (ii) and (iii)

              Ah × Ar = 3,000 × **3.90 (iii)** = $11,700

                                     Rate = 300F

              Ah × Sr = 3,000 × 4 = $12,000

                                     Efficiency = **$800A (ii)**

              Sh × Sr = 2,800* × 4 = $11,200

        * to calculate the standard hours the fixed overhead efficiency variance needs to be used:

        Actual = 3,000 × $2.50 = $7,500

        Efficiency variance = $500 Adverse

        Standard = $7,500 – $500 = $7,000

        Standard hours = $7,000/$2.50 = 2,800 hours

    (b)   A

    (c)   B

3   PLAY CO

(a)   Calculations

   (i)   ROI = $55,000/$300,000 = 18.3%

   (ii)   RI = $55,000 − 0.1 × $300,000 = $25,000

(b)   D

(c)   A

(d)   C

(e)   A

Section 7

SPECIMEN EXAM QUESTIONS

Section A – ALL 35 questions are compulsory and MUST be attempted

Each question is worth 2 marks

1   A manufacturing company benchmarks the performance of its accounts receivable department with that of a leading credit card company.

What type of benchmarking is the company using?

A   Internal benchmarking

B   Competitive benchmarking

C   Functional benchmarking

D   Strategic benchmarking

2   **Which of the following BEST describes target costing?**

A   Setting a cost by subtracting a desired profit margin from a competitive market price

B   Setting a price by adding a desired profit margin to a production cost

C   Setting a cost for the use in the calculation of variances

D   Setting a selling price for the company to aim for in the long run

3   Information relating to two processes (F and G) was as follows:

Process	Normal loss as % of input	Input (litres)	Output (litres)
F	8	65,000	58,900
G	5	37,500	35,700

For each process, was there an abnormal loss or an abnormal gain?

	Abnormal loss	Abnormal gain
Process F		
Process G		

4   The following budgeted information relates to a manufacturing company for next period:

	Units		$
Production	14,000	Fixed production costs	63,000
Sales	12,000	Fixed selling costs	12,000

The normal level of activity is 14,000 units per period.

Using absorption costing the profit for next period has been calculated as $36,000.

What would be the profit for next period using marginal costing?

$

5   The Eastland Postal Service is government owned. The government requires it to provide a parcel delivery service to every home and business in Eastland at a low price which is set by the government. Express Couriers Co is a privately owned parcel delivery company that also operates in Eastland. It is not subject to government regulation and most of its deliveries are to large businesses located in Eastland's capital city. You have been asked to assess the relative efficiency of the management of the two organisations.

Which of the following factors should NOT be allowed for when comparing the ROCE of the two organisations to assess the efficiency of their management?

A   Differences in objectives pursued

B   Differences in workforce motivation

C   Differences in geographic areas served

D   Differences in prices charged

6   **Under which sampling method does every member of the target population has an equal chance of being in the sample?**

A   Random sampling

B   Systematic sampling

C   Stratified sampling

D   Cluster sampling

7   A Company manufactures and sells one product which requires 8 kg of raw material in its manufacture. The budgeted data relating to the next period are as follows:

	Units
Sales	19,000
Opening inventory of finished goods	4,000
Closing inventory of finished goods	3,000
	Kg
Opening inventory of raw materials	50,000
Closing inventory of raw materials	53,000

What is the budgeted raw material purchases for next period (in kg)?

kg

8 Up to a given level of activity in each period the purchase price per unit of a raw material is constant. After that point a lower price per unit applies both to further units purchased and also retrospectively to all units already purchased.

Which of the following graphs depicts the total cost of the raw materials for a period?

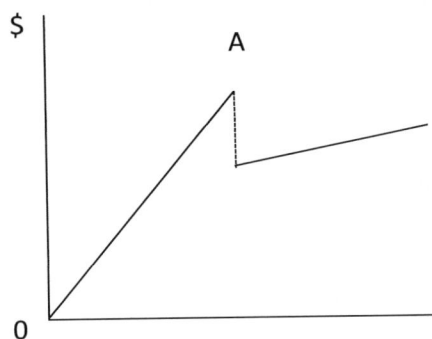

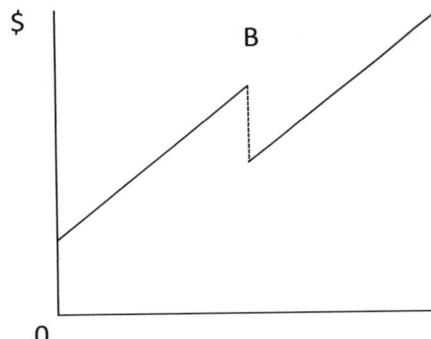

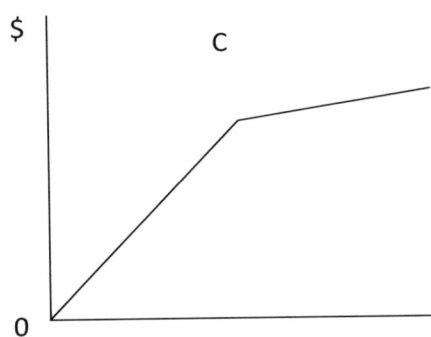

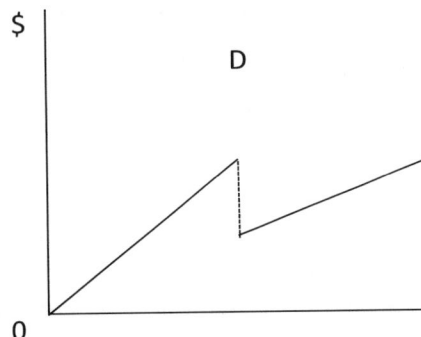

A   Graph A

B   Graph B

C   Graph C

D   Graph D

9 **Which TWO of the following are benefits of budgeting?**

It helps coordinate the activities of different departments	
It establishes a system of control	
It fulfils legal reporting obligations	
It is a starting point for strategic planning	

10   The following statements relate to the participation of junior management in setting budgets:

1   It speeds up the setting of budgets

2   It increases the motivation of junior managers

3   It reduces the level of budget padding

Which statements are true?

A   2 only

B   2 and 3 only

C   1 only

D   1, 2 and 3

11   A company has a capital employed of $200,000. It has a cost of capital of 12% per year. Its residual income is $36,000.

What is the company's return on investment?

| % |

12   A company has calculated a $10,000 adverse direct material variance by subtracting its flexed budget direct material cost from its actual direct material cost for the period.

Which TWO of the following could have caused the variance?

An increase in direct material prices	
An increase in raw material usage per unit	
Units produced being greater than budgeted	
Units sold being greater than budgeted	

13   A company has recorded the following variances for a period:

Sales volume variance	$10,000 adverse
Sales price variance	$5,000 favourable
Total cost variance	$12,000 adverse

Standard profit on actual sales for the period was $120,000.

What was the fixed budget profit for the period?

A $137,000

B $103,000

C $110,000

D $130,000

14 **Which of the following are suitable measures of performance at the strategic level?**

1   Return on investment

2   Market share

3   Number of customer complaints

A   1 and 2

B   2 only

C   2 and 3

D   1 and 3

15 **Which TWO of the following are feasible values for the correlation coefficient?**

+1.40	
+1.04	
0	
−0.94	

16 A company's operating costs are 60% variable and 40% fixed.

Which of the following variances' values would change if the company switched from standard marginal costing to standard absorption costing?

A   Direct material efficiency variance

B   Variable overhead efficiency variance

C   Sales volume variance

D   Fixed overhead expenditure variance

17 ABC Co has a manufacturing capacity of 10,000 units. The flexed production cost budget of the company is as follows:

Capacity	60%	100%
Total production costs	$11,280	$15,120

What is the budgeted total production cost if it operates at 85% capacity?

$

18 Using an interest rate of 10% per year the net present value (NPV) of a project has been correctly calculated as $50. If the interest rate is increased by 1% the NPV of the project falls by $20.

What is the internal rate of return (IRR) of the project?

A   7.5%

B   11.7%

C   12.5%

D   20.0%

19   A factory consists of two production cost centres (P and Q) and two service cost centres (X and Y). The total allocated and apportioned overhead for each is as follows:

P	Q	X	Y
$95,000	$82,000	$46,000	$30,000

It has been estimated that each service cost centre does work for other cost centres in the following proportions:

	P	Q	X	Y
Percentage of service cost centre X to	50	50	–	–
Percentage of service cost centre Y to	30	60	10	–

The reapportionment of service cost centre costs to other cost centres fully reflects the above proportions.

After the reapportionment of service cost centre costs has been carried out, what is the total overhead for production cost centre P?

A $124,500

B $126,100

C $127,000

D $128,500

20   A company always determines its order quantity for a raw material by using the Economic Order Quantity (EOQ) model.

What would be the effects on the EOQ and the total annual holding cost of a decrease in the cost of ordering a batch of raw material?

	Higher	Lower
EOQ		
Annual holding cost		

21   A company which operates a process costing system had work-in-progress at the start of last month of 300 units (valued at $1,710) which were 60% complete in respect of all costs. Last month a total of 2,000 units were completed and transferred to the finished goods warehouse. The cost per equivalent unit for costs arising last month was $10. The company uses the FIFO method of cost allocation.

What was the total value of the 2,000 units transferred to the finished goods warehouse last month?

A $19,910

B $20,000

C $20,510

D $21,710

22 Identify whether each of the following statements about the uses of big data analytics in organisations is true or false.

	True	False
It helps to better understand customer behaviour and preferences		
It helps to analyse the efficiency of business processes in real time		

23 The number of daily complaints to a local government office has a mean of 12 and a standard deviation of 3 complaints

What is the coefficient of variation as a %?

%

24 **Under which of the following labour remuneration methods will direct labour cost always be a variable cost?**

A Day rate

B Piece rate

C Differential piece rate

D Group bonus scheme

25 A company manufactures and sells a single product. In two consecutive months the following levels of production and sales (in units) occurred:

	Month 1	Month 2
Sales	3,800	4,400
Production	3,900	4,200

The opening inventory for Month 1 was 400 units. Profits or losses have been calculated for each month using both absorption and marginal costing principles.

Which of the following combination of profits and losses for the two months is consistent with the above data?

	Absorption costing profit/(loss)		Marginal costing profit/(loss)	
	Month 1	Month 2	Month 1	Month 2
	$	$	$	$
A	200	4,400	(400)	3,200
B	(400)	4,400	200	3,200
C	200	3,200	(400)	4,400
D	(400)	3,200	200	4,400

26   The following statements relate to the advantages that linear regression analysis has over the high low method in the analysis of cost behaviour:

1   the reliability of the analysis can be statistically tested

2   it takes into account all of the data

3   it assumes linear cost behaviour

Which of the above statements are TRUE?

A   1 only

B   1 and 2 only

C   2 and 3 only

D   1, 2 and 3

27   **A company operates a process in which no losses are incurred. The process account for last month, when there was no opening work-in-progress, was as follows:**

Process Account

	$		$
Costs arising	624,000	Finished output (10,000 units)	480,000
		Closing work-in-progress (4,000 units)	144,000
	————		————
	624,000		624,000
	————		————

The closing work in progress was complete to the same degree for all elements of cost.

What was the percentage degree of completion of the closing work-in-progress?

A   12%

B   30%

C   40%

D   75%

28   **Which of the following would NOT be expected to appear in an organisation's mission statement?**

A   The organisation's values and beliefs

B   The products or services offered by the organisation

C   Quantified short term targets the organisation seeks to achieve

D   The organisation's major stakeholders

29   An organisation operates a piecework system of remuneration, but also guarantees its employees 80% of a time-based rate of pay which is based on $20 per hour for an eight hour working day. Three minutes is the standard time allowed per unit of output. Piecework is paid at the rate of $18 per standard hour.

If an employee produces 200 units in eight hours on a particular day, what is the employee's gross pay for that day?

$$\boxed{\$ \qquad\qquad\qquad}$$

30   A company uses an overhead absorption rate of $3.50 per machine hour, based on 32,000 budgeted machine hours for the period. During the same period the actual total overhead expenditure amounted to $108,875 and 30,000 machine hours were recorded on actual production.

By how much was the total overhead under or over absorbed for the period?

A   Under absorbed by $3,875

B   Under absorbed by $7,000

C   Over absorbed by $3,875

D   Over absorbed by $7,000

31   **Which TWO of the following statements relating to management information are TRUE?**

No strict rules govern the way in which the information is presented	✓
There is usually a legal requirement for the information to be produced	
It is produced for parties external to the organisation	
It may be presented in monetary or non-monetary terms	✓

32   A company's sales in the last year in its three different markets were as follows

Market 1	$100,000
Market 2	$150,000
Market 3	$50,000
Total	$300,000

In a pie chart representing the proportion of sales made by each region what would be the angle of the section representing Market 3 (to the nearest whole degree)?

A   17 degrees

B   50 degrees

C   61 degrees

D   120 degrees

33 The results of a chemistry examination are normally distributed with a mean score of 56 and a standard deviation of 12.

What is the percentage probability that a student will score more than 80?

	%

34 The purchase price of an item of inventory is $25 per unit. In each three month period the usage of the item is 20,000 units. The annual holding costs associated with one unit equate to 6% of its purchase price. The cost of placing an order for the item is $20.

What is the Economic Order Quantity (EOQ) for the inventory item (to the nearest whole unit)?

35 A company uses marginal costing. The following variances occurred in the last period when the actual net profit was $40,000.

Materials	$900 adverse
Labour	$1,000 favourable
Overheads	$700 adverse
Sales price	$500 favourable
Sales volume contribution	$900 favourable

What was the budgeted net profit for the last period?

A $41,500

B $40,800

C $38,500

D $39,200

(Total: 70 marks)

Section B – ALL THREE questions are compulsory and MUST be attempted

36 Cab Co owns and runs 350 taxis and had sales of $10 million in the last year. Cab Co is considering introducing a new computerised taxi tracking system.

The expected costs and benefits of the new computerised tracking system are as follows:

(i) The system would cost $2,100,000 to implement.

(ii) Depreciation would be provided at $420,000 per annum.

(iii) $75,000 has already been spent on staff training in order to evaluate the potential of the new system. Further training costs of $425,000 would be required in the first year if the new system is implemented.

(iv) Sales are expected to rise to $11 million in Year 1 if the new system is implemented, thereafter increasing by 5% per annum. If the new system is not implemented, sales would be expected to increase by $200,000 per annum.

(v) Despite increased sales, savings in vehicle running costs are expected as a result of the new system. These are estimated at 1% of total sales.

(vi) Six new members of staff would be recruited to manage the new system at a total cost of $120,000 per annum.

(vii) Cab Co would have to take out a maintenance contract for the new system at a cost of $75,000 per annum for five years.

(viii) Interest on money borrowed to finance the project would cost $150,000 per annum.

(ix) Cab Co's cost of capital is 10% per annum.

Required:

(a) **In order to determine whether a computerised tracking system should be introduced, indicate whether each of the following is a relevant or irrelevant cost for a net present value (NPV) evaluation.**

	Relevant	Irrelevant
(i) Computerised tracking system investment of $2,100,000;		
(ii) Depreciation of $420,000 in each of the five years;		
(iii) Staff training costs of $425,000;		
(iv) New staff total salary of $120,000 per annum;		
(v) Staff training costs of $75,000;		
(vi) Interest cost of $150,000 per annum.		

(5 marks)

(b) Calculate the following values if the computerised tracking system is implemented.

(i) Incremental sales in Year 1

$\boxed{\$}$

(ii) Savings in vehicle running costs in Year 1

$\boxed{\$}$

(iii) Present value of the maintenance costs over the life of the contract

$\boxed{\$}$

Note: The following mark allocation is provided as guidance for this requirement:

(i) 1 mark

(ii) 0.5 marks

(iii) 1.5 marks   **(3 marks)**

(c) Cab Co wishes to maximise the wealth of its shareholders. It has correctly calculated the following measures for the proposed computerised tracking system project:

– The internal rate of return (IRR) is 14%,

– The return on average capital employed (ROCE) is 20% and

– The payback period is four years.

Required:

Which of the following is TRUE?

A The project is worthwhile because the IRR is a positive value

B The project is worthwhile because the IRR is greater than the cost of capital

C The project is not worthwhile because the IRR is less than the ROCE

D The project is not worthwhile because the payback is less than five years

(2 marks)

(Total: 10 marks)

37 Castilda Co manufactures toy robots. The company operates a standard marginal costing system and values inventory at standard cost.

The following is an extract of a partly completed spreadsheet for calculating variances in month 1.

	A	B	C
1	**Standard Cost of Card - Toy Robot**		**$ per robot**
2	Selling price		120
3	Direct material	1 kg of material per unit	20
4	Direct labour	6 hours at $8 per hour	48
5	Production overhead		24
6	Standard contribution		28
7	**Actual and budgeted activity levels in units**	**Budget**	**Actual**
8	Sales	25,000	25,600
9	Production	25,000	26,000
10	**Actual sales revenue and variable costs**	**$**	
11	Sales	3,066,880	
12	Direct materials (purchased and used)	532,800	
13	Direct labour (150,000 hours)	1,221,000	
14	Variable production overhead	614,000	
15	**Variances**	**$**	
16	Total direct materials variances	12,800	Adv
17	Direct labour rate variances	21,000	Adv
18	Direct labour efficiency variances	48,000	Fav
19	Total variable production overhead variances	10,000	Fav
20			

Required:

(a) Which formula will correctly calculate the direct labour efficiency variance in cell **B18**?

A =(C9*C4)-B13

B =B13-(C9*C4)

C =(C9*C4)-(150,000*8)

D =(150,000-(C9*6))*8

(2 marks)

(b) Castilda Co uses a standard cost operating statement to reconcile budgeted contribution with actual contribution. A standard cost operating statement for Month 1 is given below with some information missing.

Complete the reconciliation for the standard cost operating statement for Month 1 shown below.

Standard cost operating statement Month 1			
	$	$	
Budgeted contribution		700,000	
Sales volume variance / Total sales variance / Fixed overhead volume variance *			Adv / Fav *
Standard contribution on actual sales			
Sales price variance			Adv / Fav *
		711,680	
Cost variances			
Total direct materials variance	12,800 Adv		
Direct labour rate variance	21,000 Adv		
Direct labour efficiency variance	48,000 Fav		
Total variable production overhead variance	10,000 Fav		
		24,200	Fav
Actual contribution		735,880	

* delete where appropriate

Note: The total marks will be split equally between each part.　　**(6 marks)**

(c) Castilda's management accountant thinks that the direct labour rate and efficiency variances for Month 1 could be interrelated.

Which TWO of the following could explain their interrelationship?

A productivity bonus was paid to direct labour	
Lower grade labour performed tasks less efficiently	
Higher grade labour performed tasks more efficiently	
Actual production was less than budgeted	

(2 marks)

(Total: 10 marks)

38 Nicholson Co sells mobile telephones. It supplies its customers with telephones and wireless telephone connections. Customers pay an annual fee plus a monthly charge based on calls made.

The company has recently employed a consultant to install a balanced scorecard system of performance measurement and to benchmark the results against those of Nicholson Co's competitors. Unfortunately the consultant was called away before the work was finished. You have been asked to complete the work. The following data is available.

Nicholson Co

Operating data for the year ended 30 November 2013

Sales revenue	$480 million
Sales attributable to new products	$8 million
Average capital employed	$192 million
Profit before interest and tax	$48 million
Average numbers of customers	1,960,000
Average number of telephones returned for repair each day	10,000
Number of bill queries	12,000
Number of customer complaints	21,600
Number of customers lost	117,600
Average number of telephones unrepaired at the end of each day	804

Required:

(a) Calculate the following ratios and other statistics for Nicholson Co for the year ended 30 November 2013.

    (i) **Return on capital employed**

                                         %

    (ii) **Return on sales (net profit percentage)**

                                         %

    (iii) **Asset turnover**

                                         times

    (iv) **Average wait for telephone repair (in days)**

                                         days

                                                (6 marks)

(b) Calculate the following statistics for Nicholson Co (Give your answers to two decimal places)

    (i) **Percentage of customers lost per annum**

                                         %

    (ii) **Percentage of sales attributable to new products.**

                                         %

                                                (2 marks)

Note: The following mark allocation is provided as guidance for this requirement:

(i)   1.5 marks

(ii)   1.5 marks

(iii)   1.5 marks

(iv)   1.5 marks

(v)   1 mark

(vi)   1 mark

(8 marks)

(c)   **Complete the following explanation of a balanced score card**

A balanced scorecard measures performance from four perspectives: customer satisfaction, growth, financial success and **non-financial success / process flexibility / process efficiency.**

The scorecard is balanced in that it requires managers to **deliver performance in all four areas / offset bad performance in one area with good performance in another / achieve on an equal number of KPIs in each perspective**

(2 marks)

(Total: 10 marks)

Section 8

SPECIMEN EXAM ANSWERS

Section A

1   C

2   A

3

	Abnormal loss	Abnormal gain
Process F	✓	
Process G		✓

(litres)	Normal loss	Actual loss	Abnormal loss	Abnormal gain
Process F	5,200	6,100	900	–
Process G	1,875	1,800	–	75

4   **$27,000**

Marginal costing profit:

(36,000 – (2,000*(63,000/14,000))

$27,000

5   B

6   A

7   **147,000 KG**

Budgeted production (19,000 + 3,000 – 4,000) = 18,000 units

RM required for production (18,000*8) = 144,000 kg

RM purchases (144,000 + 53,000 – 50,000) = 147,000 kg

8   D

9

It helps coordinate the activities of different departments	✓
It establishes a system of control	✓
It fulfils legal reporting obligations	
It is a starting point for strategic planning	

10   A

11   30%

(36,000 + (200,000 × 12%))/200,000 = 30%

12

An increase in direct material prices	✓
An increase in raw material usage per unit	✓
Units produced being greater than budgeted	
Units sold being greater than budgeted	

13   D

Sales volume variance:

(budgeted sales units – actual sales units) * standard profit per unit = 10,000 adverse

Standard profit on actual sales: (actual sales units * std profit per unit) = $120,000

Fixed budget profit: (120,000 +10,000) = $130,000

14   A

15

+1.40	
+1.04	
0	✓
-0.94	✓

16   C

17 **$13,680**

Variable production cost per unit = (15,120 − 11,280)/(10,000− 6,000) = 3,840/4,000 = $0.96

Fixed cost = 11,280 − (6,000 × 0.96) = $5,520

85% capacity = 8,500 units.

Flexible budget allowance for 8,500 units = $5,520 + (8,500 × 0.96) = $13,680

18 **C**

At 13% NPV should be −10

Using interpolation: 10% + (50/60)(10% − 13%) = 12.5%

19 **D**

Direct cost	$95,000
Proportion of cost centre × (46,000 + (0.10*30,000))*0.50	$24,500
Proportion of cost centre Y (30,000*0.3)	$9,000
Total overhead cost for P	$128,500

20

	Higher	Lower
EOQ		✓
Annual holding cost		✓

21 **A**

1,700 units*10	$17,000
300 units*0.4*10	$1,200
Opening work in progress value	$1,710
Total value	$19,910

22

	True	False
It helps to better understand customer behaviour and preferences	✓	
It helps to analyse the efficiency of business processes in real time	✓	

23 **25%**

Coefficient of variation = standard deviation/mean × 100 = 3/12 × 100 = 25%

24 **B**

25   C

Month 1: production >sales	Absorption costing > marginal costing
Month 2: sales> production	marginal costing profit> absorption costing profit

A and C satisfy month 1, C and D satisfy month 2; therefore C satisfies both

26   B

27   D

Cost per equivalent unit (480,000/10,000) = $48

Degree of completion= ((144,000/48)/4,000) = 75%

28   C

29 $180

200 units*(3/60)*18 = $180

30   A

Actual cost	$108,875
Absorbed cost	$105,000
Under absorbed	$3,875

31

No strict rules govern the way in which the information is presented	✓
There is usually a legal requirement for the information to be produced	
It is produced for parties external to the organisation	
It may be presented in monetary or non-monetary terms	✓

32   C

Total number of degrees = 360

Proportion of market 3 sales: (50,000/300,000) = 0.1666 = 0.17

0.17*360 = 61 degrees

33   2.28%

Z-score = $(x-\mu)/\sigma = (80 - 56)/12 = 2$

From the normal distribution table, 2 = 0.4772

To find the probability of scoring more than 80: 0.5 – 0.4772 = 0.0228 = 2.28%

34   C

$\{(2*20*(4*20{,}000))/(0.06*25)\}^{0.5}$

1,461 units

35   D

$40,000 + $900 - $1,000 + $700 - $500 - $900 = $39,200

Section B

36   **(a)**   **(i)**   relevant

              (ii)   irrelevant

              (iii)   relevant

              (iv)   relevant

              (v)   irrelevant

              (vi)   irrelevant

    (b)   **(i)**   Increase in sales = ($11m – $10m) = $1m

                      Increase due to the project = ($1m – $0.2m) = $800,000

              (ii)   Total sales in year 1 = $11m

                      Savings ($11m*0.01) = $110,000

              (iii)   Annuity factor for five years at 10%= 3.791

                      Present value ($75,000*3.791) = $284,325

    (c)   B

ACCA marking guide			
			Marks
(a)		(i)	0.5
		(ii)	1.0
		(iii)	0.5
		(iv)	1.0
		(v)	1.0
		(vi)	1.0
(b)		(i)	1.0
		(ii)	0.5
		(iii)	1.5
(c)			2.0
Total			**10**

37 **(a)** C

(b)

Standard cost operating statement Month 1			
	$	$	
Budgeted contribution		700,000	
Sales volume variance		**16.800**	**Fav**
Standard contribution on actual sales		**716,800**	
Sales price variance		**5,120**	**Adv**
		711,680	
Cost variances			
Total direct materials variance	12,800 Adv		
Direct labour rate variance	21,000 Adv		
Direct labour efficiency variance	48,000 Fav		
Total variable production overhead variance	10,000 Fav		
		24,200	Fav
Actual contribution		735,880	

Sales volume variance:

Budgeted to sale 25,000 units but sold 25,600 units

(25,600 – 25,000)*$28

$16,800 favourable

Sales price variance:

Budgeted to sale at $120 per unit (25,600*$120) = $3,072,000

Actual sales were $3,066,880

Variance ($3,066,880 – $3,072,000) = $5,120 adverse

(c)

A productivity bonus was paid to direct labour	✓
Lower grade labour performed tasks less efficiently	
Higher grade labour performed tasks more efficiently	✓
Actual production was less than budgeted	

ACCA marking guide		
		Marks
(a)		2.0
(b)	1 mark for each correct entry	6.0
(c)		2.0
Total		**10**

38 (a) (i) Profit before interest and tax/Capital employed:

$48m ÷ $192m = 25%

(ii) Profit before interest and tax/Sales revenue: $48m – $480m = 10%

(iii) Sales revenue/capital employed = $480m – 192m = 2.5

(iv) Average number of telephones unrepaired at the end of each day/Number of telephones returned for repair: (804 – 10,000)*365 days = 29.3 days

(b) (i) Percentage of customers lost per annum = number of customers lost - total number of customers × 100% = 117,600 – 1,960,000 = 6.00%

(ii) Percentage of sales attributable to new products = Sales attributable to new products/total sales × 100% = $8m – $480m = 1.67%

(c) A balanced scorecard measures performance from four perspectives: customer satisfaction, growth, financial success and **process efficiency.**

The scorecard is balanced in that it requires managers to **deliver performance in all four areas**

ACCA marking guide		
		Marks
(a)	(i)	1.5
	(ii)	1.5
	(iii)	1.5
	(iv)	1.5
(b)	(i)	1.0
	(ii)	1.0
(c)		2.0
Total		**10**